Why Matter Matters

David P. Lang

Why Matter Matters

Philosophical and Scriptural Reflections on the Sacraments

Our Sunday Visitor Publishing Division
Our Sunday Visitor, Inc.
Huntington, Indiana 46750

ACKNOWLEDGMENTS

I hereby express my indebtedness to the following people:

To Bernard F. Cardinal Law, Archbishop of Boston, whose firm but pastoral leadership in a difficult controversy over the composition of Eucharistic bread was the inspirational occasion for the reflections and research initiating this book.

To Rev. Raymond A. Fournier, S.M., for suggesting that I write a book in the first place.

To Rev. Ronald K. Tacelli, S.J., Ph.D., Associate Professor of Philosophy at Boston College, for writing a foreword for this book.

To Dr. Peter J. Kreeft, Professor of Philosophy at Boston College, for writing a preface for this book.

To Rev. Kenneth Baker, S.J., Editor of *Homiletic and Pastoral Review*, for publishing (in the October, 2001, issue) my article "The Gnostic Resurgence: Why Matter Matters," out of which this book eventually developed.

To Tim Ryland, Editor, and Karl Keating, Publisher, of *This Rock*, for publishing (in the January, 2002, issue) my article titled "I Would Feed You with the Finest of Wheat: The Catholic Doctrine of Altar Bread."

To my friend David L. Vise, for sharing the fruits of his expertise in Scriptural exegesis: with immense gratitude for locating numerous key Scriptural texts for me, as well as illuminating some subtle, profound, and often startling interrelations among them.

To my friend Francis B. Kelly (who predicted several years ago that I would write a book), to whom I can only say, as he replied to me after he prayed about my finally beginning to write this particular book: "Numbers 6:24-26."

To the staff at Our Sunday Visitor, especially Michael Dubruiel, Acquisitions Editor, and Henry O'Brien, Senior Project Editor, for their recognition of my work and for their patience with my novice questions.

Shouting they shall mount the heights of Zion,
they shall come streaming to the Lord's blessings:
The grain, the wine, and the oil, . . .
They themselves shall be like watered gardens,
never again shall they languish.

— Jeremiah 31:12, *NAB*

CONTENTS

FOREWORD

When I heard that Dr. David Lang, my former student and good friend, was writing a book on the place of matter in the sacraments, I admit I was extremely skeptical. A whole *book*? What could *possibly* be worth saying at such length? Even someone as dauntingly knowledgeable as David Lang would have to pad a great deal, and would probably end up producing no more than a bloated pamphlet. Or so I thought. I could not have been more wrong.

Dr. Lang has produced a unique and uniquely fascinating book on the nature of the sacraments and on sacramentality as such. Even those long familiar with sacramental theology, I venture to predict, will have something important to learn from *Why Matter Matters*.

We human beings are a strange unity of matter and spirit. Our spiritual dimension cannot be reduced to matter. But it needs matter in order to express itself, in order to do what it was created to do. Our knowledge needs to be expressed in sounds and symbols; our love, in deeds and words — though neither knowledge nor love can be reduced to sounds or symbols or deeds or words. They express something deeper — but something that could not (for us) be expressed without them.

The Christmas preface reads:

> *In him we see our God made visible*
> *and so are caught up in love of the God we cannot see.*

The love of God is expressed in the life of Jesus. His deeds and words point beyond themselves, beyond their spatial and temporal location, to the timeless, transcendent Love that is their Source. God made us with this need for the bodily, the materially concrete, and He expressed His loving Word to us in just that way. He tailored both message and message-bearer to those for whom it was intended.

This, in a nutshell, is the sacramental principle: the communication of God's love through the medium of matter. This is what Dr. Lang spells out in such thorough and abundant detail.

What is so fascinating in *Why Matter Matters* is its multifaceted approach to each sacrament: not only is there a systematic marshaling of Scriptural sources, a deductive rigor in spelling out the implications of sacred texts (which one would expect from a man who holds doctorates in both philosophy and mathematics), there is also an astonishingly detailed attempt to show why *this* matter is just right for *this* sacrament. The scholastics called that sort of thing an argument *e convenientia:* "from fittingness." Anyone reading these pages will agree, I think, that the argument has never been pressed so hard or wielded so impressively (and exhaustively!) as in this book. Before reading *Why Matter Matters*, I'd never thought so much — or known so much! — about the properties of wheat, about the difference between a grain and a seed grass, about the nature of glutinous proteins, and never realized their deep significance: never fully appreciated, that is to say, the intricate, delicate, *organic* coherence of the Church's entire sacramental life. I doubt that my gratitude to the author will be unique.

Dr. Lang has some harsh things to say about Luther in particular and about Protestantism in general. But I hope that his politically incorrect bluntness will not prevent non-Catholics from reading and appreciating this book, from seeing the sacramental worldview of the Catholic Church spelled out in minute and riveting detail. For just about everyone — Catholic, Protestant, Jew, Muslim, even the interested skeptic — *Why Matter Matters* should be a rewarding, revealing, and . . . well . . . *sacramental* experience.

Ronald K. Tacelli, S.J., Ph.D.
Boston College

PREFACE

I write this Preface to convince prospective readers as quickly as possible that *Why Matter Matters* matters.

Like the hard-thinking philosopher who wrote this book, I shall give reasons for everything that I say. There are five reasons why *Why Matter Matters* matters.

First, because most of us today do not know or believe the point of this book. It always matters more to learn a new, unfashionable truth or refute a new, fashionable error than to be flattered by being assured that we were right all the time. G. K. Chesterton, asked why he became Catholic, said, "I don't need a church to tell me where I'm right; I need a Church to tell me where I'm wrong." Thus, books that surprise and shock us are our primary need, though not our primary desire. For instance, we don't need to learn that there are times when it's nice to be good (namely, those times when it's good to be nice); but we do need to learn that there are times when it's wrong to be nice (namely, those times when it's nice to be wrong).

Second, because this book's point is pervasive. It always matters more to learn a truth that is more universal, for it has more applications than a truth that is more particular. For instance, gravity matters more than gravy, for it explains why the potatoes fell along with the gravy; and grace matters more than gravity, for "everything is a grace" (as St. Thérèse of Lisieux says), including gravity and gravy.

Third, and most important of all, because its point is true, and true forever. Knowing unchangeable objective truths always matters more than knowing changeable subjective opinions or feelings. We doubt that when we watch soap operas or read pop psychology, but never when we consult road maps or surgeons.

Fourth, because its point is essential to the Catholic religion; and religion matters, and has always mattered, more than anything else, to all human cultures, times, and places up to but not including our own.

Fifth, because it is the teaching of Christ; and what God incarnate taught us matters most of all, for it always fulfills all four of the above criteria.

For all five reasons, then, it matters that matter matters.

Our culture is often called materialistic. A culture that sits in ugly, comfortable furniture watching stupid, comforting TV shows and builds churches that look like dentists' offices is not a materialistic culture; it is a spiritualistic, subjectivistic, self-cuddling, and coddling culture. We are not matter-worshipers but feeling-fondlers. We are not even *conscious* of matter, only of our consciousness of matter. We spout (and apparently even believe) such nonsense as "There is nothing to fear but fear itself" and "There is nothing either good or bad, but thinking makes it so." We are far more Buddhist than Christian.

If we could read the Bible again as if for the first time; if we could wipe clean from our mind all memories of what we learned from it and from its spiritual children; if we could blow the dust of familiarity off this most familiar of books, I think we would be deeply shocked and scandalized; and the reason has much to do with the point of the book you are now reading. Clearly, matter matters infinitely more to God than it does to us if that Book is true.

We find there, first of all, in the very first verses that matter — all matter — is deliberately willed into existence by God. *He* said, "Let it be!" Something in us resists saying "amen" to that when we go to the dentist.

And then we find God communicating Himself to the world, through His chosen people as His collective prophet, not in the esoteric ways all other religions claimed: by having "experiences," by transformations of our consciousness, whether by yoga or shamanism or mysticism or philosophy. Rather, we find public, visible, verifiable words and deeds: written records and visible, literal miracles. (Subtract all the miracles in the Bible and you have nothing left at all, nothing distinctively Jewish or Christian.) Moses' staff got real salt water on it when he parted the Red Sea.

At the culmination of all divine revelation, we find God Himself becoming a material being! That body that grew to manhood only by eating leavened bread and slaughtered animal flesh in a carpenter's home in Nazareth; that blood that really flowed down the cross and into the earth out of His broken heart (it is not a poetic metaphor!); that real flesh and those wounds that were physically touched by "Doubting Thomas" — that was (and is!) God. He even ascended to heaven in this human body. He has it now and forever. He took matter up into His divine person. *You will be able to see and touch God*, in heaven, just as literally as Thomas did, on earth.

And during His public ministry, He not only used matter to heal and save us ("the flesh is the hinge of redemption," said Tertullian) but also used specific chunks of concretely real matter, not "matter as such" (whatever that might mean). Touch the hem of another's garment and you are not healed, no matter what your state of soul; touch the hem of His garment and you are. No matter how much that may puzzle and even scandalize us, it is a fact. It is data. It is true.

And He left us Himself, most perfectly and completely and really, *not* in a book, or in ideas or values, or religious experiences, but in the Eucharist. That presence is "the *Real* Presence." If it is not, we are the most absurd of idolaters. What brain-numbing blasphemy we Catholics commit as our most essential act of worship if Protestants are right! We worship wine and bow to bread.

I still remember vividly how, forty years ago when I became Catholic, I halted, shocked, at the last hurdle, the scandal of sacramentality: that no matter how sincere your beliefs, no matter how pious your intentions, and no matter how saintly the state of your soul may be, it is not nourished by any bread or wine but only by this, because this is not bread and wine at all but God Himself in the flesh. When the priest moves that little round consecrated wafer from the left side of the altar to the right, *God is moved* from the left side of the altar to the right.

A local priest in my hometown uses cubes of leavened whole wheat bread for Communion. Crumbs inevitably fall. They are stepped on, inadvertently. The shoes that step on them have stepped in streets in which dogs have urinated. I hope this priest is only a confused heretic who does not believe in the Real Presence: I hope he is one who does not care because he does not know, rather than one who knows but does not care. But no one in the congregation is shocked. *That* fact vividly proves to me the need for this book.

This book is about not only the general principle stated in its title and this Preface, but about very specific and concrete sacramental applications and instances of that principle. For that is what matter is: specific and concrete. The particulars of how holy matter is to be treated — for example, whether the Eucharistic bread is to be unleavened — are more important than we usually think or feel. If the general principle about matter mattering is true (and if it is not, our whole faith is a superstition), then the details must matter, because matter always means details. "God is in the details." If the wine is not made from fermented grapes, then it cannot be transubstantiated into the Blood of Christ. That matters because the Blood of Christ is the greatest power in the universe, far greater than all nuclear bombs. If it matters whether the matter in a nuclear bomb is uranium or carbon, then it matters all the more whether the matter in the Eucharist is wine or grape juice.

What is at stake here? *Not* whether or not God can work outside His own sacraments. He can. Our own *Catechism of the Catholic Church* clearly says so. A more momentous philosophical principle is at stake: the refutation of gnosticism, or spiritualism, the philosophy that has been the source of nearly every major heresy in the history of the Church, including those of our own day, such as subjectivism and radical feminism.

To see this, we must back up to gain as broad a view of matter as possible. The ultimate end of all human lives, and the ultimate purpose for which God created the universe, is our eternal happiness in the Beatific Vision, the mystical marriage with God Himself in an unimaginable, unutterable, and unending ecstasy that is infinite and eternal. God created matter *for that end*. It is His Jacob's Ladder by which He comes to us and we go to Him. His angels ascend and descend upon it. Our souls meet each other — and even meet God — on this "highway to heaven."

When we obey His will regarding material things, when we do the deeds He commands with our bodies as well as our souls (they always work as one; we are not ghosts in machines), then we transform or translate or transmute our spiritual intentions, our care and love and faith, into a material thing, an instrument or medium or means or mediator of our salvation (somewhat as Christ is a mediator). Our work becomes a sacred thing, a sacramental. God transforms our souls through this material means. For He, too, transmutes His spiritual intentions toward us into this medium, so that we can meet.

For our spirits can meet only in a common field that is *not* a spirit. Pantheists do not believe that matter matters because they believe that spirits can meet in Spirit. But that meeting is melting and melding, not meeting. Imagine three spirits: A, B, and C. If A and B meet only in B, then A is assimilated to B. If A and B meet only in A, then B is assimilated to A. And if A and B meet only in C, then both A and B are assimilated to C.

God invented matter because God is love, and love loves the other, and matter is other. Ultimately, matter matters because love matters.

Peter J. Kreeft, Ph.D.
Boston College

SYMBOLS AND SACRAMENTS

God speaks to us human beings through symbols.

What is a symbol? A symbol is a perceptible sign that points to something beyond itself — a reality that the sign resembles in some way. The sign is some ordinary material object or physical action with which we are familiar, whereas the reality it signifies is usually more remote. But the similarity between them is sufficiently close that the sign is capable of leading us to a notion of the higher reality.

Why does God use symbols to speak to us? We are rational beings possessing a spiritual soul, but we also have physical bodies equipped with sensory organs. Therefore, all our knowledge during this life on earth naturally begins with sense perception and the objects of the senses: what we can see, hear, smell, taste, and touch. Our minds are not naturally attuned to direct awareness of sublime supernatural truths — too far beyond our feeble reach in their sheer brilliance. The Greek philosopher Aristotle, one of the two greatest philosophers of antiquity (the other being his teacher, Plato), compared our human minds to the eyes of bats in the brightness of daylight.[1] This is also a major lesson in Plato's famous allegory of the cave:[2] we are bedazzled when, upon departing our prison of ignorance, we are compelled to gaze at the truth (which is sometimes resisted). On account of our weakness, God graciously condescends by presenting suprasensible realities to us clothed in a language fit for our fleshly level of understanding. St. Thomas Aquinas, the superlative philosopher-theologian of the late Middle Ages, stresses precisely this point.[3] Indeed, we ourselves regularly engage in symbolic behavior: making gestures (such as handshakes), wearing uniforms connected with professional occupations, raising flags and banners, lighting candles, decorating with ribbons and wreaths, adorning with jewelry (such as wedding rings), etc.

Hence, it is not surprising that we, who interact with one another through the medium of images or symbolic representations, should encounter God in a similar manner.

Which symbols does God use to teach us? God uses the harmonious splendor of the entire physical universe, with its awesomely intricate arrangement of beautiful and beneficial things, as a gigantic sign to make Himself known to us! Three Scriptural verses emphasize this truth. First, Wisdom 13:5, *RSV*: "For from the greatness and beauty of created things / comes a corresponding perception of their Creator." Next, Psalm 19:1, *RSV*: "The heavens are telling the glory of God; / and the firmament proclaims his handiwork." Finally, Romans 1:20, *RSV*: "Ever since the creation of the world his [God's] invisible nature, namely, his eternal power and deity, has been clearly perceived in the things that have been made." St. Bonaventure, a contemporary of St. Thomas Aquinas and another illustrious philosophizing theologian, is well-known for his work *The Mind's Road to God*, in which he treats at length the ways God is reflected. For our relevant purposes here, God is mirrored through His "traces" in the physical universe open to our sensory experience, through His "image" impressed on our natural powers of intellect and will, and through His "image" in us elevated and purified by supernatural grace.

Thus, God's providential dispensation has ordered the material world to the spiritual life of humanity. In particular, our Lord Jesus Christ, the Second Person of the Blessed Trinity and the Word of God who incarnated Himself to redeem us (see John 1:1-14), instituted seven *sacraments*.[4] Most of these contain simple, commonplace material substances having the marvelous ability to elevate our minds to the realm of divine mystery. But, again, we need to experience such visible signs on account of our natural mental difficulty in beholding spiritual truths directly, especially after the further weakening caused by Original Sin.[5]

What exactly is a sacrament? The *1983 Code of Canon Law*, Can. 840, states: "The Sacraments of the New Testament were instituted by Christ the Lord and entrusted to the Church. As actions of Christ and of the Church, they are signs and means by which faith is expressed and strengthened, worship is offered to God and our sanctification is brought about." According to the *Catechism of the Catholic Church* (hereafter *CCC*), n. 1123, the sacraments are "signs [that] also instruct," which "not only presuppose faith, but by words and objects . . . also nourish, strengthen, and express it." Their purpose is to render worship to God through sanctifying individuals and building up the Body of Christ. In short, a sacrament is a symbolic rite, involving some basic physical substance or condition (its *matter*) along with a structure of words and actions (its *form*), which actually brings about the very gift that it signifies. The *CCC*, nn. 1127-1128, explains that the sacraments "act *ex opere operato* (literally: 'by the very fact of the action's being performed')." In other words, so long as the proper (or *valid*) matter and form are employed by a sacrament's legitimate minister acting according to the Church's intention, the sacramental effect immediately results through the salvific power of Christ — independently of the state of righteousness of the minister. But, of course, the degree of grace conferred depends on the "disposition" of the recipient.

It is through this conjunction of matter and form that we grasp the meaning of a sacrament and what it accomplishes. We learn that, by God's almighty power, using these humble signs as instruments, the recipient of the sacrament enters into either a different, or else a deeper, supernatural relationship with God and other people. The recipient may be empowered to carry out some new tasks that will be meritorious toward everlasting happiness in heaven.[6] (This is what happens most notably in the sacraments of Baptism, Confirmation, and Holy Orders,[7] as well as Matrimony, but each sacrament has its own unique or special purpose.) In any case, if received worthily, every sacrament imparts to the soul the gift of an enhanced participation in God's very own eternal Life — an increase in what is called *sanctifying grace*. As the first pope taught, "His divine power has granted to us all things that pertain to life and godliness, . . . that through these you may . . . become partakers of the divine nature" (2 Peter 1:3-4, *RSV*).[8]

Who could be against these wonderful blessings, the sacraments? Well, certain people throughout history have been suspicious of mixing material things with spiritual realities. Some have felt that lowly material things are incapable of being used, even by God's might, for noble spiritual purposes. Others have thought that it is beneath God's dignity and unworthy of the human soul for our heavenward journey to be contaminated by matter. All these people have been burdened with the intellectual affliction called "gnosticism."

In fact, the atmosphere surrounding certain contemporary controversies betrays some quite convincing evidence that this ancient gnostic worldview is once again attracting numerous adherents, whether or not they are explicitly aware of its influence on their thinking. This lamentable circumstance will become more apparent in due course, once we examine the proper matters for valid celebration of the various sacraments. But for now, as a preview, we claim the following situation prevails: the lands formerly under Christendom's yoke are currently plagued with a rampant relativism that considers the Church's sacramental material requirements a result of mere custom and arbitrary rules subject to change — and thus a matter of indifference or irrelevance.

One of the original tenets of gnosticism is that salvation comes through secret knowledge (called *gnosis*), accessible only to the privileged few — rather than through public divine revelation with its open invitation addressed to all mankind. Moreover, the first gnostics, equating spirit with goodness and light, deemed matter evil and submerged in darkness. Since persons are beings capable of intellectual illumination, it logically follows from this position that matter cannot pertain to the essence of a person's core identity. Therefore, any materiality attached to a person becomes extraneous and incidental to the superior spiritual aspect of consciousness.

This thinking may, at first glance, seem innocuous; perhaps surprisingly, however, it is actually fraught with dangerous ramifications. For if matter is unimportant, then it can be molded or disposed of at the whim of any prevalent intellectual current. Bodily conditions can be consigned to matters of mere expedience subject to the technologically crafty and politically cunning. If embraced by a large or powerful enough group, the gnostic attitude may stimulate the growth of totalitarian forces. Subsequently, the tyranny of grandiose utopian ideas and the ruthless drive to implement them may succeed at subjugating those whose physical constitution or ideological nonconformity does not measure up to the iron standards of the ruling elite. When man's delicately woven biological and spiritual fabric is not respected, when its Creator is not reverenced, then might makes right and hell torments earth.[9] The twentieth century witnessed on an enormous scale the emergence of some arrogantly wicked dictatorial regimes imbued with a gnostic (and often occult) worldview: Nazism, Communism, and the Sexual Revolution that spawned the Abortion Holocaust.

Even if modern neo-gnostics do not condemn matter *per se* as evil, nonetheless they (like their predecessors) persist in seeing various differences in the forms of matter as irrelevant for an enlightened understanding of reality. For them, in other words, human consciousness must be raised to the level where it is liberated from a narrow-minded entrapment in the confining categories of merely material distinctions, which supposedly hinder the maximization of individual aggrandizement. This self-centered, prideful attitude is a strong temptation during certain historical periods, especially our own era, when people are insisting on their autonomous right to "do their own thing" — even if their choices violate the moral and social norms traditionally believed to govern our human nature as embodied spirits.

Protestantism has long been infected with gnostic tendencies.[10] In fairness, though, we must note that so-called "low-church" Protestantism (such as "Fundamentalism") suffers from the gnostic mentality to a graver extent than so-called "high-church" Protestantism (such as Lutheranism and Anglicanism). In fact, long ago the low-church denominations basically eliminated ritual, so their worship services are reduced to praying, singing hymns, and hearing sermons preached on Biblical passages. As a consequence of their abandonment of material symbolism and rejection of the Holy Mass (an unbloody re-presentation of Christ's priestly sacrificial offering on Calvary), most of the sacraments (with the exceptions of Baptism and Matrimony) vanished from their multi-versions of Christianity. Actually, a certain relativism about matter affected even Lutheranism at its inception, as we shall see in Chapter 1.

By contrast, the Catholic Church has battled the periodic eruptions of gnostic ideology since the first century A.D. (for instance, Manicheanism in the early centuries, Albigensianism [or Catharism] during the Middle Ages, and nefarious revolutionary movements in more recent times). Of course, Catholicism does admit a sharp distinction between purely spiritual entities (God, angels, the human soul) and those composed of matter (the human body, animals, plants, minerals). Nevertheless, the Church refuses to erect a wall of separation between the spiritual and material realms. As we discussed earlier, the Church affirms a *sacramental* perspective on the physical world: material substances reflect and signify supernatural realities, some doing so in a more fitting manner than others. The Creator endowed things with definite natures to fulfill certain purposes, and so it cannot be a matter of indifference to Him what things are used as means to ends. As St. Paul succinctly put it in 1 Corinthians 15:39, *NAB*: "Not all bodily nature is the same." Matter matters! Indeed, God loves the way He has created material forms, according to Wisdom 11:24, *RSV*: "For thou lovest all things that exist and hast loathing for none of the things which thou hast made."

Thus, it is strangely ironic that the Church has been accused of being antiscientific. The opposite charge of taking the domain of biology (with its assortment of specific chemical compounds) too seriously is closer to the truth. But this charge is not completely accurate either, since matter is *not* all-encompassing, contrary to Marxist dogma. After all, the Church teaches (as classical philosophy likewise proves) that human beings are destined for existence beyond the grave wherein the body is corrupted. Yet, by divine omnipotence, the glorified body finally triumphs anyway in the resurrection from the dead at the end of time.

In particular, disputes over matter lie at the bottom of such seemingly unrelated issues as: (1) valid ingredients for the sacraments, (2) ordaining women priests, (3) homosexual unions, (4) artificial contraception, (5) artificial reproduction, (6) abortion, (7) euthanasia and/or assisted suicide, and (8) environmentalism and/or animal rights. The Church takes all of these human biological matters very seriously indeed — unlike certain groups of people (under the sway of gnosticism) who trivialize some of them.

This book concerns the first three items, which impinge directly on six of the seven sacraments: Baptism (Chapter 1), the Holy Eucharist (Chapter 2 and Chapter 3), Confirmation and the Anointing of the Sick (Chapter 4), Holy Orders (Chapter 5), and Matrimony (Chapter 6). The fourth, fifth, and sixth items listed are, of course, intimately related to married life, but they do not bear immediately on the valid matter of Matrimony as such. Since many comprehensive books are widely available on these topics (which, as everyone knows, have aroused much rancorous dissent in our time), any treatment of them in a book of this size would be inadequate. Hence, we declare them beyond the scope of our limited coverage, along with the topics of the seventh and eighth items (except for relegation to a brief mention in the Epilogue). In any case, even regarding the topics more extensively treated, this book does not pretend to be a scholarly dissertation on sacramental theology. Its focus, as its title implies, is restricted to the essential "material" features of the sacraments, and, in particular, to the matter required for validly bringing about (technically speaking, *confecting*) each sacrament.

Note that there is a big difference between *validity* and *liceity*. "Valid" means what is absolutely and intrinsically necessary for accomplishing a sacramental rite. "Licit" means what is permitted or lawful — something that can be relative, depending on circumstances. Liceity entails validity, but not conversely: a sacrament may be validly confected by including some feature that is prohibited for other reasons or by omitting some component that is required for other purposes. For instance, leavened wheat bread in the Latin Eucharistic rite is valid though illicit matter, since only unleavened wheat bread is traditionally allowed in the Western liturgy. For another example, flowing water alone is the valid matter for Baptism, but it is ordinarily illicit to neglect a subsequent anointing with chrism oil in the full baptismal ceremony.

Furthermore, the Sacrament of Penance (or Reconciliation) is not discussed at all in this book, because the "matter" involved there is sin,[11] which (as moral evil) is not a physical substance. Indeed, as the towering genius St. Augustine has taught us, all evil (whether physical or moral) is devoid of any positive reality; instead, it is a parasitic disorder affecting with distortion and damage something (whether body or spirit) that in itself is good. Technically speaking, evil is a *privation* of good: a lack of some perfection that ought to be present.[12]

Some remarks about our procedure in this book are called for. As its subtitle indicates, we intend to use both philosophy and theology. What's the distinction between these two fields of learning? The name "philosophy" is derived from two Greek roots, which, taken together, literally mean "love of wisdom." As an area of study, philosophy is the discipline that pursues answers to the big questions of existence (concerning God and human life) via natural reason reflecting on the common observations of mankind about ourselves and the world around us. (For example, humanity, with its immemorial awareness of such notions as "moral goodness," our "desire for immortality," and the evident "design in the universe," is driven to seek deeper insights into their implications.) By contrast, theology is the science that investigates the truth of things via meditation on divine revelation accepted in the light of supernatural faith. Although philosophy and theology share a large tract of overlap in their concerns and have the same aim (to arrive at ultimate truth), their methods differ. In short, philosophy takes a "bottom-up" approach to reality, whereas theology takes a "top-down" approach.

This author is neither professional theologian nor Scripture scholar. Hence, this book was conceived and written from a philosophical viewpoint: that is to say, from the standpoint of someone who originally wondered why the properties of certain material substances make them more pertinent for symbolizing spiritual realities than the properties of other physical things. *Wonder* is the fundamental attitude from which all philosophical inquiry begins, according to both Plato and Aristotle.[13]

Let us at the outset make the disclaimer, however, that un-aided human reason cannot strictly prove the necessity of certain materials, while excluding others, for validly enacting (or confecting) the sacraments. We depend ultimately on positive divine revelation (as traditionally interpreted by the Church's Magisterium) for definitive resolutions to whatever difficulties may arise. The *Code of Canon Law*, Can. 841, states: "Since the sacraments are the same throughout the universal Church, and belong to the divine deposit of faith, only the supreme authority in the Church can approve or define what is needed for their validity." Similarly, the *CCC*, n. 1125, warns: "No sacramental rite may be modified or manipulated at the will of the minister or the community."[14]

Yet, on the other hand, logical arguments from *suitability*, springing both from human experience with the physical world (our knowledge of the properties of material substances) and from Sacred Scripture (which Christians accept on faith as the revealed word of God), can be articulated. (Incidentally, some synonyms for "suitable" that we will regularly employ are "apt," "appropriate," "fitting," and "conducive.") To borrow a metaphor from the opening line of Pope John Paul II's encyclical *Fides et Ratio*, the conjoined efforts of reason and faith furnish us with the wings to soar to the truth. Here we obey the injunction of the first pope, who told us always to be ready with a courteous response to anyone who asks us for *reasons* why we hope or believe (see 1 Peter 3:15-16). We also follow the model of St. Augustine, who boldly proclaimed, "I believe in order that I might understand." And we further recall the proverbial motto of St. Anselm (another outstanding medieval philosopher-theologian): "Faith seeking to understand." The reader should appreciate that we have already been judiciously commingling the water of philosophy with the wine of theology.

Lastly, some critical information about Biblical interpretation should be brought to the reader's attention. St. Thomas Aquinas explains that the meaning (or *sense*) of Scripture can be reckoned on two levels: the *literal sense* and the *spiritual sense*. The literal sense is the surface meaning of the text conveyed by the words themselves. The spiritual sense is a deeper (often hidden) meaning, in which the actual persons, things, or events mentioned (called *types*) in turn signify *other* things or events. (Again we meet with symbolism!) Now, since representations can permit historical realizations in multiple ways, there may be many valid spiritual interpretations of a single Scriptural verse. They are not arbitrary, though, because they are all based on the literal narrative; furthermore, any solidly orthodox spiritual interpretation is always taught literally somewhere else in the Bible. A typical instance of the spiritual sense is the *allegorical*, wherein some person, thing, or event in the Old Testament prefigures or foreshadows a corresponding fulfillment in the New Testament.[15]

This book contains numerous Scriptural references. Although many quotations are provided in full (with the source translation designated by *RSV*, *NAB*, or *D-R*, or no designation if all three versions apply), in the interest of an economical presentation not all allusions are cited with their corresponding text. Hence, although it is certainly not necessary for comprehension of the book, if the reader wishes to derive the maximum benefit from it, the author advises a companion Bible ready at hand to look up some of the verses mentioned but not quoted. In this way the material in the book can serve more adequately as a springboard for meditative spiritual reading, as well as a work on apologetics. Likewise, it is unnecessary to pay much heed to the endnotes (unless overcome by intense curiosity); for the most part, they supply either source documentation or additional references (occasionally some greater elaboration for the more demanding reader's edification).

In sum, through a careful interweaving blend of philosophy and Biblical theology, this book will attempt to explain why certain materials are eminently suited for the various sacraments, while other forms of matter are not fitting. Consequently, we will repeatedly return to the recurring theme of appropriate symbolism, by means of which God communicates to our minds and hearts subtle intimations of lofty truths that cannot be fully expressed within the natural limits of human concepts.[16] The goal is to demonstrate that matter really matters and that the deadly lure of gnostic rationalization must therefore be resisted.

chapter one

WHY WATER?

Before doing anything else, we should first define what the term "baptism" means. The linguistic derivation (or *etymology*) of "baptize" is Greek for "plunge" or "immerse." According to the *CCC*, n. 1214, the submersion in the Sacrament of Baptism signifies "burial into Christ's death," followed by rising with His resurrection. We recall that the sacraments all employ material things as instruments for producing grace in the soul of the recipient, bringing about the very state of affairs that they signify. The rite of Baptism symbolizes and truly brings about the erasure of sin (particularly Original Sin inherited from Adam), elevating the soul to a participation in God's life through "configuration" with Christ in the suffering of His passion and the triumph of His resurrection (see the *CCC*, n. 1239). According to the *Code of Canon Law*, Can. 849, "Baptism, gateway to the sacraments, is necessary for salvation, either by actual reception or at least by desire. By it people are freed from sins, are born again as children of God and, made like to Christ by an indelible character, are incorporated into the Church."

Valid Matter

What is the correct material substance with which Baptism can be performed? The *Code of Canon Law*, Can. 849, informs us: "It is validly conferred only by a washing in real water with the proper form of words." It is a doctrine of the Catholic Faith that only "true and natural water" may be used for Baptism.[1] This dogma is based on our Savior's own pronouncement on the matter in John 3:5, *RSV*: "Truly, truly, I say to you, unless one is born of water and the Spirit, he cannot enter the kingdom of God." The footnote commentary accompanying this verse in the *New American Bible* (which, by the way, renders "born" as "begotten") stresses that, according to the

Council of Trent, Christ's wording signifies literal and not figurative water.[2]

But why should water alone be required? Isn't this prescription unnecessarily stringent? Why should it matter which liquid is used to represent the cleansing action of Baptism? Although it may be admitted that certain liquids (e.g., cocoa syrup or molasses) are symbolically unfitting due to their adherent viscosity and opaqueness, someone may object that other fluids having a more powerful dissolving and penetrating effect than pure water (say, laundry detergent or DMSO) would be even more conducive to Baptism. The more death to dirt the better!

The problem is that the fluid employed in Baptism must signify, not only a washing to efface sin, but also a rebirth. Now it is generally uncontested that only plain water can be used for Baptism, because more than any other liquid it is apt for playing the role of symbolizing the dual wholesome effects produced in the soul: both cleansing from sin and regeneration unto new spiritual life. However sanitizing they may be (e.g., the alcohol of medical antisepsis), some fluids lacking the essential character of pure water do not comport with the theme of revitalization. Conversely, other liquids, though internally invigorating (for instance, vegetable juices), do not gently wash the surface clean.

From a natural point of view, mankind has always appreciated that water is a double-edged sword (so to speak). On one hand, when imposed in sufficiently large quantity, it purifies and nurtures both vegetation and animals. On the other hand, when released in excessive quantity, it floods land, devastating crops and killing animals. Too much aquatic purification entails death by drowning. Hence, water both sustains and ruins life.

The paradoxical nature of water undoubtedly led the ancient Greek sage Thales, the first philosopher in recorded history, to posit water as the ultimate substrate of all things. He must have observed that the physical world displays cycles of degeneration and restoration, that (on the global scale) material forms are susceptible to decay and renewal. Water, which both erodes and nourishes, appears an ideal candidate for explaining the inner dynamics of natural processes — their constant ebb and flow.

Heraclitus, another ancient Greek philosopher, probably reasoned in a similar manner to conclude that fire is at the heart of cosmic change. Like water, it can account for cyclical destruction and renovation due to its volatile character of complementary antagonism. Fire provides the light and warmth to succor life, but beyond a certain range of intensity its heat devours — yet even this result can sometimes be conducive to a beneficial purgation. It seems that both Thales and Heraclitus, had they known about Judaeo-Christian revelation, would have felt at home in the Easter Vigil liturgy (with its dialectic revolving around light and water). But perhaps this is true because the liturgy involves symbols that resonate with universal human experience.

Modern biology informs us that all living tissues are actually composed primarily of water (to a remarkably high percentage of their overall content). By contrast with other beverages and foods, water is the sole alimentary substance without which the human body cannot survive for more than a very brief period. Even those who think they consume enough liquid are actually dehydrated, we are told. Thus, nutritionists and other medical professionals insist on the importance of drinking several glasses of pure water each day. Thales, therefore, came close to the truth. Indeed, water has been called a "miraculous" substance — one with an astounding array of peculiar properties that we take for granted because of their familiarity. For example, unlike other chemicals, it expands when it freezes as well as when it vaporizes. It is strongly solvent, yet emollient (mild even for sensitive skin). Naturopathic physicians recommend the prophylactic benefits of external hydrotherapy for revitalizing the entire system; they especially laud the detoxifying effects of treatments that employ alternating hot and cold water baths or showers of various kinds and durations, which are reported to alleviate organic congestion by enhancing circulation.[3]

Given all that mankind has discovered about water on the natural level, who could possibly quarrel with its uniquely irreplaceable service in the Sacrament of Baptism? Well, it seems that there is always someone who will challenge a principle — no matter how clear and firmly established it may appear. As a matter of fact, Martin Luther did dissent. He "held that any fluid suitable for ablution was permissible in case of emergency." But the Council of Trent condemned this radical thesis of exception.[4] Presumably Luther would have deemed liquid hand soap, for instance, theoretically legitimate for Baptism in special circumstances.

In actual practice, in cases of grave necessity, the Church does tolerate a mitigated dispensation from plain water for administering Baptism. Among the gradations along a spectrum of purity, how "watery" must the water be? The Church never mandates chemical analysis; rather, she is satisfied with "the estimation of ordinary people." As a guide for making this determination, it is certain that the following sources of water comprise valid matter: rain, spring, well, drain, dew (from plants or walls, etc.), melted snow or hail or ice, recondensed steam, distilled (provided only foreign elements, not constituting water as such, are subtracted), sea or mineral or sulphur water, and even muddied or otherwise adulterated water (provided the water very greatly predominates over the contaminants). The following fluids are certainly invalid matter: tears, saliva, foam, amniotic fluid, blood, milk, fruit juices, wine, beer, oil, thick broth. The following liquids are doubtfully valid matter: water from dissolved salt, water extracted from vegetation (e.g., flower petals), sap from trees or vines, thin soup, tea, coffee, weak beer. Although matter that is certainly invalid can never be used for Baptism, in cases of dire extremity (i.e., danger of death) doubtfully valid matter may be employed if regular water is inaccessible. Such a baptism, however, can be performed only conditionally, and would have to be repeated later (conditionally) when ordinary water becomes available (assuming the recipient has survived). It is always best to strive to obtain pure water.[5]

Luther probably had a more cavalier or nonchalant attitude toward water than the Catholics at the Council of Trent on account of his theory of justification. According to him, the sacraments of Baptism and Penance do not really produce an interior change in the soul. They are merely occasions for God to declare the sinner righteous — an external (or "legal") imputation of justice only, demanding simply a subjective (or "fiducial") trusting faith in Christ as Savior. In actuality (i.e., "ontologically") the soul remains mired in its unregenerate state of corruption; God just covers over the fetid swamp of sin with a white celestial canvas and some heavy supernatural deodorant (as it were). By contrast, the orthodox Catholic position is that sanctifying grace works a profound transformation within the soul, elevating it to a divinized condition consequent upon the genuine removal of sin's stain.[6]

Since Baptism does not really wipe sin clean from the soul according to Luther, logically he would not think it crucial that only plain water be used in the sacramental rite. Any liquid similar to pure water in its lavatory effects would adequately signify the supposedly superficial divine action on the soul. The lesson is that a carefree notion about the operation of salvation means a lackadaisical attitude toward the matter of the sacraments. In short, a slovenly *soteriology* makes for a sloppy *sacramentology*.

Thus, at the very inception of Lutheranism we witness evidence of a certain indifferentism to the integrity of material nature. This distorted spiritualist (or gnostic) perspective influenced the later development of Protestantism. In particular, many (if not most or all) Protestant denominations are flexible about the matter of at least some of their sacraments beyond Baptism — contrary to the more rigorous Catholic doctrine (as we shall see in each subsequent chapter).

Detailed Biblical Background

Therefore, in view of some controversy about the absolute necessity of water for sacramental Baptism, it behooves us to pass from a discussion of its natural features to Biblical accounts of its significance for salvation history. These Scriptural texts will render even more cogent why water alone can serve the requisite symbolic function in Baptism. We will first undertake a whirlwind tour of

the Easter Vigil readings. Pursuing the progression of these narratives, we will witness the constant imagery of water as a *type* of
Baptism. The Easter Vigil liturgy is an annual drama noteworthy
for its interplay of the themes of light and water, representing
Christ's victory over sin and death to be shared by the catechumens when they undergo the burial of Baptism (as St. Paul preaches
in Romans 6:3-5). The lit Paschal candle stands for the transforming light of Christ that has overcome the darkness of evil (see the
CCC, n. 1243), whereas water is a medium of submergence that
signifies purification and renewal (with connotations of chaotic
primeval forces). Moreover, one author depicts the Easter Vigil
spectacle partly in terms of a wedding or fertility rite involving the
male principle symbolized by a lit candle and a female principle
symbolized by a bowl of water. The spiritual interpretation seems
to be the mystical marriage of God to the soul by the indwelling of
the Trinity in Baptism — a union that ought to be fruitful.[7]

Creation, Flood, and Exodus

In the beginning after God created the world, when the earth was
still in darkness, "the Spirit of God was moving over the face of the
waters" (Genesis 1:2, *RSV*). A correlative verse elsewhere (Psalm 29:3,
RSV) declares in part: "The voice of the LORD is upon the waters; /
. . . the LORD, upon many waters." The "waters" in these verses can be
interpreted spiritually as the baptismal water over which the Holy
Spirit hovers, ready to sanctify the soul in the abysmal disorder of sin,
through the sacramental rite (see the *CCC*, n. 1218). Note that the
Psalms frequently use the image of water to symbolize submergence
in affliction and the threat of loss or death. (For example, in the *NAB*
edition see Psalm 18:5; Psalm 42:8; Psalm 69:2-3, 15-16; Psalm 88:8,
18; Psalm 124:4-5; also Jonah 2:4, 6.) Paradoxically, the water of Baptism represents both the lethal misery of sin and its drastic remedy: a
"trampling on death by death," as the Byzantine liturgy sings in its
Easter exultation about Christ's triumph over the tomb.

Later (as we learn from Genesis 6:5-22; 7:1-24; 8:1-19 and 2
Peter 2:5; 3:6), the Great Deluge inundated and swept away a world

that had sunk to the depths of depravity. The emergence of an earth purified by water, and once again at peace with God (Genesis 8:20-22; 9:8-17), symbolizes the soul cleansed of sin and made a friend of God (see Wisdom 7:27; John 15:13-15) by the Holy Spirit's powerful action through the instrumentality of water (see the *CCC*, n. 1219). As St. Peter instructs us in 1 Peter 3:19-21, *RSV*: "[Christ] went and preached to the spirits in prison, who formerly did not obey, when God's patience waited in the days of Noah, during the building of the ark, in which a few, that is, eight persons, were saved through water. Baptism, which corresponds to this, now saves you, not as a removal of dirt from the body but as an appeal to God for a clear conscience, through the resurrection of Jesus Christ."

Furthermore, the ark (constructed of wood) is laden with spiritual significance. Indeed, we read in Wisdom 10:4, *RSV*: "When the earth was flooded . . . , wisdom again saved it, / steering the righteous man [Noah] by a paltry piece of wood." The ark can thus be construed as a *type* of the humble wooden cross that accompanied Christ on His redemptive mission to make us righteous before God, saving us from drowning in sin. Referring to His baptism of bloody death through the cross, Christ exclaimed in Luke 12:50, *RSV*: "I have a baptism to be baptized with; and how I am constrained until it is accomplished!" The cross was heavy because we, with all our sins, were carried on it (see Isaiah 53:4-6; Romans 5:6-11; 6:6; 1 Corinthians 15:3; 2 Corinthians 5:15; Colossians 1:20, 22; 2:14; 1 Timothy 1:15; 2:6; 1 Peter 2:24).

Next (as we read in Exodus 13:21-22; 14:15-31; 15:1-21; also Psalm 66:6), God used Moses and Aaron to release the captive Israelites from slavery in Egypt. The marvelous escape of the chosen people through the yielding waters of the divided Red Sea prefigures the deliverance of the soul from bondage to sin through the baptismal water that parts when poured over the forehead (see the *CCC*, n. 1221). St. Paul comments in 1 Corinthians 10:1-2, *RSV*, with an implied analogy to the New Testament: "Our fathers were all under the cloud, and all passed through the sea, and all were baptized into Moses in the cloud and in the sea."

Moreover, immediately after crossing the Red Sea into desert land, the Israelites could find no potable water. God then told Moses to throw "a tree" into some bitter water, causing it to become "sweet" for the thirsty people to drink (see Exodus 15:22-25, *RSV*). This relatively minor incident is fraught with spiritual meaning. For baptismal water receives its efficacy to vitalize the soul only through the merits of Christ, who suffered death on "a tree" (i.e., the wooden cross), thereby rescuing us from the bitterness of sin and clearing the way to the sweet bliss of everlasting life.[8]

The Significance of the Jordan River

Still later, God appointed Joshua to lead the Israelites into the Promised Land after years of punishing delay: aimless wandering in the desert. At the command of the Lord, Joshua ordered the priests carrying the ark of the covenant to wade into the Jordan River, whereupon its flow ceased long enough for the people to cross on dry ground (see Joshua 3:7-17; 4:1-24). This event is a *type* foreshadowing the baptism of Christ in the Jordan River by St. John the Baptist (see Matthew 3:13-17 and Mark 1:9-11). Indeed, Jesus is the new Joshua, the eternal high priest bearing in Himself the Ark of the New Covenant (see Hebrews 4:14-15; 5:1-10; 7:11-28; 8:1-13; 9:11-28), whose advent enables mankind to pass unharmed from bewildered pining in a wilderness of error and sin to a state of heavenly knowledge and hope (see the *CCC*, n. 1222). An Advent hymn and a Christmas carol pensively express the contrast between the state of the human race (in general, outside Judaism) before and after the coming of Christ. A line from *O Holy Night*: "Long lay the world in sin and error pining, 'till He appeared and the soul felt its worth." A line from *O Come, Emmanuel*: "To us the paths of knowledge show, and teach us in her ways to go." Perhaps we witness here a fulfillment of what the prophet foretold in Isaiah 43:19-20, *RSV*: "Behold, I am doing a new thing; / now it springs forth, do you not perceive it? / I will make a way in the wilderness and rivers in the desert...; / for I give water in the wilderness, rivers in the desert." Compare Isaiah

35:6-7, *RSV*: "For waters shall break forth in the wilderness, / and streams in the desert; / the burning sand shall become a pool, / and the thirsty ground springs of water." See also Jeremiah 31:9, *RSV*: "I will make them walk by brooks of water, / in a straight path in which they shall not stumble."

Now Jesus did not need to be baptized unto repentance; it would be both blasphemous and logically fallacious to make such an assertion, since He Himself is the source of all grace. Rather, as St. Thomas Aquinas writes, quoting St. Ambrose, "Our Lord was baptized because He wished, not to be cleansed, but to cleanse the waters, that, being purified by the flesh of Christ that knew no sin, they might have the virtue [power] of baptism." Next, quoting St. John Chrysostom, "that He might bequeath the sanctified waters to those who were to be baptized afterwards." And quoting St. Gregory Nazianzen, "Christ was baptized that He might plunge the old Adam entirely into the water."[9]

But why should the Jordan River have been the site of Christ's baptism? Aquinas explains that, just as the Israelites entered the Promised Land through the Jordan River, so the Sacrament of Baptism instituted by Christ would bring admittance into the kingdom of God.[10] St. Thomas also alludes to the incident when the prophet Elijah, in the company of the prophet Elisha, divided the Jordan River by striking the water with his rolled-up cloak (see 2 Kings 2:8), after which he was taken up into the heavens on a flaming chariot-with-horses borne aloft in a whirlwind (see 2 Kings 2:9-14 and Sirach 48:9, 12). According to Aquinas, this episode signifies that the road to heaven is opened by the "fire" of the Holy Spirit, who sanctifies the waters of Baptism due to Christ's redemptive merits.

Along these lines, recalling that John 3:5 mandates rebirth through both water and the Holy Spirit, we note that in John 1:26-34 the Baptist contrasts his own water baptism with Christ's Baptism in the power of the Holy Spirit. Regarding the "fire" of the Holy Spirit and its connection with Baptism, we hear John's prophetic utterance (in Matthew 3:11 and Luke 3:16, *RSV*): "He will

baptize you with the Holy Spirit and with fire." A visible fulfillment of the Baptist's promise occurs, of course, in Acts 2:3, which
records the Pentecostal descent of the Holy Spirit upon the Apostles
in the form of tongues of fire. Christ expresses His desire that the
Spirit's ardent charity (which entails zeal for truth) be enkindled
in the hearts of all people: "I came to cast fire upon the earth; and
would that it were already kindled! I have a baptism to be baptized
with; and how I am constrained until it is accomplished!" (Luke
12:49-50, *RSV*). Obviously, Christ alludes in verse 50, not to His
water baptism by John in the Jordan, but rather His baptism of
bloody death.[11]

It is paradoxical that the Holy Spirit, symbolized by fire, should
first operate on the soul through the medium of water. The dialectic of fire (candlelight) and water permeating the Easter Vigil evokes
memory of the ancient philosophical controversy between Thales
and Heraclitus over the relative priority of these cosmic elements.
Perhaps their conjunction in Baptism signifies that the thirst for
saving faith of the soul lost in the desert of sin and disbelief must
first be slaked with confessional or creedal truth before it can tolerate the fervor of charity. At this point, St. Paul enjoins us in 1
Thessalonians 5:19, *RSV*: "Do not quench the Spirit." That is, once
you have been inundated with the cleansing and cooling water of
Baptism, do not fear the incendiary action of the Holy Spirit on
your heart.

Let us linger a bit longer at the Jordan River, pondering its
meaning with the Angelic Doctor. Aquinas elaborates on the symbolic distinction between the crossing of the Red Sea and the crossing of the Jordan River. The first foreshadowed Baptism by
representing purification from sin, whereas the second prefigured
Baptism by representing the opening of the gates to heaven. Since
the second of these events signifies the chief (more important) effect of Baptism, whose sole cause is Christ (without the aid of ministers), it was more appropriate that He be baptized in the Jordan
River than the Red Sea.[12] Indeed, the sky opened at Christ's baptism to indicate the second meaning.[13] Nevertheless, it is interest-

ing to observe that Naaman was cured of leprosy by plunging seven times into the Jordan (see 2 Kings 5:9-14). How can we not view this episode through spiritual lenses as a prefigurement of Baptism's cleansing from the disease of sin?

Harking back to the beginning lines of Genesis, we witness the Holy Spirit once again descending and "hovering" over the waters — this time the waters of the Jordan at Christ's baptism, when the skies were rolled back to reveal the Spirit in the visible form of a dove (see Matthew 3:16; Mark 1:10; Luke 3:21-22; John 1:32-33). Interestingly, a dove played a key role in the Great Deluge narrative, informing Noah of the completion of the earth's cleansing, with the restoration of harmony on earth symbolized by an olive leaf in the dove's beak (see Genesis 8:8-12). Perhaps a reconciliation between God and humanity is likewise being heralded at the Jordan River. Furthermore, Christ tacitly equated His might with the power of the Holy Spirit. Indeed, He "moved" or "hovered" over the waters in His humanity by walking on top of the sea (see Matthew 14:22-33; Mark 6:45-52; John 6:16-21). Moreover, He reprimanded a storm (recall Psalm 29:3, *RSV* [28:3 in *D-R*]: "The voice of the LORD is upon the waters"), subduing tumultuous seas (see Matthew 8:23-27; Mark 4:35-41; Luke 8:22-25). Jesus thereby showed how His power renders the wild turbulence of water a tame and healing sacramental channel: "He gathered the waters of the sea as in a bottle; / he put the deeps in storehouses" (Psalm 33:7, *RSV*). These Gospel displays of divine power imply an assimilation of Christ and the Holy Spirit, as it is written in Song of Solomon 5:12, *RSV*: "His eyes are like doves / beside springs of water."

In sum, all these "Easter Vigil" readings and their ramifications prove that only water can suitably serve as the valid matter for Baptism.

Water: Symbol of Life-Giving Grace

According to 1 Corinthians 12:13, *RSV*, "we were all baptized into one body [i.e., the Church]" through "one Spirit," of which "all were made to drink." The *CCC*, n. 694, asserts that "the Spirit is also personally the living water welling up from Christ crucified as its source and welling up in us to eternal life." Indeed, many Scriptural passages state or imply that Christ Himself is the source of the saving "water" of unending life — "water" symbolizing the sanctifying grace of the Holy Spirit. For example, He tells the Samaritan woman at the Shechem well that He provides "water" springing up like a fountain unto everlasting life. (See John 4:10-15, and compare with Psalm 36:10; Isaiah 12:3; Revelation 7:17, 21:6.) Furthermore, He explicitly proclaims in John 7:37-38, *RSV*: "If any one thirst, let him come to me and drink. He who believes in me, as the scripture has said, 'Out of his heart shall flow rivers of living water.'" This echoes Isaiah 55:1, *RSV*, which invites "every one who thirsts" to "come to the waters." In fact, Isaiah 55:10-11, *RSV*, prophetically compares Christ, the "word" sent from God, with "rain . . . come down from heaven" to "water the earth" for the sake of "giving . . . bread." And Joel 2:23, *NAB*, further identifies this "rain" with "the teacher of justice," who is, of course, our Redeemer. (See also Jeremiah 2:13, *RSV*, wherein God refers to "me, the fountain of living waters.") To graphically illustrate this truth, Jesus literally allowed water to pour forth from His pierced side, as depicted in John 19:34 and alluded to in Ephesians 5:25-26. As it is written in Zechariah 14:8, *RSV*: "On that day living waters shall flow out from Jerusalem."

A foreshadowing of Christ as the source of living water occurred in the episode when the Israelites complained to Moses about the absence of water in the desert. Obeying God, Moses struck with his staff a rock from which gushed plentiful water. (See Exodus 17:1-7 and Numbers 20:2-11, along with Psalms 78:15-16, 20; 114:8.) According to St. Paul, in a spiritual sense "the Rock was Christ." (See 1 Corinthians 10:1-2, 4, along with Psalms 18:2, 31, 46; 62:7; 92:15, *RSV*.) Paul could confidently propose this interpretation, because Christ founded His Church on Peter, whom He designated the "Rock" — responsible for holding the primary jurisdiction of the sacraments, which are subsumed under "the keys of the kingdom of heaven" (Matthew 16:19, *RSV*). Now if the visible head of the Church on earth (i.e., the Vicar of Christ, or the pope) is the "Rock" entrusted with the authoritative dispensation of the sacraments, then *a fortiori* the Founder Himself is the pre-eminent "Rock." Since "water" flows from this "Rock" as the symbol of everlasting life and since Baptism is the sacrament of initiation into this life, we infer that the only valid matter conducive to Baptism is plain water.

Another important aquarian metaphor is contained in parallel visions from the Old and New Testaments. In Ezekiel 47:1-12, *RSV*, the prophet beheld "water . . . issuing from below the threshold of the temple." The pellucid stream grew to such depths that it had the power to freshen even the sea and to support bountiful living creatures. This flow from the sanctuary watered trees that grew along the banks of the river, perpetually ("every month") causing them to bear "fruit for food" and sprout "leaves for healing." In a transparent recapitulation and explication of this visual prophetic theme, St. John the Evangelist was shown "the river of life-giving water, clear as crystal, which issued from the throne of God and of the Lamb" (Revelation 22:1, *NAB*). He also saw along the riverbanks "the trees of life which produce fruit twelve times a year, once each month" and whose "leaves serve as medicine for the nations" (Revelation 22:2, *NAB*). St. John's mystical scene makes perfectly clear that this "life-giving water" represents sanctifying grace bestowed by the Holy Spirit (see the *CCC*, n. 1137), who proceeds from the Father and the Son. The riverbanks perhaps symbolize the solidity of the Church, which unfailingly channels grace to us. We infer from Revelation 21:12, 14 that the number "twelve" signifies the Apostles, whose successors down through the centuries preserve and continually administer the sacraments ("the trees of life") for the healing benefit of wounded humanity. Since Baptism is chronologically the first sacrament to be received, and in a way flows into the other sacraments, it is fitting that water (preferably "crystal clear") be the only valid matter for its ritual enactment.

We behold a similar picture in Isaiah 44:3-4, *RSV*: "I will pour water on the thirsty land, / and streams on the dry ground; / I will pour my Spirit upon your descendants, / and my blessing on your offspring. / They shall spring up like grass amid waters, / like willows by flowing streams." Another foreshadowing of Baptism appears in Ezekiel 36:25, 27, *RSV*: "I will sprinkle clean water upon you, and you shall be clean from all your uncleannesses" and "I will put my spirit within you."

No references to the conferral of Baptism by the early Church ever mention any physical substance other than plain water. (We take it that Acts 8:36-39 and 10:47 narrate typical accounts, with due allowances made for changes in particular circumstances.) Hence, it would be brazen and rash to suggest that another liquid resembling water in certain features could function as valid matter for this sacrament; in fact, such an error would be heretical. In God's sacramental plan for mankind, the symbolism of natural water is so crucial for signifying what Baptism works in the soul that any other fluid would fail to bring about its salutary effects in our minds and hearts. To transport a verse from the Epistles into this context, "Let . . . our hearts [be] sprinkled clean . . . and our bodies washed with pure water" (Hebrews 10:22, *RSV*). May no renegade priests or deacons ever substitute their judgment for the Church's by attempting to administer (or "celebrate," as they now say) Baptism with champagne!

This concludes our reflections on Baptism and water. Our thirst (but not the Spirit) quenched, we hunger for bread.

chapter two

WHY WHEAT BREAD?

The Holy Eucharist is called the "Blessed Sacrament," on account of its supremacy among the sacraments; it is the "Sacrament of sacraments." Although, unlike Baptism, it is not strictly necessary for salvation, nevertheless it surpasses Baptism and the other sacraments in its sublime excellence. All the sacraments confer grace, but only the Blessed Sacrament contains our Lord Jesus Christ Himself — the very Author of grace. In this exalted sacrament, He is truly present in His entirety (Body, Blood, Soul, and Divinity), veiled under the appearances of physical things. (See the *CCC*, nn. 1324-1332, 1374.)

Valid Matter

Which physical things? The *CCC*, n. 1412, teaches that one of the "essential signs of the Eucharistic sacrament" is "wheat bread." The *Code of Canon Law*, Can. 924, mandates: "The most holy Sacrifice of the Eucharist must be celebrated in bread. . . . The bread must be wheaten only, and recently made, so that there is no danger of corruption." The *Instruction Concerning Worship of the Eucharistic Mystery* elaborates: "The bread for the celebration of the Eucharist, in accordance with the tradition of the whole Church, must be made solely of wheat, and, in accordance with the tradition proper to the Latin Church, it must be unleavened."[1] Thus, it is a definitive doctrine of the Church (which must be held on faith by all who wish to remain loyal Catholics) that only bread made of pure wheat flour can be used as valid matter for conversion into the Body of Christ.[2] This complete change of substance (called *transubstantiation*), in which only the appearances of bread remain,[3] occurs at the Consecration of the Mass, when the priest, acting in the person and at the command of Christ, pronounces the words spoken by Christ at the Last Supper: "This is my body." (See Matthew 26:26; Mark 14:22; Luke 22:15-16, 19; 1 Corinthians 11:23-24; also the *CCC*, nn. 1337-1342, 1375-1377.)

It is a difficult enterprise to discern why only wheat bread may serve as the material substance willed by Christ for transubstantiation into His sacred Body. In the final analysis the answer must remain mysterious to us during this life, since we have no direct insight into the unfathomable divine mind nor can we boast exhaustive comprehension of the properties of physical things. Our mental poverty having been confessed, however, it does not follow that God has abandoned us like intellectual "orphans" so that we are left without reasonable clues in the matter. (Such "orphaning" would violate Christ's promise in John 14:16-18, *D-R.*) Here is where the importance of sacramental symbolism enters. We must explore the significance of both *bread* and *wheat*.

Why Bread?

In the first place, why *bread?* This is the easier of the two questions. Given that our Lord wanted us to eat His flesh under the appearances of some earthly food (John 6:27, 31-35, 48-51, 58), it was fitting that He accomplish His desire with the simplest and purest form of nourishment. After all, a line has to be drawn somewhere; otherwise, the words of consecration could be uttered over anything edible — a grossly unedifying situation. Bread baked from an unadulterated grain makes perfect sense on account of its immemorial reputation for functioning virtually universally as mankind's staple food, the stuff of life. (The Biblical significance of bread is discussed in the *CCC*, nn. 1333-1335.)

It might be objected that meat (like bread) has a hearty texture but in addition has the attribute of carnality, which would seem to be more conducive to representing Christ's flesh. Nevertheless, it would be extremely unfitting for the rapidly putrescent flesh of brute animals to serve as a sign of our Lord's untainted, immortal, and spiritualized Body (see 1 Corinthians 15:42-44). Besides, in the beginning, man was apparently vegetarian; it was only after the

Great Flood that God gave permission to eat animal flesh. (Contrast Genesis 1:29-30 with Genesis 9:3-4.) Since Christ came to restore man to original justice, it would be unsuitable for anything not consumed in a relatively primordial stage of human history to function as a symbol of Christ's pristine flesh. Thus, a *plant* food that is *substantial* (like hearty bread but unlike light fruits or even vegetables) would be more apt for signifying divinized human flesh.

In addition, the many grains that comprise a loaf of bread signify the unity of all believers in the Church with the Savior, as St. Paul says in 1 Corinthians 10:17, *RSV*: "Because there is one bread, we who are many are one body, for we all partake of the one bread."[4] Hence, wishing to be the pure and simple staff of our spiritual life, Christ chose bread as the most appropriate symbolic vehicle. Humanity, cursed in Adam to arduously till the soil and reap its yield, has been blessed in Jesus by the transformation of pain into a "pledge of future glory" (see the *CCC*, nn. 1402, 1404, 1405).

Why Wheat?

Now we address the second and far more puzzling question: why *wheat* bread? Some actual controversy over the grain used to make Eucharistic bread has erupted in certain dioceses. A very pertinent and practical reason has motivated this dispute: namely, the problem of sprue (or celiac disease). This illness consists in a severe condition of gluten intolerance, in which the ingestion of any grain containing a particular protein (alpha-gliadin) causes an allergic reaction resulting in serious intestinal damage. Many people have been perplexed when the Church's pastors refused to grant any dispensation from the traditional policy prohibiting substitution of a grain other than wheat. (For instance, rice — unlike the grains wheat, barley, oats, and rye — does not contain gluten. Another nonglutinous and hypoallergenic grain is millet.) To them it seemed arbitrary, rigid, and harsh for the Church to recommend that those afflicted with this sickness resort to the alternative of receiving Holy Communion only under the form of sacramental wine. Indeed, this counsel seems "discriminatory" and "judgmental," because in effect it denies the consecrated Host to the sufferers, depriving them of a benefit accessible to nearly everyone else.

Why should it matter, they wondered, which grains are used? Would it make any difference to Jesus what kind of altar bread is converted into the substance of His Body at the Consecration of the Mass? It is a natural human response to raise this question out of compassion in the face of misery. We must be wary, however, of succumbing to a false sense of charity by committing the gnostic error of trivializing material differences.

Just as there is a natural reason why bread should be the only food fit for conversion into the substance of Christ's Body, so also there would seem to be a practical reason why God chose only one particular grain as legitimate for Eucharistic bread. Imagine if any grain were allowed. Inevitably, questions would arise over which cereal foods are really grains, because some that are commonly perceived as grains are actually seed grasses (e.g., wild rice and buckwheat). Ecclesiastical policies would then be intrinsically and inextricably hostage to the accuracy of current botanical determinations. Moreover, developments in hybridization of true grains with other seeds or grasses would further blur distinctions and complicate matters. If the Church capitulated and proclaimed the flour from all these broad cereal groups to be licit ingredients of Eucharistic bread (assuming a well-defined classification could be relied upon), some people would predictably test the boundaries of the liberalized Canon Law and protest the exclusion of other starchy foods (for instance, potatoes or beans). An interminable debate would beset sacramental theology and its pastoral applications — far worse than now. In His infinite wisdom and compassion God has authoritatively settled the matter once and for all by selecting pure wheat as the sole grain for altar bread. (Exceptions for hard cases, such as allergies, would make a mess of things here and would wind up destroying the general principle.)

The Church's official doctrine permitting only wheat flour as valid matter for composing Eucharistic bread cannot, of course, be strictly proved by unaided human reasoning. It can, however, be somewhat logically defended on the basis of agricultural observation and even more persuasively justified on the basis of Scripture. Let us again recall that the sacraments employ material things as channels of grace, actually bringing about in reality what they signify. Furthermore, it is a plain fact that some materials are more suited than others for playing a specific symbolic role. We saw, for example, the intimate connection between water and Baptism in Chapter 1.

Why, among all grains, is wheat the most appropriate for the Holy Eucharist, in which Christ's Body is truly present under the appearances of bread? Wheat alone bears to a superlative degree both the agricultural *and* Biblical connotations of being sown, fallen, crushed, buried, and then risen after harvest into life-giving bread to be broken and shared. These are all symbols of Christ's passion, death, resurrection, and Real Presence to us in the Holy Sacrifice of the Mass. No grain other than wheat carries all these meanings to such a high peak of intensity.

Moreover, Christ instituted the sacraments containing matter in commonplace use among mankind, as ordinary (albeit highly significant) water in Baptism exemplifies.[5] St. Thomas Aquinas asserts: "Now among other breads wheaten bread is more commonly used by men"; in fact, other grains' breads are usually eaten only when wheat bread is unavailable.[6] And according to one authority on the subject, wheat "covers more of the earth's surface than any other grain crop."[7] Therefore, it seems that wheat, more than any other grain, aptly symbolizes the universality of Christ's call to partake of His Body under the form of bread (as we read in John 6:32-35, 41, 48-59).

Another relevant facet open to ordinary human observation is the shimmering beauty of a field of standing wheat shining like gold in bright sunlight. But the gleam of untarnished gold signifies the pure glory of the divine majesty[8] — an effulgence that radiates toward God's royal subjects, transforming them and their surroundings (much as the worthy reception of the Blessed Sacrament in Holy Communion transforms). For instance, in Job 22:25-26, *RSV,* we read: "If the Almighty is your gold, . . . / then you will delight yourself in the Almighty, / and lift up your face to God." It is remarkable that the first and last specific elementary mineral substance mentioned in Sacred Scripture is *gold* (see Genesis 2:11 and Revelation 21:21, prescinding from the subsequent more generic descriptors "glass" and "crystal"); thus, gold is "the Alpha and the Omega" of minerals representing God Himself (Revelation 22:13).[9] It is also important to note that the sacred vessels in which consecrated Hosts are kept (reposed in the ciborium and solemnly exposed in the monstrance) are made of gold, a precious metal that has come to be associated with the Blessed Sacrament. This fact is prefigured by Solomon's lavish adornment with gold overlaying the temple's inner sanctuary, where the ark of the covenant rested, in 1 Kings 6:19-22. Hence, wheat and the Holy Eucharist are symbolically related via the medium of gold — a fascinating point that we shall have occasion to recall more than once in the sequel. (A linguistic curiosity: the English words "wheat" and "white," corresponding to the German *weizen* and *weiss*, respectively, are derived from Middle and Old Anglo-Saxon roots meaning "to gleam.")

Detailed Biblical Background

To allay any doubt in the matter, many Scriptural passages can be cited to support the thesis that no grain except wheat is appropriate for the Holy Eucharist. Of the following texts, the first group of verses (from the four Gospels) is critical, whereas the remaining ones (mostly from the Old Testament) lend auxiliary support.

First, Jesus compares His own body with wheat, when He declares in John 12:24, *RSV*: "Truly, truly, I say to you, unless a grain of wheat falls into the earth and dies, it remains alone; but if it dies, it bears much fruit."[10] Obviously He is figuratively alluding here to His own passion, death, and resurrection, as well as the salvific fruits for mankind resulting from His redemptive self-sacrifice; nevertheless, the self-reference to wheat is explicit.

Second, He compares Peter (and implicitly the other Apostles) with wheat, when He admonishes him in Luke 22:31-32, *RSV*:

"Simon, Simon, behold, Satan demanded to have you, that he might sift you like wheat, but I have prayed for you that your faith may not fail; and when you have turned again, strengthen your brethren." These profoundly rich verses indicate a participation of the Church's hierarchy (successors of the Apostles) in our Lord's redemptive suffering, along with a share in His supreme authority to teach the Faith infallibly and to sanctify the community. In particular, therefore, the passage suggestively teaches the indefectibility of the Church's belief in the material composition (wheat bread) of the Eucharistic Sacrament, as well as in the chief formal effect of this supernatural food (the spiritual fortification of the individual and thence the community).

Next, in the parable of the wheat and the weeds (Matthew 13:24-30), which ends with the command "gather the wheat into my barn," three verses (25, 29, 30) explicitly specify wheat (instead of some other grain). Here Jesus compares to wheat His own chosen people (the "elect"), who eschatologically (at the end of time) comprise His Mystical Body. The "wheat" is the food of ultimate significance; evidently, the other herbage has no everlasting worth, as explained in Matthew 13:36-43. We remind ourselves that Psalm 1:4 calls the wicked "chaff" — the refuse or empty husks separated during the grain-threshing process (most often associated with wheat). St. John the Baptist had prophetically anticipated this analogy, announcing to the crowds the advent of one who would "clear his threshing floor and gather his wheat into the granary" but burn the "chaff" (Matthew 3:12; see also Luke 3:17, *RSV*).

Finally, in a parallel text (Mark 4:26-29), our Lord likens the growth of the Church as a whole to the gradual maturation of "ripe wheat in the ear" (Mark 4:28, *NAB*). Note that in Ephesians 1:22-23 and 5:23 St. Paul calls the Church Christ's "body," of which He is the "head."

Thus, throughout these quotations, we hear Christ provide the unifying metaphor of wheat for Himself, the Head of the body, together with the members of His Church (both clergy and laity). Indeed, due to our Savior's headship, the Church in all its parts (both individually and collectively) takes on the symbolic aspect of wheat; in a spiritual sense, according to Him, it *is* wheat. Because He mentions no other grain in this context, the symbolism conveyed is unmistakable. Since the Eucharist is preeminently the sacrament of unity,[11] we are forced to conclude that its proper matter, willed by the very Founder of the Church, is unadulterated wheat flour.

In fact, it is precisely the plentiful glutinous proteins naturally present in wheat that make wheat bread dough very viscid in consistency and thus highly cohesive — more so than barley, rye, and oats, and especially the nonglutinous rice and millet.[12] In Psalm 122:3 we find that Jerusalem, which can be mystically understood as the Church, is described as "bound firmly together" (*RSV*) "with compact unity" (*NAB*) — just like a loaf of wheat bread. Furthermore, Colossians 1:17, *RSV*, asserts that "in him all things hold together"; that is, through Christ everything agglutinates, as in wheat flour batter. Hence, wheat bread is a more fitting symbol for the spiritual coherence or oneness of the Mystical Body of Christ than bread made from other grain flours. As the *Instruction Concerning Worship of the Eucharistic Mystery* makes clear, "By reason of the sign, the matter of the Eucharistic celebration should appear as actual food. This is to be understood as linked to the consistency of the bread, and not to its form, which remains the traditional one. No other ingredients are to be added to the wheaten flour and water."[13] Thus, the wafer shape is irrelevant; what matters is the *nature* of the flour itself.

Our Lord's wheat imagery must have made a deep impression on the early Church and must have enjoyed wide circulation in serious Christian speech. As a notable example, we quote the famous metaphor of St. Ignatius of Antioch, uttered before his martyrdom at Rome in the year 107: "I am the wheat of Christ, ground by the teeth of beasts to become pure bread."[14]

These citations by themselves would fairly decisively settle (or "clinch") the matter once and for all, even if there were no other supporting Scriptural evidence. But there is actually a significant background of texts from the Old Testament making the sacramental substitution of any other grain for wheat virtually inconceivable. We devote the remainder of this chapter to expounding this thesis.

Old Testament Typology

As an important first instance, we find further corroboration in 1 Chronicles 21, which tells the story of King David's prideful distrust of God (displayed by the deed of taking a census of Israel) and his subsequent repentance for his sin. An integral part of his penance consisted in making sacrificial atonement to God on an altar of *holocausts*[15] erected on the threshing floor of Ornan the Jebusite. Speaking deferentially to King David in 1 Chronicles 21:23, *RSV*, Ornan said: "I . . . give . . . the wheat for a cereal offering." David, a fair and honest man, refused to accept Ornan's property as a gift, insisting on paying for the wheat, some wood, and the threshing floor with a large sum of gold. So an interesting connection between wheat and gold emerges here, consonant with our previous agricultural observation.

Yet much more is at stake in this narrative. Indeed, Jebus was the original site of Jerusalem, according to 1 Chronicles 11:4 and 2 Samuel 5:6. Moreover, according to 2 Chronicles 3:1, Solomon constructed the Jerusalem temple on Mount Moriah, covering (as David instructed) the very spot where Ornan's threshing floor stood. But, according to Genesis 22:2, it was on Mount Moriah where Abraham intended to immolate his son Isaac, atop a pile of wood that had been carried by Isaac himself (see Genesis 22:3, 6, 7, 9). We thus witness an astonishing analogy of proportionality: just as Abraham spiritually sacrificed *his* son Isaac on a stack of wood out of obedience to God, so did David mystically offer up Jesus Christ (*his* Son, according to Matthew 1:1) in the form of threshed (or beaten) wheat on a wood-laden altar as atonement for sin. And both sacrifices took place at Jerusalem, where our Lord actually delivered up the temple of His own bruised flesh as unblemished victim on the altar of the wooden cross in expiation for our sins.

This tale and its ramifications are marvelously replete with the symbolism of *types* and *allegory*. In particular, the wood procured by both Abraham and David is a *type* of Christ's cross, and the threshed wheat is a *type* representing our Lord's crushed Body. (Of course, Isaac is also a *type* of Jesus, as the author suggests in Hebrews 11:17-19.) Furthermore, David's holocaust oblation is an *allegory* foreshadowing the sacrifice of Calvary. Once again (discovered this time by an intricate chain of reasoning[16]), Christ's Body is compared with wheat, mystically valued as costly gold — confirming the association mentioned earlier between the Eucharist and that precious metal. In light of this historical typology, it is extremely unlikely that Christ would have used any bread other than wheat for the institution of the Holy Eucharist at the Last Supper.

Incidentally, another episode in which the themes of atonement, gold, and wheat were interwoven had occurred previously in 1 Samuel 4-6. We learn that the Philistines, punished with plagues by the Almighty for capturing the ark of the covenant, determined to appease God's wrath (and thereby end their misery) by returning the gilded ark to Israel on a cow-driven cart along with a box containing a guilt offering of golden items. The two milch cows (no doubt under divine guidance) headed directly for the Israelite settlement Bethshemesh, where the inhabitants "were reaping their wheat harvest in the valley" (1 Samuel 6:13, *RSV*). Overjoyed at the arrival of the ark, the people through their Levite priests used the wagon-wood to offer holocausts at a large stone, on which the priests also put the golden tokens. We shall give an elaborate exegesis of this text in a later (and more appropriate) section, exhibiting its profound symbolism.

Why Not Barley?

The only other viable contender in the Bible for the grain constituting Eucharistic bread would be barley. It is crucial to rule out barley flour as valid matter for confecting the Blessed Sacrament, because someone might object that the multiplication of loaves prior to the Passover feast in John 6:1-13 (a miracle immediately preceding Christ's Bread-of-Life discourse and which itself prefigures the Eucharist) was accomplished using barley. Although barley has already been tacitly eliminated via the above citations, a more explicit exclusion rests on the fact that the unleavened bread eaten by the Israelites at the original Passover meal,[17] anticipating the Last Supper and Good Friday, was quite probably not composed of barley. Indeed, barley had been destroyed during two earlier Egyptian plagues: by hail when nearly ripe for harvest and then by locusts in all storage bins (see Exodus 9:22-25; 10:4-6, 12-15). In particular, we read in Exodus 9:31-32, *RSV*: "The flax and the barley were ruined, for the barley was in the ear and the flax was in bud. But the wheat and the spelt were not ruined, for they are late in coming up." At any rate, there is a prophetic overtone here, since the adverb "late" carries the deep significance of the division between the Old and New Covenants: barley, the grain of the Old (unto earthly nourishment); and wheat, the grain of the New (unto heavenly food).

St. Thomas Aquinas concurs, writing that the "hardness" of barley bread signifies the "hardness of the Old Law." Quoting St. Augustine, he explains further: "The flour within the barley, wrapped up as it is within a most tenacious fiber, denotes either the Law itself, which was given in such a manner as to be vested in bodily sacraments; or else it denotes the people themselves, who were not yet despoiled of carnal desires, which clung to their hearts like fibre." By contrast, according to the Angelic Doctor, the softness of wheat flour more suitably represents the "sweet yoke" binding a "spiritual people" to Christ in the Blessed Sacrament.[18] Augustine's and Aquinas's assessments are accurate on merely culinary grounds, because barley pearls are like little pebbles that must be soaked in water for many hours and then preferably pressure-cooked to render them sufficiently tender for eating. Wheat berries, even the so-called "hard" variety, do not require subjection to such drastic treatment.

Along similar lines, we read in Revelation 6:6, *RSV*: "A quart of wheat for a denarius, and three quarts of barley for a denarius."

The implication is that wheat has three times the value of barley. Now "three," of course, is the number of Persons in the Blessed Trinity, whose existence was not explicitly revealed until New Testament times, whereas during the Old Testament era the Jews knew God only as a single Personality. The one-to-three ratio indicates that barley was meant to relinquish whatever influential role it may once have played in salvation history, giving way to wheat in the New Covenant of Christianity. In fact, though, as we shall continue to see, barley never exhibited the symbolic importance of wheat. Like John the Baptist, barley always functioned as a precursor: it would decrease, so that wheat could increase (see John 3:30).

A number of other significant Biblical events, besides the original Passover meal and the retrieval of the ark of the covenant, happened in connection with wheat. For instance, we might mention the call of Gideon while threshing wheat (in Judges 6:11), an episode we will later examine in greater detail. We can furnish additional examples, such as the story of Joseph and his brothers (Genesis 37, 39-50), a tale fraught with the whole emotional spectrum of human drama. At the time of the famine that gripped the Middle East, Joseph was installed as the highest-ranking ruler under the Egyptian pharaoh — among other duties, in charge of dispensing food over the entire region. Recounting the events in Genesis 41-47, the sacred text is replete with references to grain. Most often the term is generic: it could (and probably does) mean either wheat or barley. Yet there are two specific mentions of wheat (in the *Douay-Rheims* translation of Genesis 42:25; 44:2), though none of barley. We shall also have the opportunity to revisit this Josephite narrative in the sequel. On the other hand, although barley figures prominently in Ruth, the poignant book of loyalty, love, and grain (see, in particular, Ruth 1:22; 3:15-17), wheat is also mentioned (see Ruth 2:23). Since the peasant Ruth was King David's great-grandmother (see Ruth 4:17, 21-22; Matthew 1:5-6), a transition from the destitute, earthly Old Law to the royal, heavenly New Law seems to be foreshadowed here. In 2 Samuel 14:30 a son of King David actually orders a field of barley to be burned with fire —

perhaps dimly forecasting the destruction of the Old Covenant in favor of the New (compare Luke 12:49).

To buttress the conclusion relegating barley to the Old Covenant and assigning wheat to the New, we can glean additional agricultural-historical facts about these grains from the contemporary author Reese Dubin:

> Barley and wheat were the most important grains grown throughout the Holy Land ("a land of wheat and barley," Deuteronomy 8:8). Barley was more popular because it could grow in poorer soil and survive heat and drought better. Wheat was for the rich. Barley, the tougher, chewier, and less durable of the two, was for the poor — a universal symbol of poverty and humility. [Even after much cooking, barley retains its "tough" or "chewy" texture.] [19]

Dubin then goes so far as to make the bold claim: "Wheat symbolized eternal life."[20]

Thus, the Eucharist, which anticipates Christ's final coming in magnificent power and His Mystical Body's assimilation into His glory, fittingly sheds the coarse, indigent garment of barley associated with His first advent in the lowly stable of Bethlehem (the birthing "house of bread"), as well as with His public ministry before the culminating events of Passion week. Instead, the Blessed Sacrament dons the resplendent regal robe of the softest, finest wheat — the grain of the new and everlasting covenant wherein the Church partakes of the prodigious wealth of Christ. Therefore, we conclude that Jesus must have used wheat bread for the institution of the Eucharist on Holy Thursday.

Our Lady, the Church, and Wheat

Not only is wheat emblematic of opulence, it is also "symbolic of fertility," as a footnote commentary in the *New American Bible* informs us.[21] This textual gloss concerns the following verse: "Your body is a heap of wheat encircled with lilies." (See Song of Songs

7:3, *NAB*; both the *Douay-Rheims* version of Canticle of Canticles and the *Revised Standard Version* of the Song of Solomon number the verse in question as the second sentence of 7:2, rendering it essentially the same, except that both translate "body" as "belly.") This extravagant praise, lavished on the bride by the chorus (the "Daughters of Jerusalem") in the famous love poem, can be interpreted (according to traditional Catholic exegesis) as referring to either the Blessed Virgin Mary or the Church. In either case, the white lily is a classical symbol of purity. If appropriated to our Lady, the verse implicitly compares Christ with wheat, since He (as the Son of God with no earthly father) took His flesh entirely from His most holy Mother's virginal flesh: He (and He alone) is "seed of woman" (see Genesis 3:15, *D-R/RSV*). If ascribed to the Church, again the verse tacitly compares Christ with wheat, since the Church is the Bride of Christ ("without spot or wrinkle," "holy and without blemish," according to Ephesians 5:27, *RSV*, and Revelation 21:2) who gives us from her abundance the Body of Christ in the Eucharist. Because "in the blessed Eucharist is contained the whole spiritual good of the Church, namely Christ himself" (*CCC*, n. 1324), the Church (the Mystical Body of Christ) is indeed a "heap of wheat." At any rate, in both cases the Woman-Bride-Mother manifests the spiritual fecundity of bringing forth the new life of Christ, signified by wheat.

A brief aside about the lily symbolism. We read in Song of Solomon 2:1-2, *RSV*: "I am a rose of Sharon, / a lily of the valleys. / As a lily among brambles, / so is my love among maidens." These verses unquestionably refer to our Lady, the former in the grammatical first person singular and the latter in the second or third person singular. But in Luke 12:27, *RSV*, regarding the lilies of the field, our Lord exclaims that "even Solomon in all his glory was not arrayed like one of these." In view of the context (Luke 12:22-31) of Christ's metaphor, together with the imagery of Song of Solomon, the particular verse Luke 12:27 may contain a cryptic exaltation of His Blessed Mother's glories. For the lily represents simultaneously the perfectly pure soul who would surrender to total trust in God's providence (as did the lowly maiden in Luke 1:37-38, 45-55) and supernal beauty surpassing (in a spiritual sense) the splendor of Solomon. Two further ideas are suggested: both Solomon's legendary gold (noting that lilies have been artistically depicted as gilded) and his renowned wisdom. Psalm 45:9, 13, *RSV*, undoubtedly describes our Lady: "At your right hand stands the queen in gold of Ophir. . . . / The princess is decked in her chamber with gold-woven robes." In other words, the Blessed Virgin Mother of God is at once the pure humble maiden (white lily) and the celestial Queen (golden-robed) who is endowed with the requisite wisdom to rule at the King's "right hand." Since the wheat bread of the Eucharist is associated with gold (as we have already seen), there seems to be forged a key link joining Mary to both Eucharistic wheat bread and the virtue of wisdom.

Indeed, St. Thomas Aquinas explains that it pertains to the Holy Spirit's gift of wisdom to judge rightly about divine things from a "connaturality" with them — an affinity caused by charity.[22] As St. Paul says in 1 Corinthians 2:14-16, *RSV*, the "spiritual man," having received "the gifts of the Spirit of God," is one who "judges all things" in the light of "the mind of Christ." Now, since the Holy Eucharist is the superlative sacrament of charity, there must be an intimate bond between the Blessed Sacrament and the supernatural gift of wisdom. Our Lady certainly possesses both charity and wisdom to a degree exceeding all other intellectual creatures, whether angels or men.

We hereby enter into a deeper and more complex network of notions. It is written in the book of Proverbs (attributed to Solomon): "Wisdom has built her house, / she has set up her seven columns; / She has dressed her meat. . . . / Come, eat of my food" (Proverbs 9:1-2, 5, *NAB*). (The *D-R* translation renders "columns" as "pillars," "dressed her meat" as "slain her victims," and "food" as "bread.") What is the spiritual meaning hidden in this abstruse passage? How is it to be interpreted in light of Song of Songs 7:3 and the Eucharist? We notice that it provokes the thought of several correlative Biblical verses. Let us do a point-by-point exegesis (while imploring the reader's indulgent patience with what might seem to be a tedious digression).

First, as St. Paul proclaims, Christ is "the wisdom of God" (1 Corinthians 1:24). In fact, Proverbs 8:22-23, *D-R* (in the chapter immediately before the quoted passage) reveals Wisdom's self-description: "The Lord possessed me in the beginning of his ways, before he made any thing. . . . I was set up from eternity, and of old before the earth was made." A parallel text is Sirach 24:3, 9, *RSV*: "I [Wisdom] came forth from the mouth of the Most High. . . . / From eternity, in the beginning, he created me, / and for eternity I shall not cease to exist." Since the term "created" cannot literally refer to the Second Person of the Trinity, it must mean "begot" here, or else it could mystically refer to the Blessed Virgin Mary (as we shall see below). These verses recall God's oath in Psalm 2:7, *RSV*: "You are my son, / today I have begotten you."[23] And St. John announces about Jesus in John 1:1, *RSV*: "In the beginning was the Word, and the Word was with God, and the Word was God."[24] According to Christ's own testimony in Matthew 12:42, *RSV*: "The queen of the South . . . came from the ends of the earth to hear the wisdom of Solomon, and behold, something greater than Solomon is here." Thus, Christ is precisely the "Wisdom" *par excellence* about which Solomon discoursed in the text from Proverbs under our scrutiny.

But, if "Wisdom" in the quoted passage is the Second Person of the Blessed Trinity, then why the feminine pronouns? Well, from what we discussed in a previous paragraph, there is an intimate union between Christ and His Mother. Moreover, Jesus identified Himself with the Church when, striking St. Paul (the infant Church's nemesis before his conversion) to the ground in a blinding flash, He asked: "Saul, Saul, why do you persecute me?" (Acts 9:4; 26:14, *NAB/RSV*). Now the Church is also feminine in relation to Christ, according to Ephesians 5:27 and Revelation 21:2. Thus, because of His intimate association with these feminine entities, both Mary and the Catholic Church can be considered (in a mystical, not literal, sense) to have existed in Christ from eternity

— somewhat analogous to the way in which Eve preexisted in Adam before she was actually formed in the flesh herself. (Ephesians 3:9-11 is relevant here.) Appropriately, then, our Lady is invoked as "Seat of Wisdom" in the Litany of Loreto, for she "sat" mysteriously with Eternal Wisdom and Wisdom Incarnate literally sat on her lap as a Child.

Second, we maintain that the "house" set up by Wisdom is the Catholic Church founded by Christ in time. The proof of this claim begins with 1 Timothy 3:15, *D-R*: "the house of God, which is the church of the living God, the pillar and ground of the truth." Moreover, in Matthew 7:24, *RSV*, Christ says: "Every one then who hears these words of mine and does them will be like a wise man who built his house upon the rock." Now, we saw above that Jesus Christ, the Son of God and Son of Mary, is preeminently the "wise man." Hence, we should expect that He would build *His* "house" on "rock." But that is exactly what He did. For in Matthew 16:13-18, He declared that He would build His *Church* on the "rock" who was St. Peter, the first pope of the Catholic Church. It follows that the Catholic Church is the enduring "house" established by the "Wisdom" of God. (See also Hebrews 3:3-6, *RSV*, which calls Jesus the "builder" of "God's house," along with Ephesians 2:19-20, *RSV*, which speaks of "fellow citizens with the saints and members of the household of God, built upon the foundation of the apostles and prophets, Christ Jesus himself being the cornerstone.") As a corollary, the "scribe instructed in the kingdom of heaven" in Matthew 13:52, *D-R*, who knows how to bring forth "old things" from his "treasure" for application to "new" situations, must be whichever pope is currently reigning, since he is the "householder" in God's kingdom on earth.

We remark that our Lady can be considered a co-foundress of the Church in virtue of her incomparably close cooperation with her Son in His redemptive mission: most notably, her *fiat* (assent at the Annunciation) bringing Him down to earth (see Luke 1:31-35, 38), her instigation of His first public miracle at the Cana wedding feast (see John 2:1-5, 11), and her inexpressible anguish over his passion and death on the cross (see Luke 2:34-35; John 19:25-27), making her the Queen of Martyrs and co-redemptrix of the human race.

Next, the "seven columns" (or "seven pillars") represent the seven sacraments instituted by Christ, which our Lady (as mediatrix of all graces[25]) and the Catholic Church ("the pillar and bulwark of the truth" according to 1 Timothy 3:15, *RSV*) both help dispense in their respective ways. In particular, the "dressed meat" is the Eucharistic Body of Christ, as He Himself avowed in John 6:56, *D-R*: "For my flesh is meat indeed." The fact that the "meat" is "dressed" in the *NAB* translation evidently refers to the pre-resurrection burial of Jesus with herbs, spices, and perfumed oils (see John 19:39-41). If we instead substitute the *D-R* rendition, "slain her victims," the verse seems to apply to Jesus as the "worthy Lamb" that was "slain" in Revelation 5:9; indeed, "Wisdom" offered Himself up as the Victim on the tree where His temporary wooden "house" was constructed (the birthplace of the Church). The use of the plural "victims" would then signify an extension to Mary, the "Seat of Wisdom," who spiritually sacrificed herself with Jesus at the foot of the cross.

Finally, the beckon "Come, eat of my food!" recalls two similar-sounding invitations: "Come, receive grain and eat" (Isaiah 55:1-2, *NAB*) and "I am the bread of life; he who comes to me shall not hunger" (John 6:35, *RSV*). So Jesus Christ, the "Wisdom" of God who constructed the Church as His house, is the grain bread (our spiritual "meat"or "food") to be consumed at the divine banquet of the Eucharist. And, on account of their inseparable union with our Lord, when we eat His flesh at Holy Communion, we mystically partake of the flesh of our Lady and the "flesh" of the Church (all other members conjoined in the Mystical Body). This explains why the chorus (the "Daughters of Jerusalem") in the Song of Songs calls the Bride's body "a heap of wheat." For Jesus (the Head), Mary (His most exalted disciple), and all the other members of His Church (taken as a whole) are unified under the aspect of wheat bread in the Holy Eucharist. In addition, this mysterious unity explains why "Wisdom," though quintessentially the God-Man Jesus Christ, can be personified in the feminine gender under the inspiration of the Holy Spirit.

We comment briefly on the "Daughters of Jerusalem." In Luke 23:27-28, the "Daughters of Jerusalem" bewail Christ's passion: the threshing of the wheat (the fulfillment of the allegorical prophecy in 1 Chronicles 21) or "breaking of the bread" (alluded to in Luke 24:35). But he rebuffs or reverses their lament for Him, warning that they must endure affliction, too. In Song of Songs 7:3, the "Daughters of Jerusalem" chant the glories of our Lady and the Church for their share in the paradox of virginal and maternal suffering for the sake of giving the Bread of Life to mankind; thus, they are perforce extolling our victorious risen Lord. Therefore, the "Daughters of Jerusalem" seem to represent the followers of Jesus and adherents of His Church — the faithful who are devotees of Mary, as well.

We can establish yet another connection of our Lady with wheat by returning to the story of Gideon in Judges 6:11-23, *RSV*. While he was "beating out wheat," "the angel of the LORD appeared to him and said to him, 'The LORD is with you, you mighty man of valor.'" (The *D-R* translation of the angel's epithet for Gideon is "O most valiant of men.") Gideon, acting with humble prudence, expeditiously presented an offering of unleavened cakes made from flour (probably wheat), which the angel caused to be consumed by fire from a rock as a sign of a genuine divine manifestation and God's favor toward Gideon. This incident, interpreted as a foreshadowing, should elicit the thought of a parallel scene in the New Testament: namely, the Annunciation (see Luke 1:26-38). When the Archangel Gabriel appeared to Mary, he saluted her similarly, though of course even more respectfully, with reverent appellations uniquely proper to her. Not only did the messenger greet her by "The Lord is with thee" (Luke 1:28, *D-R*) and call her "blessed among women" (see Luke 1:28), but he also addressed her using the awesome title "full of grace" (Luke 1:28, *RSV/D-R*). With profound humility and heroism exceeding even Gideon's, she consented to God's plan to make her very own body a "heap of wheat," since the Bread that she would bear would later be crushed by the Passion, and finally consumed by the fire of excruciating anguish on the rocks of Gabbatha and Golgotha as a sacrifice acceptable to God.

Finally, let us revert to 1 Samuel 6:1-18, which we remember narrates the story of the Philistines' desperate (and eventually successful) attempt to send the captured ark of the covenant back to Israel. We recall that they harnessed two milking cows (which had never been yoked before) to a cart, upon which they loaded the ark along with a box of gold objects in expiation for their crime. (The golden figures were fashioned according to the images of the rodents and bodily tumors that had ravaged their territories.) When the wagon hitched to the cows was released, it arrived without delay and without human guidance at the Israelite city of Bethshemesh, where the townsfolk "were reaping their wheat harvest in the valley" (1 Samuel 6:13, *RSV*). Jubilantly greeting the ark, the people through their Levite priests used the cart wood to offer burnt sacrifices at a large stone, on which the priests also set up the golden tokens.

How does all this relate to our Lady?

First, she is invoked in the Litany of Loreto as "Ark of the Covenant" — a mystical title prefigured by the gilded Mosaic ark containing a golden urn with some manna inside, along with Aaron's blossomed rod and the stone tablets of the ten commandments (see Exodus 16:31-34; 25:16, 21; Numbers 17; Hebrews 9:4). Indeed, the Church accommodates to Mary the verses found in Revelation 11:19; 12:1, *RSV*, which describe "a woman clothed with the sun" who is evidently "the ark of [God's] covenant." This assimilation of the ark with the Blessed Virgin is most fitting, for she bore in her womb the heavenly Manna, who (as the new Moses) presents mankind with the New Law fulfilling the Old Testament. The escape of the ark from the pagan Philistines may signify Mary's immunity to Satan's clutches (see Genesis 3:15 and Revelation 12:6). The cows pulling the ark, who had never been restrained with a yoke and who had not suckled their calves, lend an added maternal (yet virginal) dimension: perhaps they connote the Blessed Mother's Immaculate Conception (preservation from the burden of sin) and her feminine integrity. Their departure with unrelenting immediacy for Bethshemesh almost certainly represents the fact that "Mary arose and went in haste into the hill country, to a city of Judah" (Luke 1:39, *RSV*). The exultation of the people on viewing the ark with its gold-enshrined manna evokes the scene of the Visitation, when, upon Mary's greeting of Elizabeth, John the Baptist leapt for joy in his mother's womb over the advent of the Bread of Life (see Luke 1:40-44) — just as King David danced for joy before the ark (see 2 Samuel 6:3-5, 9, 12-15).

Second, the Hebrew word *Bethshemesh* means "House of the Sun" or "House of Light." Now Christ is "the light of the world" (John 8:12; 9:5; see John 12:46). Thus, it is appropriate that the ark, representing our Lady, should carry the manna, foreshadowing our Lord, into a place designated by the motif of light. Moreover, both our Lord and His Mother can be symbolically compared to a blossomed branch (see Isaiah 11:1 and Song of Solomon 2:1) — an image of the lambent beauty of purity.

Third, it is highly significant that upon the arrival of the ark the people "were reaping their wheat harvest in the valley." Since wheat glimmers most like gold when it is ripe for harvest and when the sun is shining, the manna surrounded with gold in the ark at the "House of the Sun" — and therefore Jesus, the heavenly Bread — becomes identified with the wheat itself. (King David's exuberance about the ark was also connected with wheat: note the "threshing floor" in 2 Samuel 6:6.) Hence, our Lady's mystical title "House of Gold" in the Litany of Loreto signifies the presence of the golden "Wheat of Life" within her, as Song of Solomon 7:2, *RSV*, also implies: "Your belly is a heap of wheat, / encircled with lilies."

The fact that the people were laboring to reap their harvest suggests the Offertory prayer at Mass regarding the altar bread, "which earth has given and human hands have made" (see also Genesis 3:17, 19). The wheat gathered in the presence of the ark implies that such altar bread, destined to be transformed into "the Bread of Life," must itself be wheaten. The modifying phrase "in the valley" might refer to our need for the Blessed Sacrament in this earthly "valley of tears"; or else it may indicate the advent of the ark symbolizing our Lady, who is the golden "lily of the valley" (Song of Solomon 2:1; 7:2).

Lastly, the golden tokens with verminous and repulsively diseased shapes perhaps represent our sinless Savior, who (as St. Paul says in 2 Corinthians 5:21, *RSV*) for our sake was made sin "so that in him we might become the righteousness of God." (See also Psalm 22:6, *RSV*: "But I am a worm, and no man.") Because the priests in 1 Samuel 6:15 put up the gold figures on the great stone where they sacrificed burnt offerings, the stone probably symbolizes Mount Calvary, upon which our Redeemer was "lifted up" (John 3:14; 8:28; 12:32, 34), and the wood undoubtedly signifies the cross.[26]

St. Joseph and Wheat

It is interesting that Reuben, Jacob's firstborn son, was symbolically instrumental in the conception of his half-brother Joseph on the occasion of a wheat harvest. Genesis 30:14-24 tells the story of Reuben's discovery of some mandrake plants (reputed to enhance fertility, according to a *New American Bible* footnote gloss) in a field during the wheat harvest season; the passage also records the repercussions of this providential serendipity. His aunt Rachel, the sister of his mother, Leah, evidently somehow used the herb: perhaps she merely inhaled its aroma, since "mandrakes give forth fragrance" (Song of Solomon 7:13, *RSV*).[27] In any event, she subsequently gave birth to her firstborn son Joseph. Now it was Reuben (along with Judah) who contrived a scheme to save Joseph's life after the rest of his half-brothers decided to kill him (see Genesis 37:12-30). Hence, Reuben was responsible twice for Joseph's life: once indirectly (concerning his conception) and once directly (concerning his deliverance from a murderous plot).

But Joseph compensated Reuben (while rescuing the rest of his father's family, too) — through the medium of grain. We recall that at the time of the great famine that seized the Middle East, Joseph was appointed the highest-ranking official under the Egyptian pharaoh. Among other duties, he controlled the rationing of food throughout the whole region. Narrating the Josephite events of Genesis 39-47, the inspired text is laden with references to grain. Most often the term is generic here: it could (and probably does) mean wheat or barley. Yet there are two explicit mentions of wheat (in the *D-R* translation of Genesis 42:25; 44:2), though none of barley. Since Joseph's relationship to Reuben is linked originally to a wheat harvest, it would not be presumptuous to conclude that the primary grain in Genesis 41-47 is really wheat.

This is significant, because the Church considers the Old Testament Joseph, son of Jacob, a *type* of St. Joseph, who prudently provided for Mary and Jesus. (Compare Genesis 41:39-44, 55; 45:8; 49:22-26 with Matthew 1:18-25; 2:13-15, 19-23; Luke 2:4-7, 16, 22-33, 39-46.) The first Joseph guarded like a "father" and "lord of all his house" (Genesis 45:8, *RSV*) the grain that spared the lives of the Israelite people. Similarly, the second Joseph took paternal care of the Grain of Life, while protecting his lilylike spouse — described thus in Song of Solomon 2:2, *RSV*: "As a lily among brambles, / so is my love among maidens." Since Christ is the "heap of wheat, / encircled with lilies" inside the "belly" (Song of Solomon 7:2, *RSV*) of His all-fair Mother, St. Joseph therefore received both "the blessings of fresh grain and blossoms" (Genesis 49:26, *NAB*). In religious art St. Joseph is often portrayed holding a flowering branch, which is typically a lily — probably symbolizing his familial association with Jesus and Mary, as well as his chastity.

Whereas the first Joseph dreamt (see Genesis 37:5-7) that his brothers' sheaves of grain (probably wheat) paid homage by bowing down to his sheaf (an event figuratively fulfilled later, in Genesis 42:6-9), the second Joseph was directed via dreams to become the foster father of the Son of God, actually experiencing the willingly respectful obedience of the Heavenly Heap of Wheat (see Luke 2:48-51) whom he in turn adored. The New Testament Joseph was privileged with the custody of the Living Wheat Bread sent to save both Israel and the Gentiles from the spiritual famine of sin — later symbolized by captivity or bondage in Egypt (although initially this land proved a haven from death for Jacob's family, as it was when the Holy Family fled the clutches of Herod's murderous designs, recounted in Matthew 2:13-15, 19-20).

The Holy Sacrifice of the Mass

After this lengthy elaboration on the roles of the Blessed Virgin, the Church, and St. Joseph in the Blessed Sacrament, let us relate wheat to the Mass with further details by using prophecy embedded in Scriptural verses. A famous text (Malachi 1:11, D-R), which Catholic commentators have for many centuries viewed as prophesying about the Mass, reads: "For from the rising of the sun even to the going down, my name is great among the Gentiles, and in every place there is sacrifice, and there is offered to my name a clean oblation."

How does this tie in with wheat? Well, God commanded the Israelites in Exodus 34:22, *RSV*: "You shall observe the feast of weeks, the first fruits of wheat harvest, and the feast of ingathering at the year's end." Now the celebration of Weeks consisted in a festival of thanksgiving for the harvest. It can, then, be considered a *type* of the "ingathering" at Mass for the Eucharist, a term whose etymology is Greek for "good gift" or "thanksgiving" (see the *CCC*, n. 1360): namely, gratitude for the inexhaustible yield of grace gained by our Lord's redemptive merits. Indeed, according to St. Paul (1 Corinthians 15:20, *RSV*), "Christ has been raised from the dead, the first fruits of those who have fallen asleep." Furthermore, in 1 Corinthians 15:37, *RSV*, St. Paul explicitly mentions "wheat" as a "kernel" to be sown. It later rises as a mature "body," which signifies a state of "power" and "glory" (verse 43). Recalling Christ's self-comparison (in John 12:24) with a grain of wheat that is fallen, buried, and risen to produce abundant fruit, while keeping St. Paul's words in mind, we can appreciate that *Christ* is truly "the first fruits of [the] wheat harvest." Hence, the verse cited concerning the feast of Weeks may be construed along the lines of Malachi 1:11 as:

"You shall offer the Holy Eucharist with the pure sacrifice of the Wheat of Life." And this unblemished oblation is to be perpetuated throughout the weeks of the "times of the Gentiles" (Luke 21:24, *RSV*) as a "daily sacrifice" (Daniel 11:31; 12:11, *NAB*).

The Apostles themselves later comprised, and also gathered together, a secondary portion of the fruitful "wheat harvest." For Christ told them in John 16:20, *RSV*: "You will weep and lament. . . ; you will be sorrowful, but your sorrow will turn into joy." This promise evokes the prophecy of Psalm 126:6, *RSV*: "He that goes forth weeping, / bearing the seed for sowing, / shall come home with shouts of joy, / bringing his sheaves with him." Now ordinarily in this context "sheaves" would mean bundles of *wheat*. Thus, the Apostles are rewarded for their labors in supporting the early Church, which (we recall from our exegesis of Song of Songs 7:3) is a "heap of wheat" — formed (like bundles tied together) into cohesive communities by the first bishops. Of course, the "sheaf" metaphor applies as well to all who would toil in the fields of the Lord. (See Matthew 9:37-38; Luke 10:2; John 4:36-38.)

Another concealed allusion to the Mass involving wheat occurs in the context of divinely detailed prescriptions to Moses for consecrating Aaron and his sons as priests. Among a number of imperatives for this rite, God issues the particular command (in Exodus 29:2, *RSV*): "You shall make them [unleavened cakes and unleavened wafers] of fine wheat flour." This ritual contains a *typical* foreshadowing of what regularly transpires in the New Covenant: the Church across the centuries continually obeys the Lord's injunction to make "unleavened wafers" out of "fine wheat flour" through her provident preparation for the Eucharistic sacrifice offered by her priests. Moreover, we infer that the "fine flour" prescribed in Numbers 28:5, 9, 12, 20, 28; 29:3, 9, 14, *RSV*, for the daily sacrifices (both morning and evening), as well as for the Sabbath and other special annual feasts, was probably wheat rather than barley. The verses in Leviticus 2:1, 2, 4, 5, 7; 6:15, 19; 7:12, *RSV*, concerning cereal offerings also contain numerous references to "fine flour," which is probably wheat.

Yet another series of episodes betokening the Mass arises with the decrees of the Persian kings Cyrus and Darius authorizing the Jews to rebuild the Jerusalem temple after the Babylonian captivity and exile. One of these official notices was: "And whatever is needed — young bulls, rams, or sheep for burnt offerings to the God of heaven, *wheat*, salt, wine, and oil, as the priests at Jerusalem require — let that be given to them day by day without fail, that they may offer pleasing sacrifices to the God of heaven, and pray for the life of the king and his sons" (Ezra 6:9-10, *RSV*, emphasis added). Moreover, the Persian king Artaxerxes, ratifying the approval of his predecessors, issued a similar ordinance to his treasurers: "Whatever Ezra the priest, the scribe of the law of the God of heaven, requires of you, be it done with all diligence, up to a hundred talents of silver, a hundred cors of *wheat*, a hundred baths of wine, a hundred baths of oil, and salt without prescribing how much" (Ezra 7:21-22, *RSV*, emphasis added). The decrees of the Persian kings supply additional external confirmation of our interpretation of the "fine flour" commanded for the divine worship sacrifices in Leviticus 2, 6, 7 and Numbers 28-29 as *wheat*. These passages from Ezra indicate that *wheat* was the grain employed (if not exclusively, then at least principally) in the daily priestly sacrifices offered in worship of God — once again a prefigurement of the perfectly pleasing daily Sacrifice of the Mass foretold by the prophet Malachi. Since barley is not even mentioned, wheat is the only possible matter fitting for symbolizing the Body of Christ.

In view of such key passages as those cited from Exodus 34, 1 Samuel 6, and 1 Chronicles 21 (with the hindsight lens of Ezra 6-7 focused on Leviticus 2, 6, 7 and Numbers 28-29), it seems almost certain that the "holy bread . . . of the Presence," of which David and his men partook in 1 Samuel 21:1-6, *RSV*, was wheaten. Now Jesus alluded to this incident in Matthew 12:1-8, Mark 2:23-28, and Luke 6:1-5, when the Pharisees accused Him and His hungry disciples of violating the Sabbath by picking ears of grain in a field to roll in their hands for eating. Exonerating David on the grounds of the necessity to feed his famished men, He then called

Himself the "Lord of the Sabbath." That is, since Christ is the Davidic shepherd who feeds His flock with the requisite nourishment (see Isaiah 40:11; Ezekiel 34:11-16; John 10:1-16, 27-28; Hebrews 13:20; Revelation 7:17), He has the authority to institute a new Sabbath meal. Hence, this event, narrated in all three Synoptic gospels, prefigured the Last Supper, where for the first time He fed His chief disciples with the Real Presence of His very own flesh under the appearance of bread. Therefore, if the holy bread consumed by David and his men was in fact wheaten (as is highly probable), it seems reasonable to conclude that the standing grain mentioned by the Synoptic evangelists in all three passages was likewise wheat. But even if it happened to be barley, the ultimate fulfillment of the foreshadowing in 1 Samuel 21 would dictate that the bread used during the Passover meal of Holy Thursday be wheat alone. It follows that the Holy Sacrifice offered on the new Sabbath of Sunday — and, by extension, every Mass on any day of the week — must employ altar bread derived solely from wheat.

Other Scriptural passages also herald the advent of this celestial banquet. First, we read in Psalm 81:16, *RSV*: "I would feed you with the finest of the wheat." The pronoun "you" here evidently refers to "Israel," as the *NAB* translation (of the corresponding verse numbered 81:17) makes fully explicit. Now St. Paul and St. Peter imply (in Romans 9:24-26; 11:7, Galatians 3:23-29; 4:22-28, and 1 Peter 2:9-10) that the Catholic Church is the New Israel — an exegesis corroborated by Isaiah 2:2-3, *RSV*: "It shall come to pass in the latter days / that the mountain of the house of the LORD / shall be established as the highest of the mountains. . . ; / and all the nations shall flow to it, / and many peoples shall come, and say: / 'Come, let us go up to the mountain of the LORD, / to the house of the God of Jacob; / that he may teach us his ways / and that we may walk in his paths.' / For out of Zion shall go forth the law, / and the word of the LORD from Jerusalem." But the fulfillment of Isaiah's prophecy must be the Catholic Church, for we have already observed that "the house of the LORD" is the Church. Since this phrase is in parallel synonymy with "the house of the God of

Jacob" and since Jacob's new name was *Israel* (see Genesis 32:28–29), the Church is God's *new* Israel. Hence, Psalm 81:16 announces God's Eucharistic plan for the Church, in which Christ becomes for us the "finest wheat."

Subsequently, we find in Psalm 147:12, 14, *RSV*: "Praise the LORD, O Jerusalem! / Praise your God, O Zion! . . . / He fills you with the finest of the wheat." These verses proclaim the fulfillment, through Holy Communion, of the divine intention expressed in Psalm 81:16. In this connection, see also Psalm 132:15, *RSV*: "I will abundantly bless her [Zion — i.e., the New Israel or the Catholic Church] provisions; / I will satisfy her poor with bread [i.e., the Body of Christ in the Holy Eucharist]."

Surely, in both texts (Psalm 81:16 and Psalm 147:14) the Holy Spirit means for us to take the spiritual sense of "the finest of the wheat" as the Body of Christ. Jesus, who (in John 6:35, 48, 51, 58) calls Himself the "Bread of Life" from heaven, is (more specifically and inextricably) the "Wheat of Life." Thus, no bread other than wheaten can be logically justified as valid matter for Eucharistic transubstantiation.

Wheat Versus 'Grain'

Although "grain" is often mentioned generically in Biblical passages without any further specification, some texts utilize the literary device of parallelism to imply that *wheat* is meant. For example, we read in a context of commercial transaction (Amos 8:5, *RSV*) "that we may sell grain . . . that we may offer wheat for sale." Moreover, we can compare the worldly business dealings in Luke 16:7 and Revelation 18:13: "wheat" figures in the former, while the phrase "fine flour and wheat" (*RSV*) occurs in the latter. In view of these data and our foregoing discussions taken collectively, it is far from an exaggeration to assert that wheat is the paradigmatic or prototypical grain in the Bible. On the contrary, this conclusion is entirely warranted by a convergence of overwhelming evidence.

The only other grain that could even enter the debate over the issue of valid matter for Eucharistic bread would be barley, which is frequently included in lists of valuable foodstuffs (along with the ubiquitous wheat, wine, and oil). We have already seen a reference to Deuteronomy 8:8, *RSV*: "a land of wheat and barley, of vines and fig trees and pomegranates, a land of olive trees and honey." Note, as an additional example, 2 Chronicles 2:10, *RSV*: "I will give for your servants, the hewers who cut timber, twenty thousand cors of crushed wheat, twenty thousand cors of barley, twenty thousand baths of wine, and twenty thousand baths of oil." Also see verse 15: "Now therefore the wheat and barley, oil and wine, of which my lord has spoken, let him send to his servants." Further, we learn from 2 Samuel 17:28, *RSV*, that King David and his hungry men were brought "wheat, barley, meal, parched grain, beans and lentils." Moreover, Ezekiel 45:13-17 dictates that wheat and barley should constitute the cereal offerings of atonement for the appointed feasts of the house of Israel. Again, in Joel 1:10-11, *RSV*, we read a cry of lament about "the wheat and the barley" due to the destruction of the "grain" harvest. Lastly and perhaps most remarkably, in 1 Kings 5:11, *RSV*, where Solomon allotted Hiram's household "twenty thousand cors of wheat" annually, barley is never mentioned at all. Even in those verses containing references to both wheat and barley, though, wheat takes precedence over barley in order of enumeration. There are very few exceptions where barley predominates over wheat (e.g., in Ruth and possibly 1 Kings 17:11-16, both of which narratives concern the peasant class) or where barley excludes wheat (for instance, 2 Kings 4:42-44, where the miraculous multiplication of barley loaves by the prophet Elisha seems to prefigure an even greater proliferation of barley loaves by Jesus in John 6:1-13).

There seems to be a pervasive Old Testament contrast between "fine flour" and "barley," indicating that the "fine flour" could very well mean *wheat*. See, for example, 2 Kings 7:1, 16, 18, *NAB*, where "fine flour" is twice as expensive as "barley." Admittedly, the latter particular verses taken by themselves are inconclusive, since the distinction could theoretically obtain between finely processed barley flour as opposed to whole coarse barley grain. But the preceding explications of Exodus 9:31-32; 29:2; 34:22, Leviticus 2,

Numbers 28-29, Ezra 6:9-10; 7:21-22, Amos 8:5, as well as Luke 16:7 and Revelation 6:6; 18:13, still retain their force and cogency.

Our scrutiny of relevant verses from both Old and New Testaments has revealed that barley finishes a distant second place behind wheat in order of prominence. And if barley cannot be admitted to the Eucharistic table as valid matter for altar bread, then certainly the door of the sanctuary is closed to grains such as rye, oats, rice, and millet, which have virtually no supporting Biblical basis for this purpose.

Wheat and Wine

Let us return for a moment to 1 Samuel 4-6, which recounts the tale of the Philistines' capture of the ark. They desired to possess this precious artifact, not from a sense of devoted faith, but rather out of superstitious greed as some sort of magical talisman. As a penalty God afflicted them with such tormenting pestilence that they had to scheme a plot to remove it from their midst. In other words, their original intention to achieve power backfired on them, and what should have been a blessing became a curse instead. Since the ark of the covenant contained manna symbolizing Christ, we are reminded of 1 Corinthians 11:23-29 (especially verses 27-29), where St. Paul warns against unworthy reception of Holy Communion. In light of his serious admonition, we should interpret in a spiritual sense Hosea 7:14, *NAB*: "They have not cried to me from their hearts / when they wailed upon their beds; / For wheat and wine they lacerated themselves, / while they rebelled against me." The "wheat and wine," which here redound to the punitive anguish of their consumers, depict seemingly plain and common foods. Yet they display extraordinary value, because they will nourish only those who do not revolt against God.[28] In other words, they must signify some divinely directed goods above and beyond the natural plane. Eucharistic imagery is evidently implied: Jesus can be received in Holy Communion under the elemental aspects (species) of either *wheat* bread or wine (and not bread from another grain).

Along these lines, we observe that the call of Gideon came when he "was beating out wheat in the wine press" (Judges 6:11, *RSV*). This incident foreshadowed the scourging of Christ, in which His Body was disfigured by the same weapons that drained His Blood. The verse furnishes another close connection between the two material species of the Blessed Sacrament, which would be instituted by Christ centuries after the time of the Judges.

Having amply discussed the "wheat" element in the Blessed Sacrament of the Holy Eucharist, we turn our attention in the next chapter to the "wine." But what *kind* of wine?

chapter three

WHY GRAPE WINE?

Let us briefly revisit the beginning of the preceding chapter. There we saw that, among all the sacraments, only the Holy Eucharist contains our Lord Jesus Christ Himself — the very Author of the grace transmitted by the other sacraments. In this sublime sacrament, He is truly present in His entirety (Body, Blood, Soul, and Divinity), veiled under the appearances of physical things. (See the *CCC*, nn. 1324-1328, 1374.)

Valid Matter

We pose the same question as before. *Which* physical things? Previously we concentrated on bread; now we will see what other material substance the Church prescribes for a valid Mass. The *Code of Canon Law* (Can. 924) states: "The most holy Sacrifice of the Eucharist must be celebrated . . . in wine to which a small quantity of water is to be added. . . . The wine must be natural, made from grapes of the vine, and not corrupt." As mentioned previously, the *CCC*, n. 1412, also teaches that one of the "essential signs of the Eucharistic sacrament" is "grape wine." It is a definitive doctrine of the Catholic Church that only pure and natural grape wine can be used as valid matter for conversion into the Blood of Christ.[1] This complete change of substance (called *transubstantiation*), in which only the appearances of wine remain, occurs at the Consecration of the Mass, when the priest, acting in the person and at the command of Christ, pronounces the words spoken by Christ at the Last Supper: "This is My Blood." (See Matthew 26:27-28; Mark 14:23-24; Luke 22:17-18, 20; 1 Corinthians 11:25; also the *CCC*, nn. 1375-1377.) A consecration of wine, terminating in a conversion to Christ's Blood, must take place for a Mass to be valid, because on Calvary (which the Mass mystically reenacts in an unbloody manner) Christ's Blood was separated from His Body, as recorded in John 19:31-37, especially verse 34 (see also 1 John 5:6). Finally, it should be emphasized that grape juice in itself is not necessarily valid matter; it must be at minimum raw or fresh grape juice susceptible to *fermentation* (i.e., akin to wine).[2]

As was the case with wheat bread, it is not a simple project to ascertain why only grape wine may serve as the material substance willed by Christ for transubstantiation into His precious Blood. In the final analysis the answer must remain mysterious to us during this life, since we have no direct insight into the unfathomable divine mind nor can we boast exhaustive comprehension of the properties of physical things. Our mental poverty having been confessed, however, it does not follow that God has abandoned us like intellectual "orphans" so that we are left without reasonable clues in the matter. (Such "orphaning" would violate Christ's promise in John 14:16-18, *D-R*.) Here is where the importance of sacramental symbolism enters. We must explore the significance of both *wine* and *grapes*.

Why Wine?

In the first place, why *wine*? This is the easier of the two questions to answer. Now, a line has to be drawn somewhere; otherwise, the words of the second part of the Consecration could be uttered over anything potable (say, black tea or carbonated soft drinks or clam juice) — a symbolically unpalatable situation. After all, aesthetic value cannot be dismissed. Given that our Lord wanted us to drink His Blood under the appearances of some earthly liquid (John 6:53-56), it was fitting that He accomplish His aim with a full-bodied beverage usually perceived as resembling the crimson color of human blood. It might be objected that animal blood would seem to have precisely the accurate value desired for representing Christ's Blood. Nevertheless, it would be extremely unsuitable for the rapidly putrefactive blood of brute animals to serve as a sign of His untainted, immortal, and spiritualized Blood. Besides, in the beginning, man was apparently vegetarian; it was only after the Great Flood that God gave permission to eat animal flesh, but even then imbibing animal blood was prohibited. (Contrast Genesis 1:29-30 with Genesis 9:3-4 and also see Leviticus 7:26-27; 17:12-14.) Since Christ came to restore man to original justice, it would be unsuitable for anything not consumed in a relatively primordial stage of human history to function as a symbol of Christ's pristine Blood. Thus, a *plant* juice would be more apt for signifying divinized human blood.

Indeed, the aged juice naturally pressed from pure fruit makes sense for several reasons. One of them is the Biblical association of wine with important events in salvation history. (The *CCC*, nn. 1333-1335, discusses the Biblical significance of wine in some detail.) For example, we can mention the incident involving Abraham and Melchizedek (Genesis 14:18-20), the Passover celebration (Leviticus 23:13), and the wedding feast at Cana publicly inaugurating Christ's miraculous ministry (John 2:1-11). (Deuteronomy 16:13-15 also shows that wine has connotations of merry-making.) Another reason is that the reddish-purplish hue and consistency of certain fruit juices suggest the color and viscosity of human blood. A third aspect in this picture is the bittersweet flavor of wine, simultaneously signifying both the pleasure of a healthy life and the pain of suffering and death. A fourth factor to ponder is that the fermentation of fruit juice into wine implies a time element; in particular, God the Son descended to earth and underwent His passion in the "fullness of time" (*D-R*), or the "right time" and "proper time" (*RSV*), or the "fitting time" (*NAB*) — see Ecclesiastes 3:1; 8:6; Wisdom 18:14-15; Romans 5:6; Galatians 4:4; 1 Timothy 2:6; Hebrews 1:1-2. A fifth feature of wine is its connotation of romantic love, even to the point of a lush sensuousness — see, for instance, Song of Songs 1:2, 4; 5:1; 7:3, 9-10; 8:2, 11-12, *NAB* (although pomegranates are also featured in a number of verses). Interestingly, there is a recurrent refrain reminiscent of the time element referred to in the passages cited in the preceding sentence: "Do not . . . stir up love before its own time." Mystically, the wine of Divinity (God's love) was fully poured out on the water of humanity (our weakness) only when the time was ripe. (See John 1:12-17.) Finally, the fact that from many pieces of fruit there flows one drink signifies the unity of all the Church's believers with the Lord.[3] Hence, wishing to be the passionately rich and vivifying drink of our spiritual life come to ripe maturity in union with Him, Christ chose wine as the most appropriate symbolic vehicle.

Why Grape?

Now we address the second and more puzzling question: why *grape* wine? Why should it matter which vegetable or fruit juice (of an appropriate color) is used? For instance, why not carrot, tomato, or beet, or cherry, cranberry, strawberry, raspberry, mulberry, pomegranate, blueberry, elderberry, blackberry, or plum juice? This is not an absurd, idle, or frivolous question. For instance, mulberry wine is explicitly mentioned along with grape wine in 1 Maccabees 6:34. And there are numerous references to pomegranates and their juice, in juxtaposition with (grape) wine, in Song of Songs, most notably 8:2. Each of these many juices also has (to a greater or lesser extent) the sanguine attributes of a sufficiently reddish-orange or reddish-purple color with the requisite texture. Certainly the last ten fruit juices listed are susceptible to fermentation into wine. Moreover, their pigmentation is always closer to that of human blood than some varieties of grape (which can be "white" or pale green). Would it make any difference to Jesus what kind of altar wine is converted into the substance of His Blood at the Consecration of the Mass? It would be a spontaneous human response to raise this question out of compassion in the face of some ailment (say, an allergy requiring abstention from grape wine). We must be wary, however, of succumbing to a false sense of charity by committing the gnostic error of trivializing material differences.

Just as there is a natural reason why wine should be the only drink symbolically fit for conversion into the substance of Christ's Blood, so also there would seem to be a practical reason why God chose only one particular fruit as legitimate for Eucharistic wine. Imagine if any fruit wine were allowed. Inevitably, questions would arise over which plants are technically fruits and which are technically vegetables, because some that are commonly perceived as vegetables are actually fruits (e.g., tomatoes) — and the reverse scenario may be conceivable. Moreover, developments in hybridization of true fruits with vegetables would further blur distinctions and complicate matters. Ecclesiastical policies would then be intrinsically and inextricably held hostage to the accuracy of current botanical determinations.

If the Church relented and proclaimed the juices from certain broad fruit-vegetable groups to be licit ingredients of altar wine (assuming a well-defined classification could be relied upon), some people would predictably test the limits of Church discipline by protesting the exclusion of other fermented liquids (for instance, bean or coconut) and alcoholic beverages (say, gin from juniper berries, rum from sugar cane, or vodka from potatoes). In particular, why not liquor distilled from *grains*, such as corn, rye, barley, and rice (i.e., whiskey, beer, saki, etc.)? Why should the type of spirits matter? In fact, would it not be veritably more fitting and consonant with the matter of the first part of the Consecration to use malted *wheat*? That would make matters neat and complete! Causing the wheat whiskey/wine to look like blood would require merely the admixture of a crimson dye (say, from beets). Who could ask for anything more? (Except perhaps the folks who crave hot chocolate for winter Masses and iced coffee or lemonade for summer Masses.)

Given the human propensity to extend the territory of a libertine agenda, some wave-makers would petulantly complain: why the restriction to plant foods, when there are people who would prefer fermented dairy products (e.g., kefir or buttermilk) as beneficial for maintaining healthy intestinal flora? For that matter, why not seafood juices? (After all, some of the Apostles were fishermen.) How unfair, judgmental, and rejecting of diversity! An interminable debate would beset sacramental theology and its pastoral applications — far worse than now. If one is repelled by the repercussions of laxity in this area, then one gratefully appreciates that God, in His infinite wisdom and compassion, has authoritatively settled the matter for all time by appointing unadulterated grape juice as the sole ingredient of altar wine. (Exceptions for hard cases, such as allergies, would make a wreck of things here and would wind up destroying the general precept.)

The Church's official doctrine permitting only grape juice as valid matter for constituting Eucharistic wine cannot, of course, be strictly proved by unaided human logic. It can, however, be somewhat rationally defended on the basis of biological knowledge and even more convincingly justified on the basis of Scripture.

Grapes display some "convenient" attributes on the natural level. Reese Dubin discusses the therapeutic power of grapes, stemming in large measure from their high content of antibiotic and antioxidant chemical constituents (notably polyphenols and procyanidins). Although most edible fruits have purifying properties to some extent, among them all grapes excel at building strong blood as well (tantamount to a "blood transfusion").[4] And it is *blood* that must be symbolized in the Eucharist. Also, John Heinerman reports current medical thinking that grape wine in moderation can help reduce the risk of heart attack.[5]

Let us recall yet again that the sacraments employ material things as channels of grace, actually bringing about in reality what they signify. Furthermore, it is a plain fact that some materials are more suited than others for playing a specific symbolic role. We saw, for example, the intimate connection between water and Baptism in Chapter 1, and between wheat and the Eucharistic Body of Christ in Chapter 2. Why, among all fruits, are grapes the most appropriate for the Holy Eucharist, in which Christ's Blood is truly present under the semblances of wine?

For one thing, grape wine is the most universal kind of wine; other fermented plant beverages are called "wine" only by a derivative affiliation with grape wine.[6] Furthermore, Heinerman reports: "Apocryphal and ancient Jewish rabbinical sources all seem to suggest that the forbidden fruit consumed by Adam and Eve in the Garden of Eden was, in reality, a bunch of grapes and not the proverbial apple!"[7] This antiquated opinion appears far-fetched, but, if it were true, it would be a delicious or a bitter irony (depending on one's perspective). Mankind's original lust for grapes would be symbolically "satisfied," and punishment for disobedience expiated, in overflowing measure by the sacrificial blood of animals throughout the Old Testament and by the sacrificial Blood of the Lamb of God at the dawn of the New Covenant.

Detailed Biblical Background

Of course, the above reasoning is not conclusive in itself. We infer that grapes (instead of other fruits) are the most fitting source for altar wine mainly by relying on key canonical Biblical references. Some passages associate grapes with oppressively laborious suffering to the point of a massive spilling of blood, in order to satisfy God's justice by atonement for the offense of sin. These indicate the agonizing and sorrowful connotations of grape wine. Other passages depict the ebullient inauguration of a luxuriously prosperous era of abundant refreshment and vigorous vitality. These signify the joyous and sensuous aspects of grape wine. We analyze (or at least comment on) some crucial proof-texts in the sequel.

The Biblical mandate that blood be shed in expiation for sin (see Exodus 12:21-23; 24:6-8; Leviticus 17:11; Hebrews 9:7, 12-14, 18-22; 10:19) leads us to contemplate the divine dispensation (foreshadowed in the Old Covenant) that the Blood of Christ be shed in propitiation for our sins (see Romans 3:25; 5:8-9; Ephesians 2:13; Colossians 1:20; 1 Peter 1:2, 18-19; Revelation 5:9; 7:14). Indeed, the Lord Himself declared at the Last Supper (Matthew 26:28-29, *RSV*): "This is my blood of the covenant, which is poured out for many for the forgiveness of sins. I tell you I shall not drink again of this fruit of the vine until that day when I drink it new with you in my Father's kingdom." (See also Mark 14:24-25 and Luke 22:17-18.) The "fruit of the vine" is, of course, grapes (as will be irrefutably demonstrated below). Hence, Jesus is intimately binding the symbolism of grape wine with His own Blood at this first Mass, when He converted grape wine into His Precious Blood, while foretelling His bloody sacrificial death.

Before continuing with the topic of the Mass, we digress to highlight one of Christ's principal metaphors for Himself (and for us). Not only did He call Himself the "Bread of Life" (in John 6:35, 51), but He also declared in John 15:1, 4-5, *RSV*: "I am the true vine and my Father is the vinedresser. . . . Abide in me, and I in you. As the branch cannot bear fruit by itself, unless it abides in the vine, neither can you, unless you abide in me. I am the vine, you are the branches. He who abides in me, and I in him, he it is that bears much fruit, for apart from me you can do nothing." This passage fulfills the psalmist's prophecy (in Psalm 80:14-15, 17, *RSV*) designating the Messiah, the "son of man" who is "planted" (like a "vine") at God's "right hand": "Turn again, O God of hosts! / Look down from heaven, and see; / have regard for this vine, / the stock which thy right hand planted. . . . / But let thy hand be upon the man of thy right hand, / the son of man whom thou hast made strong for thyself!" The symbolism of "the vine and the branches" has critical ramifications for the valid matter of Eucharistic wine, as well as for the theme of participation in Christ's life and work.

Equivalence of 'Fruit of the Vine' and 'Grapes'

With regard to the "fruit of the vine" mentioned by Jesus at the Last Supper and in the parable of "the vine and the branches," someone may object that tomatoes, raspberries, and blackberries are fruits growing on vines, so maybe they could also fit His metaphor. Never mind the fact that these fruits would not have figured in the illustrative literary devices of a Jewish rabbi (i.e., "teacher," according to Matthew 23:8, 10 and John 13:13-14), since tomatoes probably stemmed from South America (thus unavailable in Palestine during the Biblical era) and the other fruits lacked the agricultural prominence of grapes. More importantly, from other Scriptural contexts in which the term "vine" appears, we can assert with near certitude that, virtually whenever the metaphor of "vine" is employed in the Bible, it denotes a *grape* vine. And thus when "wine" occurs in association with "vine," it means *grape* wine.

As proof from the Old Testament, we first adduce Genesis 40:9-10, *RSV*: "There was a vine before me, and on the vine there were three branches; as soon as it budded, its blossoms shot forth, and the clusters ripened into *grapes*" (emphasis added). Next, we hear the warning by Moses to the Israelites in Deuteronomy 28:39, *RSV*, if they fail to observe God's commandments: "You shall plant vineyards and dress them, but you shall neither drink of the wine nor gather the grapes." Moreover, the allegorical "Vineyard Song" in Isaiah 5:1-7, *RSV/D-R*, refers to "grapes" several times (in verses 2, 4), and not surprisingly concludes with an allusion to "bloodshed" contrasted with "justice" or "righteousness" (in verse 7). Furthermore, the verses Isaiah 16:10; 17:6, *D-R*, link "vineyards" and "wine" explicitly with "grapes": "There shall be no rejoicing nor shouting in the vineyards. He shall not tread out wine in the press that was wont to tread it out: the voice of the treaders I have taken away. . . . And the fruit thereof that shall be left upon it, shall be as one cluster of grapes." (A mention of "grape" also occurs in 17:11.) Lastly, we read in Joel 1:5, *RSV*: "Wail, all you drinkers of wine, / because of the sweet wine, / for it is cut off from your mouth." The *NAB* renders "sweet wine" as "juice of the grape" and in verse 10 mentions "must," which denotes grape juice incompletely fermented.

For proof from our Lord's words elsewhere in the New Testament itself, consider the parable of the vineyard owner, the tenants, and the owner's son in Matthew 21:33-42. Near the beginning of the story, we are told that the owner sent servants to procure "*grapes*" (verse 34, *NAB*; emphasis added) from the vineyard. Further, near the end of this thinly veiled condemnation of the Pharisees (who quickly understood its intended application to them, perhaps in conjunction with the "Vineyard Song"), we hear the owner threaten to transfer management of his vineyard to men who will ensure his possession of "*grapes* at vintage time" (verse 41, *NAB*; emphasis added). Thus, when Christ calls Himself a "vine," He means a *grape* vine — likewise when He mentioned the "fruit of the vine" at the Last Supper in Matthew 26:28-29, Mark 14:24-25, and Luke 22:17-18. Since His life-giving Blood (the sap of the divine "vine") flows through the Eucharist into the bodies and souls of His faithful (the vine's "branches"), the only valid matter for the consecration of altar wine at Mass is the juice of *grapes*.

Regarding the theme of participation in Christ's life and work expressed in the simile of "the vine and the branches," we should observe not only that the branches are lifeless apart from the vine, but also that grapes hang from vines in clusters. In other words, there is a communitarian coherence among the individual pieces of fruit — quite unlike the way in which other vined fruits (say, tomatoes, raspberries, and blackberries) grow. The color of the grapes (whether purplish or pale) is basically irrelevant (although a crimson hue is *typical*); the deeper and more essential fact about grapes seems to be that all varieties grow in clusters. Interpreted in a spiritual sense, the clusters may represent all those individuals in a particular time and place who are bonded for a common supernatural purpose on their heavenward journey (for instance, networks of relatives and friends, parishes, religious orders, apostolates in the Church, etc., as suggested in 1 Corinthians 12.) Hence, just as we saw in Chapter 2 the unifying metaphor of *wheat* for the Head and members (clergy and laity) of Christ's Mystical Body, so here we witness the unifying metaphors of the envined branches and the clustered *grapes*. Just as Christ is the "(Wheat) Bread of Life," so also is He the "(Grape) Wine of Life." And just as no productive branch is separated from the vine as a whole (with no grape growing in splendid isolation from other grapes), so also the members of the Mystical Body share one lifeline of grace emanating from the Head (with each individual assisting others to remain in the family). The upshot, once again, is that only the wine of grapes can serve as valid matter for confecting the Eucharist.

The Mass

Let us return, where we left off, to the topic of the Holy Sacrifice of the Mass, first offered at the Last Supper in anticipation of the Good Friday holocaust. The connection between grapes and the consecration of wine at Mass had actually been prophesied centuries before its original realization during the epochal event on Holy Thursday — which was marked by a mixed atmosphere of religious solemnity, celebratory friendship, and somber portent about Good Friday. (See John 13:1-3, 21, 34-35; 14:27-28; 15:9-15; 16:6, 20; 17:24.) There are a number of significant passages from the Old Testament in this connection, mirroring these features of divine worship, spiritual joy, and sacrificial oblation.

We meditate first on the deep meaning of Isaiah 62:9, *NAB*: "You who gather the grapes shall drink the wine / in the courts of my sanctuary." This compact oracular utterance contains a stunning prophecy about the latter times (the New Testament) couched in mystical symbolic terms. The key to unlocking the riddle consists in the insight that the "courts of my [God's] sanctuary" include the interior of any Catholic church — more particularly, the worship space both in front of and immediately surrounding the altar (the "sanctuary"). Indeed, the Father is the King whose "courtly" subjects are His people gathered at Mass in the congregation, together with His ministers offering the holy sacrifice of His Son at the altar itself. The Church's members "gather the grapes" (literally, in pre-celebration preparation, and figuratively, at the Offertory presentation). During the Mass, some of the faithful (at least the priest) have the opportunity to drink from the chalice of Christ's Blood (the "wine"). Thus, sacramental wine must be derived from grapes and not from some other fruit — a provision first entirely fulfilled at the Last Supper.

Second, we reflect on Amos 9:13-14, *NAB*: "The juice of grapes shall drip down the mountains, / and all the hills shall run with it. . . . / Plant vineyards and drink the wine." These verses, too, are profound. According to traditional exegesis, the "mountains" or "hills" should be interpreted as the Catholic Church.[8] Hence, this prophecy can also be construed as referring to the Consecration and Communion at Mass, where the Precious Blood of Christ flows prolifically. (Of course, His Blood initially flowed on *Mount* Calvary, thence taking its course from Jerusalem to the "hills" of Rome.) At any rate, in order to drink Christ's Blood ("the wine"), grapes are needed, since the fruit must be picked from "vineyards." It follows that the valid matter for constituting Eucharistic wine is grape juice alone.

A further thought. The exhortation to "drink the wine" recalls Christ's command in the Johannine Eucharistic discourse (see John 6:53-56). The injunction in the present instance, though, rather than sounding a warning, is imbued with a generous atmosphere of contented satisfaction, as though the Father were entreating His children with this implicit final exclamation: ". . . and enjoy!" (See the *CCC*, n. 1334, which relates "an eschatological dimension" of "messianic expectation" to "the festive joy of wine.") In other words, Jesus wants to make His Blood our spiritual drink for the sake of our own happiness.

A consonant passage in this respect is Jeremiah 31:4-5, *RSV*, addressed to "virgin Israel": "Again you shall adorn yourself with timbrels, / and shall go forth in the dance of the merrymakers. / Again you shall plant vineyards / upon the mountains of Samaria; / the planters shall plant, / and shall enjoy the fruit." Using our interpretive key, we discover the spiritual meaning: "virgin Israel" represents the Catholic Church, which will spread the grace of the one true Faith of her divine vine ("plant vineyards upon the mountains") to the schismatic or apostate lands that have lost it (signified by "again" and "Samaria"). We find here terms of jubilation ("adorn with timbrels," "dance," "merrymakers," "enjoy") associated with the "fruit" of the "vineyards" (namely, grapes and grape wine, as previously justified). Symbolically understood, these verses proclaim that the Blood of Christ, if and when it is poured into the hearts of mankind, causes peace and joy.

Another pertinent verse is Psalm 4:7, *RSV*: "Thou hast put more joy in my heart / than they have when their grain and wine abound." Also compare Zechariah 9:17, *RSV* ("Yea, how good and how fair it shall be! / Grain shall make the young men flourish, / and new wine the maidens") with 10:7: "Their hearts shall be glad as with wine." Taken in a spiritual sense, all these verses convey definite images about the transforming effect of the Blessed Sacrament on the soul.

Continuing this theme of invitation to delight in the Eucharist, we read in Proverbs 9:1, 2, 5, *RSV*: "Wisdom has built her house, / she has set up her seven pillars. . . . / She has mixed her wine. . . . / 'Come, . . . / drink of the wine I have mixed.'" (The *D-R* version translates "mixed" as "mingled.") In review, we saw in Chapter 2 that Christ is "the wisdom of God" (1 Corinthians 1:24). Moreover, the feminine pronouns forcefully indicate such an intimate union between Christ and His Mother, as well as between Christ and His Church (which is also feminine in relation to Him), that both Mary and the Catholic Church can be considered, in a mystical (not literal) sense, to have existed in Christ from eternity. Furthermore, the "house" set up by Wisdom is the Catholic Church founded by Christ in time, of which our Lady can be considered a co-foundress in virtue of her incomparably close cooperation with her Son in His redemptive mission (making her the Queen of Martyrs and co-redemptrix of the human race). In connection with the present passage, we emphasize the formation of His Body from her blood in her virginal womb,[9] her instigation of His first public miracle (changing water to wine) at the Cana wedding feast (see John 2:1-5, 11), and the ineffable sorrow of *her* pierced heart (see Luke 2:34-35) at the sight of His scourged body, crucifixion, and death, when *He* was finally pierced with a lance and drained of His lifeblood (see John 19:34, 37).

Additionally, we remember that the "seven pillars" represent the seven sacraments instituted by Christ, which our Lady (as mediatrix of all graces[10]) and the Catholic Church ("the pillar and bulwark of the truth," according to 1 Timothy 3:15, *RSV*) both help dispense in their respective ways. In particular, the "mixed wine" is the Eucharistic Blood of Christ, as He Himself avows in John 6:55, *RSV*: "For . . . my blood is drink indeed." The fact that the wine is "mixed" may foreshadow the commingling of wine with a small amount of water at the Offertory of the Mass.[11] An interpretation might be based on Song of Solomon 7:2, *RSV*, where the Daughters of Jerusalem praise the Bride: "Your navel is a rounded bowl / that never lacks mixed wine." If applied to Mary, this verse could refer to the intimate union ("mixing") between her Immaculate Heart and the Sacred Heart of Jesus. But if applied to the Church, it could refer to the centrality ("navel") of her Mass, with its perpetual mingling of water and wine in sacred vessels ("bowls") — an Offertory rite that in turn represents the elevation of the human race ("water") through the Incarnation of Divinity ("wine"). The entire conversion of this slightly watered-down wine into the Blood of Christ at the second part of the Consecration is prefigured by Christ's first public miracle at the Cana wedding feast, when He changed pure water into delectable wine (see John 2:1-11).[12]

Another possible interpretation requires a cross-reference to 2 Maccabees 15:39, *RSV*: "It is harmful to drink wine alone, or, again, to drink water alone, while wine mixed with water is sweet and delicious and enhances one's enjoyment." This undoubtedly sage admonition from a physician of the soul seems to presuppose the inability of our weak human nature to bear the strength of undiluted Divinity. Although it would be spiritually lethal for us to remain immersed in the bland "water" of a merely natural human existence, on the other hand we cannot sustain the energy to soar consistently amidst the azure heavens of vintage ecstasy. In this life of mundane toil we are not granted the gift of resting in uninterrupted bliss, which would (unlike the Beatific Vision) make us oblivious to the needs of earthly wayfarers. This Scriptural insight harmonizes remarkably with Aristotle's recommendation that a virtuous human life in our present condition should incorporate a judicious interplay between practical and contemplative activities: this is the "blend" our nature demands as the most "pleasant" or "delightful."[13] After all, God Himself said about Adam, who was blessed with the consolation of continual divine companionship, "It is not good that the man should be alone" (Genesis 2:18, *RSV*).

Perhaps even more appropriately, though, we can construe the "mixed" wine as signifying the addition of a particle of the fractured consecrated Host to the chalice containing the Precious Blood after the "Lamb of God" invocation, while the priest prays quietly: "May this mingling of the Body and Blood of our Lord Jesus Christ bring eternal life to us who receive it." This exegesis is prompted by a footnote commentary in the *NAB* on Psalm 75:9, a verse that features the phrase "spiced . . . wine." The gloss elucidates that the literal meaning of "spiced" is "mixed" — that is, laced with narcotic spices having the potency to induce greater intoxication. This intensification of Eucharistic imagery would lead us to augment our notion of the feminine "round bowl" symbol in Song of Solomon 7:2 as indicating the Church's ultimate worship (at her "navel" or deepest core) of the resurrected Christ, expressed at Mass by enacting for our edification the reunion of both sacramental species before the priest's Communion. After all, as St. Paul scolds the Corinthians, "If Christ has not been raised, your faith is futile" (1 Corinthians 15:17, *RSV*).

Finally, the words "Come, drink of the wine" recall some similar-sounding invitations from other places in the Bible:

1. "Every one who thirsts, / come. . . ! / Come, buy wine . . . / without money and without price" (Isaiah 55:1, *RSV*).
2. "Like a vine I caused loveliness to bud, / and my blossoms became glorious and abundant fruit. . . . / Come to me, you who desire me, / and eat your fill of my produce" (Sirach 24:17, 19, *RSV*, foreshadowing John 15:1, where Christ compares Himself with a "vine").
3. "The time of pruning the vines has come" (Song of Songs 2:12, *NAB*).
4. "Come, my beloved. . . . / Let us go out early to the vineyards, / and see whether the vines have budded, / whether the grape blossoms have opened" (Song of Solomon 7:11-12, *RSV*).
5. "Come to me, all who labor and are heavy laden, and I will give you rest" (Matthew 11:28, *RSV*).

Every verse quoted, except for the last, issues an explicit invitation either to come to grape vines or to drink wine; the fourth passage is the most specific in its employment of the adjective "grape." Nevertheless, the last verse, where Christ Himself speaks, contains an implicit invitation to drink "wine," since He calls Himself the "vine." Thus, the Precious Blood of Jesus Christ (the "Wisdom" of God who constructed the Church as His house) is our spiritually refreshing drink to be consumed at the divine banquet of the Holy Eucharist — and the proper matter of this "wine" is derived from the fruit of grape vines. Moreover, the factor of "time" in the third quotation (and implied in the fourth) conjures up the idea of correct age. It is written elsewhere that "the teeth of him who eats the un-ripe grapes shall be set on edge" (Jeremiah 31:30, *NAB*). Hence, the normative matter for confecting the Blood of Christ is *fermented* grape juice.

Divine Justice and Sacrificial Atonement

Some Scriptural passages juxtapose the themes of grape wine, bloody libation, and punishment for sin. (Isaiah 1:18, *D-R*, depicts sins as the color of "scarlet," "red," and "crimson," thereby suggest-ing that offenses against God's Majesty betray a gory or even deadly aspect — murder of the divinely established order of things.)

One glaring example is Revelation 14:18-20, *RSV* (compare Joel 3:13): " 'Put in your sickle, and gather the clusters of the vine of the earth, for its grapes are ripe.' So the angel swung his sickle on the earth and gathered the vintage of the earth, and threw it into the great wine press of the wrath of God; and the wine press was trodden outside the city, and blood flowed from the wine press, as high as a horse's bridle, for one thousand six hundred stadia [about two hundred miles]." Here we witness God's fury unleashed against groups of people ("clusters of the vine of the earth") whose sin has reached such a limit of negative maturation that they are virtually fixed in a state of unrepentance. Thus, they are almost begging, at the peak of their allotted time to do evil (the "grapes are ripe"), for divine retribution, which reduces them to pulp and wrings them dry (in "the great wine press of the wrath of God"). Their blood, shed to satisfy divine justice against hardened wickedness, is compared to wine ("flowed from the wine press"). Yet the grape juice, running unrestrained along the ground without benefit of containing barrels ("for . . . stadia"), is wasted and will eventually rot — preventing the valuable spiritual fermentation that should have occurred.

Another example in the same vein is Micah 6:13, 15, *RSV*: "I have begun to smite you, / making you desolate because of your sins. . . . / You shall tread grapes, but not drink wine." Here, the phrase "you shall tread grapes" suggests some *self*-destruction: a bloody penalty inflicted partly by the sinners on themselves as a consequence of their own actions. Again we see that evildoing frustrates the fruitfulness of spiritual maturity ("but not drink wine"). Their suffering bears no merit; they derive no good from their misfortunes. These verses recall St. Paul's warning in 1 Corinthians 11:27-30 to those who would drink the Precious Blood of Christ sacrilegiously.

Next, we have the excerpt from Deuteronomy 32:14, *NAB*: "With the cream of its finest wheat, / and the foaming blood of its grapes you drank." This verse contains striking Eucharistic imagery. As we know from Chapter 2, the "finest wheat" represents Christ's Body in the Blessed Sacrament (here, with the additional rich feature of "cream"). Therefore, the parallel phrase must also apply to the Holy Eucharist, whose secondary species is wine. But the corresponding (second) phrase in this verse mentions the "blood of grapes." Consequently, the sacramental wine that will be converted to Christ's Blood must be obtained solely from the juice of grapes.

Another relevant aspect here is the use of the adjective "foaming" to modify the noun "blood." This graphic word conjures up images of surging waves in an ocean storm, molten lava gushing from a volcano, and water in a pot furiously threatening to boil over. Thus, it carries connotations of the frenzied wrath of natural forces. In human terms (at least in the English language), we speak of someone enraged to the point of sputtering and "foaming" at the mouth. Transported to the supernatural realm, it seems to signify God's righteous anger in demanding reparation for offenses against His holy majesty. For instance, note Psalm 75:9, *NAB*: "A cup is in the LORD's hand, / full of spiced and foaming wine" and Jeremiah 25:15-16, *NAB*: "Take this cup of foaming wine from my

hand, and have all the nations . . . drink it" — along with Hebrews
10:26-31. The "foaming blood of grapes," then, represents Christ's
Blood shed in a terrible sacrifice to atone for mankind's sins.

More is true, however. The "foaming blood" evidently also indicates Christ's own intense wish to deliver Himself up for us, because He said in Luke 22:15, *RSV*: "I have *earnestly desired* to eat
this passover with you before I suffer" (emphasis added). It appears
that His Blood was already surging; in fact, He sweat drops of
blood during the Agony in the Garden before the physical tortures
even began (see Luke 22:44). This "foaming blood" contains so
much energy that, once outpoured and "sprinkled," it rises directly
from the ground and "speaks more graciously than the blood of
Abel" (Hebrews 12:24, *RSV*). The crowning with thorns (see Matthew 27:29, Mark 15:17, John 19:2) drew more blood, thus showing the monstrosity of the crime committed against Him; for,
contrary to the norm of nature He articulated in Matthew 7:16,
D-R, in this case "men [did] gather grapes of thorns" (taking blood
in a figurative sense as the juice of "grapes," but "thorns" literally).

Still another sentence (Genesis 49:11, *D-R*) in a similar vein
reads: "He shall wash his robe in wine, and his garment in the
blood of the grape." In this verse Jacob is uttering a deathbed prophecy about his son Judah, who here probably represents the Jewish
nation during the bloody passion and death of Christ. (See Matthew 27:25.) It seems applicable, however, not only to Judah's ge-
netic descendants who accepted Christ as the Savior by His
expiatory death, but also to Judah's spiritual offspring who "have
washed their robes . . . in the blood of the Lamb" (Revelation 7:14,
RSV). Furthermore, we read in Isaiah 63:2, *RSV*: "Why is thy ap-
parel red, / and thy garments like his that treads in the wine press?"
A continuation of this image into 63:3 makes evident the com-
parison between grape juice and blood. See also 1 Maccabees 6:34,
D-R, which mentions "the blood of grapes" (though mulberry wine
figures secondarily). At any rate, we witness repeatedly the strong
Scriptural assimilation of the two substances grape juice and blood.
Therefore, it would be impossible for the Church to allow the sub-

stitution of any wine other than grape for the second part of the Consecration in the Mass.

Lastly, it is written in Zechariah 9:15, *RSV*: "They shall drink their blood like wine, / and be full like a bowl, / drenched like the corners of the altar." The *D-R* translates this verse: "Drinking they shall be inebriated as it were with wine, and they shall be filled as bowls, and as the horns of the altar." Like most of the preceding passages, this verse (which appears in a prophecy about the victorious Messianic dominion) symbolically ties blood together with wine, undoubtedly from grapes (a thesis sufficiently defended). Like them, as well, it seems to resonate with the same satiating plenitude ("full," "drenched," "filled").

But the blood drunk here is that of the vanquished. Thus, this verse emphasizes (to an even stronger extent, if possible, than the previous passages) explicit sacrificial notes, using the salient terms "bowl" and "altar." (The *NAB* modifies "bowls" with the adjective "libation.") The connotation is that the imbibers of the grape wine become (as it were) secondary vessels of wrath, configured to the "bowls" and the "corners of the altar." The spiritual interpretation might be that those who drink the Eucharistic Blood of Christ partake in His vicarious redemptive suffering, since He became the Victim for our sins. St. Paul professes some definite teaching along this line. In 2 Corinthians 5:21, *RSV*, he writes: "For our sake he [God] made him [Jesus] to be sin who knew no sin, so that in him we might become the righteousness of God." (See also Isaiah 53:4-6 and Galatians 3:13.) On the other hand, St. Paul insists in Colossians 1:24, *RSV*: "In my flesh I complete what is lacking in Christ's afflictions for the sake of his body, that is, the church."[14] (See also 1 Corinthians 4:9-13 and 2 Corinthians 4:8-11; 6:4-10.)

Furthermore, Zechariah 9:15 (*D-R* rendition) may rouse memory of the traditional prayer called "*Anima Christi*" (dating from the fourteenth century, composed by an unknown author). One of its invocations beseeches our Lord with the plea "Blood of Christ, inebriate me"; that is, inundate me with your zealous charity for souls and with fiery (even ecstatic) love for you. Thus, in this

Scriptural verse God foretells that many people (pilgrim-saints) will be drunk on the Blood of the Lamb slain in apparent defeat; for those who regularly adore Christ in the Blessed Sacrament drink intoxicating draughts of His Spirit as a foretaste of heavenly bliss.[15] We hope that we, too, may receive the grace of this union to the limits of our capacity.

In sum, for many reasons no fruit can replace grapes as the source of sacramental wine in the Eucharist. Over and over again we are confronted with the symbolic relevance of the distinctions among material substances for the sacraments. But the matter of oil in the sacraments of Confirmation and the Anointing of the Sick awaits handling.

chapter four

WHY OLIVE OIL?

Because olive oil is a substance used regularly as the primary matter in two distinct sacraments, this chapter is divided into two sections, with the first part devoted to a discussion of Confirmation and the second to a separate treatment of the Anointing of the Sick (formerly called "Extreme Unction," nomenclature that we will occasionally continue to use ourselves when we deem it appropriate). Although anointing with blessed oil plays a customary auxiliary role in Baptism, oil is not this sacrament's essential valid matter, which is water (covered in Chapter 1); nevertheless, we will discuss the symbolic purpose of olive oil for Baptism in a brief appendix to the current chapter.

PART I

According to the *CCC*, n. 1285, and the *1983 Code of Canon Law*, Can. 879, the Sacrament of Confirmation renders the baptized "more perfectly bound to the Church" and enriches them "with a special strength of the Holy Spirit." It completes the grace initiated at Baptism, enabling the baptized to carry out their obligation of witnessing to Christ, spreading the Faith, and defending it by word and deed. Besides enhancing the interior presence of the Holy Spirit "for the inner strengthening of the supernatural life and for the courageous outward profession of Faith," Confirmation *per se* increases sanctifying grace and "imprints an indelible spiritual mark" on the soul.[1] This *seal* authoritatively signifies a "total belonging to Christ," an "enrollment in his service for ever," and "the promise of divine protection in the great eschatological trial" (*CCC*, nn. 1295-1296, with references to Revelation 7:2-3; 9:4 and Ezekiel 9:4-6; see also the *CCC*, n. 1304).

Valid Matter

Along with imposition of hands and pronunciation of the prescribed formula, the Confirmation rite requires anointing on the forehead with consecrated *chrism* — a perfumed oil traditionally made by combining olive oil and balsam (an aromatic tree resin).[2] Actually, according to Ludwig Ott: "There is no official dogmatic decision regarding the essential matter of the Sacrament of Confirmation."[3] Most reputable theologians, however, concur with the creditable position that it is indeed chrism.[4]

In fact, though, the revised *Code of Canon Law*, Can. 847, declares: "In administering sacraments in which holy oils are to be used, the minister must use oil made from olives or other plants." Thus, by contrast with her dogmatically immutable teaching on the valid matter of the other sacraments, the Church has allowed a relaxation in the formerly stricter discipline governing the matter of Confirmation. (See Matthew 16:19 on the pope's prerogative of the keys to bind and loose, along with Isaiah 55:8-9 on the mystery of God's particular dispensations in human history.) Nevertheless, olive oil retains its pride of place, because it is the only plant specifically named in this decree. Indeed, olive is the paradigmatic, or prototypical, kind of oil. On this point, St. Thomas Aquinas comments: "This oil [i.e., olive] is called oil properly, and is very much in use, wherever it is to be had. And whatever other liquid is so called, derives its name from its likeness to this oil: nor are [other oils] commonly used, unless it be to supply the want of olive oil."[5]

Of course, utterly impassable boundaries persist: neither mineral oils (e.g., petroleum preparations) nor animal oils (say, fatty secretions from birds such as the emu) are valid even under the more latitudinarian norms. Hence, although the valid material substance for Confirmation is evidently not so absolute and unexceptionable as the valid matter for Baptism and the Holy Eucharist, olive oil remains paramount: it still seems the desirable and ideal choice. Therefore, it behooves us to explore the significance of the olive — the king of plant oils — in its traditional connection with Confirmation.

It is not difficult to understand the chrismal meaning of fragrant balsam, a regal symbol. For Confirmation more fully incorporates the individual recipient into the "royal priesthood" about which St. Peter eloquently discourses and St. John hears sung in his apocalyptic rapture. (See 1 Peter 2:5, 9 and Revelation 5:10; also the *CCC*, nn. 908, 1305.) Aquinas asserts that a fragrant balm is combined with oil because it makes the odor spread, citing St. Paul in 2 Corinthians 2:15, *RSV*: "For we are the aroma of Christ to God." Note, as well, 2:14, *RSV*: "God . . . through us spreads the fragrance of the knowledge of him [Christ] everywhere." (See also the cross-reference description of Christ in Ephesians 5:2, *RSV*, as "a fragrant offering and sacrifice to God.") After they received the Holy Spirit under the form of tongues, the Apostles spread the Faith by speech. The diffusion of the balsamic scent symbolically recalls the Gospel's promulgation of the heavenly kingdom.[6]

But why should *olive oil* be the primary physical substance directed as constituting the ordinary matter of Confirmation? We first inquire: why *oil* at all?

Why Oil?

Oil has deep relevance for Confirmation. Oil signifies a certain richness or abundance, which is appropriate because Confirmation bestows a greater fullness of the gifts of the Holy Spirit. Moreover, since oil loosens or limbers the muscles and joints, a crucial state of fitness for athletes in contest and soldiers in battle, it symbolizes the readiness for spiritual combat that must mark mature Christians as soldiers of Christ (see the *CCC*, n. 1293). Pertinent Scriptural references include: 1 Corinthians 9:24-27 ("run that you may obtain it [the prize]," verse 24, *RSV*); Philippians 3:12-15 ("I press on toward the goal for the prize of the upward call of God in Christ Jesus," verse 14, *RSV*); 1 Timothy 1:18-19 ("wage the good warfare, holding faith and a good conscience," *RSV*); 2 Timothy 2:3-5 ("Take your share of suffering as a good soldier of Christ Jesus," verse 3, *RSV*); and 1 Peter 5:8-10 (which speaks of being confirmed or strengthened in opposing the diabolical enemy). In addition, oil lubricates metal parts, minimizing friction to facilitate smooth mechanical functioning. Therefore, if we envision warriors outfitted with armor (helmet, breastplate, belt, footgear, sword), a vivid picture portrayed by St. Paul in Ephesians 6:10-17, we appreciate their need for a supply of oil to maintain their versatility when contending with foes. The analogous situation must prevail for the adequately equipped Christian, who should cultivate a supernatural flexibility or prudence in knowing how to face and respond to spiritual dangers. (See also Matthew 7:15; 10:16-17 and Luke 14:28-33.)

Furthermore, oil is used as fuel to keep lamps burning. Since Christians must be "the light of the world," whose "light must shine before men" in visible testimony to the glory of God (as our Lord urges in Matthew 5:14-16 and implies in Mark 4:21; Luke 8:16; 11:33-36), it is fitting that the sacrament of faithful witness should employ oil for its matter.

Concerning the restriction of sacramental oil to plants, we speculate that mineral sources are excluded because Confirmation is a sacrament of living witness, enabling the evangelical propagation of the message of abundant life. (See John 1:4; 3:15-16; 4:14; 6:40, 47, 51, 54, 57-58; 10:10; 11:25-26; 14:6; 20:31; 1 John 1:1-3; 2:25; 5:11-13.) Thus, the lush vitality characterizing the effluence of vegetation has more suitable connotations for the sacramental rite than the exudations of inert minerals. On the other hand, sebaceous animal excretions, being carnal and usually susceptible to more rapid decay (even putrefaction) than plant oils, would not befit the spiritual theme of eternal life conveyed by the authentic promotion of Christ's Gospel.

Why Olive Oil?

On account of the prominence still granted to the olive even in the revised *Code of Canon Law*, we shall try to ascertain an answer to a question far more subtle and profound than the more general issue of oil for Confirmation. Why is it that this sacrament's ordinary oil should be pressed from *olives*? First, we will examine some distinctive natural properties of olive oil that may help to elucidate the matter. But, since biochemistry and philosophical deduction cannot irrefutably resolve the problem, we will subsequently have to resort to Scriptural exegesis.

Reese Dubin extols the virtues of olive oil in glowing terms: "Olive oil is the most important food in the Bible, where it is mentioned more than 200 times and is the symbol of goodness, purity, and — especially — long life. . . . The olive tree grows slowly and attains a great age."[7] According to Dubin, the ancient Egyptians reportedly employed olive oil for numerous purposes — food, fuel, medicine for nearly all ailments, sacrificial offerings, and coronations. Furthermore, he continues with some rather audacious statements:

> The ancient Hebrews regarded olive oil as the key to long life and rejuvenated mental powers. Often attaining life spans of 100, 200, 300 years or more, they not only consumed olive oil, but virtually all of them — male or female, rich and poor alike — used oil embrocations [liniments] daily. According to the Psalmists, the oil directly penetrated the body when rubbed on, relieving aches and pains, restoring strength.[8]

Regarding Dubin's reference to the "Psalmists," we can find at least one supporting verse in Psalm 109:18, *RSV*: "May it soak into his body like water, like oil into his bones!"

Jean Barilla concurs with many of these contentions, in particular that the olive tree "symbolizes longevity." Her book on olive oil reports a plethora of astounding historical and biological facts (as well as legends and myths replete with symbolism) about the olive, culled from the literature of the Egyptians, Greeks, Romans, Hebrews, and Arabs.[9]

Dubin claims modern medicine has discovered that olive oil reduces high blood pressure, rectifies low blood pressure, and protects the circulatory system. It aids the heart and blood vessels by lowering harmful (LDL) cholesterol, raising beneficial (HDL) cholesterol, and (due to its high content of oleic acid) preventing blood platelets from conglomerating into blood clots. Since it is absorbed through the skin, when used topically it alleviates arthritic complaints, and can have the same advantages for arthritis symptoms if taken internally. Additionally, statistical studies have shown that olive oil consumption diminishes the risk of contracting all major diseases, including cancer. It has, asserts Dubin, a reputation as "the longevity food," which he explains on the basis of antioxidants present in it. These compounds retard the aging process by prolonging the life of somatic cells.[10] They evidently ward off attacks from free radicals that can derange cells and thereby make them more vulnerable to carcinogenesis. Apparently, olive oil is more stable than other oils, which can go rancid (or oxidize) more quickly.

Of course, we make the disclaimer that the foregoing is not intended as medical advice. The association between a high consumption of olive oil and low incidence of cardiovascular illness in certain Mediterranean regions may be merely a statistical correlation rather than a causative connection. The lower disease rates are perhaps a reflection of the replacement of dietary animal fat with good quality natural vegetable oil. The reduced pathology would then be a direct result of abstention from animal fat, and only incidentally related to olive oil as such. Therefore, the reader should probably regard the theoretical claims about olive oil's intrinsic therapeutic worth as tentative scientific hypotheses. On the other hand, practically speaking, it seems unlikely that the prophylactic addition of olive oil to the diet would harm most people.

But, if we do accept Dubin's descriptive assessment of olive oil's natural biological value, we see that its salient feature is the promotion of physical longevity or endurance, especially by strengthening the heart. This characteristic, transferred to the supernatural realm, represents persevering resistance against forces that threaten dissolution of personal integrity, with preservation from dis*heart*enment in the struggle. The sacramental significance of olive oil for Confirmation is obvious: steadfast patience, stalwart fortitude, and a resolute "heart" when confronting evil, in order to survive its onslaught spiritually intact.

Detailed Biblical Background

Yet physiological considerations, though intriguing as auxiliary arguments, cannot conclusively prove that oil pressed from olives is the most suitable oil for the Sacrament of Confirmation. At best they can serve only as adjuncts to more convincing demonstrations. After all, an oil with even greater therapeutic virtues could conceivably be discovered and recommended by health professionals in the future. Therefore, we must rely on Scriptural symbolism in salvation history to furnish a more cogent apologetical defense.

General Equivalence of 'Oil' and 'Olive Oil'

It is safe to make the generalization that whenever "oil" is mentioned in the Bible without further explicit qualification,[11] it means *olive* oil. This sweeping conclusion seems to follow from a warning by Moses to the Israelites, if they fail to observe God's commandments: "You shall have olive trees throughout all your territory, but you shall not anoint yourself with the oil; for your olives shall drop off" (Deuteronomy 28:40, *RSV*). A similar curse in Micah 6:15, *RSV*, corroborates the point: "You shall tread olives, but not anoint yourselves with oil." Moreover, 1 Kings 8:13-14, *D-R* (equivalent to 1 Samuel 8:13-14, *NAB*) links "ointments" with "olive-yards." These verses patently assume the ubiquitousness of olive trees, implying that the Israelites customarily, if not exclusively, derived their liniments, salves, and other oil-based products from olive oil (just as Dubin claims regarding their "daily embrocations"). On the other hand, when Moses blessed the Israelites before his death (in Deuteronomy 33:24, *NAB*) he prayed that the oil of olive trees would flow bountifully. (See also 2 Kings 5:26, *RSV*, which mentions "olive orchards" along with "vineyards.") This allusion, as well, appears to entail the widespread availability of olives, and hence the commonplace use of olive oil. Let us further point out that, in a footnote comment on the clause "He shall see no streams of oil"

(Job 20:17, *NAB*), the *New American Bible* unhesitatingly affirms that the "oil" means "olive oil."

Earlier we noted the connection between oil as a lubricant for the bodies and accouterments of contestants (athletic competitors or warrior combatants) and oil to confirm the aspiring militant Christian. (See again 1 Corinthians 9:24-27; Philippians 3:12-15; 1 Timothy 1:18-19; 2 Timothy 2:3-5; Ephesians 6:10-17.) We now learn that the only oil with the relevant Biblical precedents is olive oil. In order that the Christian may respond to the call of battle with alacrity, yet suave deftness, "the oil of . . . olive trees [should run] over his feet" (Deuteronomy 33:24, *NAB*). Moreover, the supernatural war cannot be successfully joined without the acute spiritual vision to discern where the enemy of salvation lurks, as our Lord directs in Revelation 3:18, *RSV*: "I counsel you to buy from me . . . salve to anoint your eyes, that you may see." In light of the Old Testament precedents (especially 1 Kings 8:13-14, *D-R*) the "salve" (or "ointment" in 1 Kings 8:13-14, *D-R*) would probably be based on olive oil. Dubin gives anecdotal evidence vindicating the naturally therapeutic value of olive oil for healing the eyes (and ears, too).[12] Interpreting "see" in a spiritual sense (as discerning the truth), compare James 1:5; 1 Timothy 2:4; Colossians 1:9-11; Philippians 1:9-10.

But we are far from finished. Besides the undoubtedly routine ingestion of olive oil (raw or in cooked food), as well as its sundry topical applications, it found another use as fuel to maintain lamps shining brightly in the dwelling of the Lord. Two verses stand out. First, Exodus 27:20, *RSV*, reads: "And you shall command the people of Israel that they bring to you pure beaten olive oil for the light, that a lamp may be set up to burn continually." Second, Leviticus 24:2, *RSV*, reiterates: "Command the people of Israel to bring you pure oil from beaten olives for the lamp, that a light may be kept burning continually." (The *NAB* translation has "clear oil of crushed olives.") Earlier we cited our Lord's exhortation that His disciples act as "the light of the world," as lamps to illuminate the whole "house" (see again Matthew 5:14-16 and Luke 11:33-36). We now know, based on Scriptural antecedents, that their conspicuous lamps must be fueled with the grace of Confirmation, which has been traditionally imparted by anointing with olive oil. Furthermore, this divine mandate to Moses seems to serve as a *typical* prefigurement of the sanctuary lamp that always burns before the tabernacle in Catholic churches, indicating the Real Presence of Jesus Christ.

An even more remarkable adumbration of the "royal priesthood" (see 1 Peter 2:5, 9 and Revelation 1:6; 5:10) anointing in Confirmation occurs when God ordered Moses to consecrate His dwelling tent and to anoint Aaron along with his sons. Moses had to prepare the ointment for these sacred tasks by combining olive oil with aromatic spices. (See Exodus 30:22-33, especially verse 24, along with Leviticus 8:10-12.) The Lord forbade the manufacture of this holy unction for any other purpose. Since the "ordinary anointing of the body" (verse 32, *NAB*) with olive oil was not prohibited, the reason for the restriction must have been the rare herbs in this perfumed mixture, to be associated only with the consecration ritual. Analogously, Confirmation chrism, which contains fragrant balsam along with olive oil, must be consecrated by a bishop and can be used only for this sacrament, according to the *Code of Canon Law*, Can. 880, and the *CCC*, n. 1297.

To further support the contention that "oil" in the Bible generally means "olive oil" and, in addition, that olive oil is the archetypal sacramental oil, we can adduce several verses listing sequentially the three sacramental substances of bread, wine, and oil.

1. Tobit 1:7, *NAB*: "To the Levites who were doing service in Jerusalem I would give the tithe of grain, wine, olive oil." We see here that all three chief substances are included in a religious context. Although the kind of grain is not specified, the wine (from what we learned in Chapter 3) must be grape and the oil is explicitly olive.

2. Nehemiah 5:11, *RSV*: "Return to them this very day their fields, their vineyards, their olive orchards, and their houses, and the hundredth of money, grain, wine, and oil which you have been exacting of them." Again we see that all three principal substances are enumerated, this time in a moral context of social justice.

Although the kind of grain is again not specified, the wine is definitely grape and the oil is obviously olive.

3. Deuteronomy 8:7-8, *RSV*: "For the LORD, your God, is bringing you into a good land, a land of brooks of water, of fountains and springs, flowing forth in valleys and hills, a land of wheat and barley, of vines and fig trees and pomegranates, a land of olive trees and honey." This passage, occurring in the context of a Mosaic sermon on God's providence, the blessings of obedience to His commandments, and the perils of affluent prosperity, is striking. It can be construed as an allegorical foreshadowing of the sacramental dispensation of the New Covenant ("a good land"). Clearly, the "flowing fountains and springs of water" signify Baptism (from Chapter 1). To correctly interpret the remaining sacramental materials, however, we must abide by a certain hermeneutical methodology. Since sacramental substances take priority over other foodstuffs due to their superior affinity with the supernatural level, we must select the *first* item indicated in each member of the ensuing triplet (after the aquatic imagery); the remainder have secondary importance (i.e., they are nonsacramental). When we follow these directions, lo and behold! We extract the words "wheat," "vines," and "olive trees." The "wheat" represents the Eucharistic Body of Christ (from Chapter 2) and "vines" (meaning "grapes") symbolize the Eucharistic Blood of Christ (from Chapter 3). It follows that the oil of "olive trees" constitutes the quintessential valid matter for the other sacraments in which oil is mandated.

We further observe that 1 Samuel 8:14-15, *RSV*, ties together "grain" ("the best of your fields") with "vineyards and olive orchards," and that 2 Kings 18:31-32, *RSV*, refers to bountiful water and "a land of grain and wine, a land of bread and vineyards, a land of olive trees and honey." The *D-R* translation of the corresponding passage in 4 Kings 18 renders the last phrase quoted as "a land of olives, and oil and honey." The triad of "gather the ears of corn" (probably wheat), "cluster of grapes," and "olive tree" also arises in Isaiah 17:5-6, *D-R*. Thus, in the *RSV* rendition of 2 Chronicles 2:10, 15, two verses that list wheat, barley, wine, and oil as vital foodstuffs (cited in Chapter 2 concerning the wheat-barley question), the "oil" almost certainly means *olive* oil.

Moreover, consider Revelation 18:13. The *NAB* translation of this verse contains the list of sacramental substances "wine and olive oil, fine flour and grain," whereas the *RSV* translates the list as "wine, oil, fine flour and wheat." Synthesizing the two renditions, we deduce that the grain is wheat and the oil is olive. Hence, the "oil" of Luke 16:6 is indubitably the "olive oil" of Revelation 18:13, *NAB*, since both verses occur in the context of worldly business dealings involving wheat and oil.

4. Revelation 6:6, *NAB*: "A day's pay for a ration of wheat and the same for three of barley! But spare the olive oil and the wine!" This verse occurs in a prophecy about war, famine, and probably vicious persecution. We have already seen (in Chapter 2) that "wheat" is the Eucharistic grain, whereas "barley" was the grain of the Old Covenant. Thus, the passage seems to imply the severe scarcity of one of the crucial elements (namely, wheat bread) for celebrating the Holy Sacrifice of the Mass. (See Daniel 8:11-12; 9:27; 11:31; 12:11-12.) Yet there will not be a total reversion to the times before the New Covenant, because Mass will still be offered, thanks to the sufficiency of grape wine (even though much less frequently and never openly). The reason why may be that wine (unlike grain) is relatively unaffected by the vicissitudes of disastrous weather patterns and disruptive sociopolitical conflict, since its alcoholic content protects it from spoilage virtually indefinitely in storage. Similarly, an abundance of grace will be poured out through other sacraments involving the matter of olive oil. In particular, the strength of Confirmation will be required to endure the enormous suffering (see the *CCC*, n. 1296).

Olive Oil and the Mass

Continuing with the theme of the Mass just broached, we encounter some astounding passages (in Numbers 28-29) in which the Lord prescribes for the Israelites, through His servant Moses, exact details for carrying out divine worship.[13] There are relatively minor variations in these precise instructions among the appointed occasions, which cover daily and Sabbath worship, as well as the special feasts of the New Moon, Passover, Pentecost, New Year's Day, Atonement Day, and Booths; however, the similarities among them predominate. Hence, we will concentrate our attention on the elements of the daily sacrifice described in Numbers 28:2-8, *RSV*:

> Command the people of Israel. . . . And you shall say to them, This is the offering by fire which you shall offer to the LORD: two male lambs a year old without blemish, day by day, as a continual offering. The one lamb you shall offer in the morning, and the other lamb you shall offer in the evening; also a tenth of an ephah of fine flour for a cereal offering, mixed with a fourth of a hin of *beaten oil* [emphasis added]. It is a continual burnt offering, which was ordained at Mount Sinai for a pleasing odor, an offering by fire to the LORD. Its drink offering shall be a fourth of a hin for each lamb; in the holy place you shall pour out a drink offering of strong drink to the LORD. The other lamb you shall offer in the evening; like the cereal offering of the morning, and like its drink offering, you shall offer it as an offering by fire, a pleasing odor to the LORD. [According to verse 14, the "strong drink" is "wine."]

There are amazing parallels here with the Mass and the sacraments, making the Mosaic rite a *type* of the Mass. The morning holocaust of the "lamb without blemish" symbolizes the sacrifice of Jesus Christ, the Lamb slain (mystically) since the foundation of the world (see 1 Peter 1:19-20; Revelation 5:9, 12; 13:8). The morning and evening holocausts together signify the daily offering throughout the world (as the time zones are traversed) of the Holy Sacrifice of the Mass foretold in Malachi 1:11. The evening holocaust itself represents the perpetuation of the Mass (and consequently the real physical presence of Christ) down through the ages "even to the consummation of the world" (Matthew 28:20,

D-R). Moreover, we note that the daily sacrifice in both the Old and New Covenants involves "fine flour" (probably wheat, as we saw in Chapter 2, since barley is coarse)[14] and "wine" (evidently from grapes, as we saw in Chapter 3).

Finally, most pertinent to the present chapter, we observe the presence of olive oil in the Mosaic ritual. The "beaten oil" in verse 5 is definitely olive; in fact, the *NAB* renders the phrase as "oil of crushed olives." (A footnote on verse 5 in the *NAB* regarding the "oil of crushed olives" comments that "this oil, made in a mortar, was purer and more expensive than oil extracted in the olive press." Perhaps we could therefore call it "super-extra-virgin" olive oil.) Now oil is not literally or materially used during the Mass. Olive oil is involved in the Mass symbolically, though, since it represents the Holy Spirit, whose power is invoked (at the *epiclesis*) to transubstantiate bread and wine into the Body and Blood of Christ. More on this point shortly. At any rate, its use in any other sacrament (such as Confirmation) would dictate its traditional or normal derivation from olives; the Scriptural precedent makes this the most suitable kind of oil.

The Root of the Olive Tree

Next, we explicate the most astonishing thing of all about the ultimate significance of the olive tree. St. Paul writes to the Gentile converts about the Jews (Romans 11:16-21, 23-24, *RSV*):

> If the dough offered as first fruits is holy, so is the whole lump; and if the root is holy, so are the branches.
>
> But if some of the branches were broken off, and you, a wild olive shoot, were grafted in their place to share the richness of the olive tree, do not boast over the branches. If you do boast, remember it is not you that support the root, but the root that supports you. You will say, "Branches were broken off so that I might be grafted in." That is true. They were broken off because of their unbelief, but you stand fast only through faith. So do not become proud, but stand in

awe. For if God did not spare the natural branches, neither will he spare you. . . . And even the others, if they do not persist in their unbelief, will be grafted in, for God has the power to graft them in again. For if you have been cut from what is by nature a wild olive tree, and grafted, contrary to nature, into a cultivated olive tree, how much more will these natural branches be grafted back into their own olive tree.

Here is our exegesis of this profound extended metaphor. The "natural" olive tree represents the kingdom of God, the Church, mystically present ("wild" or unstructured) in the world from the creation of Adam and Eve, but more fully articulated during the epoch of the Old Covenant, and firmly established (or "cultivated") with the era of the New Covenant. (Consult the *CCC*, nn. 760-765, here.) It follows from what St. Paul himself indicates (in verses 13 and 14 earlier) that the olive tree's "natural" branches symbolize the Jewish nation, the first chosen people, whereas the "ingrafted" branches (of the "cultivated" olive) symbolize the Gentiles, chosen with Christ's arrival.

But what does the "root" signify? St. Paul describes it as "holy" ("consecrated" in verse 16, *NAB*), "rich," and the "support" of both Gentiles and Jews. A key to its interpretation is Revelation 22:16, *RSV*: "I Jesus have sent my angel to you with this testimony for the churches. I am the root and the offspring of David, the bright morning star." Compare Revelation 5:5, *RSV*: "The Lion of the tribe of Judah, the Root of David, has conquered." These verses evoke the recollection of other prophecies.

1. Isaiah 11:1, *RSV*: "There shall come forth a shoot from the stump of Jesse, / and a branch shall grow out of his roots."
2. Isaiah 11:10, *RSV*: "In that day the root of Jesse shall stand as an ensign to the peoples; him shall the nations seek, and his dwellings shall be glorious."
3. Isaiah 4:2, *RSV*: "In that day the branch of the LORD shall be beautiful and glorious, and the fruit of the land shall be the pride and glory of the survivors of Israel."

4. Jeremiah 23:5, *RSV* (compare with Isaiah 9:5-6 and Luke 1:3): "Behold, the days are coming, says the LORD, when I will raise up for David a righteous Branch, and he shall reign as king and deal wisely, and shall execute justice and righteousness in the land."

5. Zechariah 3:8; 6:12-13, *RSV*: "Behold, I will bring my servant the Branch. . . . Thus says the LORD of hosts, 'Behold, the man whose name is the Branch: for he shall grow up in his place, and he shall build the temple of the LORD. It is he who shall build the temple of the LORD, and shall bear royal honor, and shall sit and rule upon his throne."

6. Isaiah 53:2, *RSV*: "For he grew up before him like a young plant, / and like a root out of dry ground."

7. Matthew 2:23, *RSV*: "He shall be called a Nazarene." (In Hebrew, *nezer* means "branch" or "shoot," probably signifying olive in this case.)

Taken together, all these texts yield the undeniable conclusion that the "holy root" supporting the olive tree is Jesus Himself. He is the "Root" of the kingdom of God with respect to His nature as divine and uncreated; He is the "Shoot" or "Branch" of the Jews with respect to His human nature and descent. That He is "rich" is signified by the luxuriance of olive oil, with which He abounds as its very source. In other words, He is eternally (like the "morning star") "bright" with the fuel of His own infinite Being (see Revelation 21:23), dwelling in "inaccessible light" (see 1 Timothy 6:16, *D-R*) and splendor.

This exegesis is implicitly vindicated by St. Paul himself in Romans 15:12, where he quotes Isaiah's "root of Jesse" prophecy with respect to Christ. Another clue verifying our interpretation lies in the fact that St. Paul speaks in parallelism of the "first fruits" offered under the form of (bread) "dough," along with the "root," as "holy." But in 1 Corinthians 15:20, *RSV*, he calls Christ "the first fruits of those who have fallen asleep" — nomenclature that Jesus essentially applied to Himself in John 12:24. Thus, Eucharistic references are latent in this passage, as well. For the "first fruits" spreads its consecration to the "whole lump" of dough. Bread made from cohesive wheat flour, signifying the unity of the Mystical Body on the foundation of Christ, is suggested (see 1 Corinthians 10:16-17 and Psalm 122:3). This is reinforced when St. Paul stresses that the "root supports you," implying utter dependence of everyone on it. But Christ also warned in the parable of the vine and the branches (John 15:5, *RSV*): "Apart from me you can do nothing." From our treatment of this metaphor in Chapter 3 on grape wine, we infer that we are dealing symbolically with the Eucharistic Blood of Christ here. In sum, we deduce the tacit presence in this Pauline passage of wheat bread and grape wine, along with olive oil.

So, having recognized that Jesus is metaphorically the Root of the olive tree, we can appreciate that He is symbolically filled with its oil, like an inexhaustible reservoir. Now He is the "King of kings and Lord of lords" (see 1 Timothy 6:15; Revelation 17:14; 19:11-16; also Isaiah 9:5-6; Luke 1:32-33; John 18:37), as well as the "Messiah" or "Christ" or "Anointed One" (see Matthew 1:1; 16:16; Mark 8:29; Luke 4:41; 9:20; 24:26, 46; John 1:41; 11:27; Acts 2:36; 3:20; 10:38). It follows that *His* regal oil should be the proper oil of anointing. Because Confirmation is the sacrament that "perfects the common priesthood of the faithful, received in Baptism" (*CCC*, n. 1305), consecrating "a chosen race, a royal priesthood, a holy nation" (1 Peter 2:9, *RSV*), its matter is most fittingly olive oil.

Olive Oil and the Holy Spirit

Hence, we can infer with almost total certitude that the oil of anointing for the priests and kings of Israel was olive oil, even when the kind of oil is not specified. (See, for example, Exodus 29:7; Leviticus 21:10, 12; 1 Samuel 10:1; 16:13; Psalm 89:20-21.) Their consecration would constitute a *type* prefiguring the anointing of Confirmation. In fact, we are told (in 1 Samuel 16:13, *RSV*) that, from the day of King David's anointing by Samuel, "the Spirit of the LORD came mightily upon David." The sealing with chrism in Confirmation therefore brings about a fullness ("mighty coming") of the Holy Spirit within the soul, and the Holy Spirit becomes symbolically identified with the oil of anointing — that is, olive oil. (The *CCC*, n. 695, goes so far as to say that anointing with oil has become "a synonym for the Holy Spirit.") That is why the anointing with chrism on the forehead in Confirmation is accompanied by the essential formula (see the *CCC*, n. 1300): "Be sealed with the Gift of the Holy Spirit." (In 2 Corinthians 1:21-22, *NAB*, St. Paul writes: "God is the one who firmly establishes us along with you in Christ; it is he who anointed us and has sealed us, thereby depositing the first payment, the Spirit, in our hearts." See also 1 John 2:20, 27, *RSV*, about the "anointing" by the "Holy One," along with Acts 10:38.)

All this makes sense from a Trinitarian perspective. Since the Holy Spirit proceeds from the Son (as well as from the Father)[15] and since the olive tree (more concretely, its root) represents Jesus Christ, we conclude that the fruitful effusion of the tree — namely, olive oil — aptly signifies the Holy Spirit. Conversely, Christ is figuratively filled with olive oil because He is literally consubstantial with the Holy Spirit (as He and the Father are one) in the unity of the Blessed Trinity.

Returning for a moment to the account of the morning and evening sacrifices prescribed for the Israelites through Moses, we note that (in Numbers 28:5, *NAB*) God ordered the "fine flour" to be "mixed with . . . oil of crushed olives." The Lord also commanded (in Exodus 29:2, *RSV*) that unleavened cakes and bread wafers made of "fine wheat flour" be "mixed with oil." Compare Leviticus 2:1-2, 4, *RSV*: "When any one brings a cereal offering as an offering to the LORD, his offering shall be of fine flour; he shall pour oil upon it, and put frankincense on it, and bring it to Aaron's sons the priests. And he shall take from it a handful of the fine flour and oil, with all of its frankincense; and the priest shall burn this as its memorial portion upon the altar, an offering by fire, a pleasing odor to the LORD. . . . When you bring a cereal offering baked in the oven as an offering, it shall be unleavened cakes of fine flour mixed with oil, or unleavened wafers spread with oil." Frankincense was, of course, one of the gifts presented by the Magi to the Infant King in Matthew 2:11. Thus, Leviticus seems to foreshadow this worship of Christ by the Gentiles, since their offering of gold (as we saw in Chapter 2) symbolizes the "fine [wheat] flour" of the Eucharistic Bread, along with the sacred vessels (ciborium and monstrance) in which the Host is reposed and exposed. Indeed, frankincense is burned before the Blessed Sacrament at solemn occasions, such as the culmination of adoration preceding benediction.

Since olive oil represents the Holy Spirit, this "mixing" of flour with olive oil is a *type* foreshadowing the invocation (*epiclesis*) and descent of the Holy Spirit at the Mass's Consecration to penetrate (like liniment, as it were) the wheat bread down to its very ontological depths, converting it into the substance of Christ's Body.[16] Because of the mutual indwelling of the three Persons of the Blessed Trinity, the Holy Spirit is spiritually united with Jesus in the Eucharistic Host. Consequently, the "olive oil" (signifying the Holy Spirit) mystically becomes "mixed" (due to transubstantiation and circumincession) with the "fine flour" (signifying the Body of Christ). No gnostic reticence or repugnance over "mixing" the spiritual and the material here! In this regard, we should ponder Luke 1:35, where the Holy Spirit overshadowed Mary, a "heap of wheat" like the Church (as we learned in Chapter 2 from Song of Solomon 7:2), miraculously bringing about the physical presence of Jesus in her body.

Thus, the "oil" of the Holy Spirit further cements the already cohesive glutinous bread into an ineffably strong bond of unity. Even after the Consecration, the Church petitions the Father for the unifying fruits of the Holy Spirit's chrismal charism. Here are examples from three Eucharistic prayers:

> Eucharistic Prayer II: "May all of us who share in the body and blood of Christ / be brought together in unity by the Holy Spirit."
> Eucharistic Prayer III: "Grant that we, who are nourished by his body and blood, / may be filled with his Holy Spirit, and become one body, one spirit in Christ."

Eucharistic Prayer IV: "By your Holy Spirit, gather all who share this one bread and one cup / into the one body of Christ."

The Mount of Olives and Gethsemani

Let us press on to investigate additional olive symbolism. Some critical events are associated with the Mount of Olives. The *Bible Dictionary* appended to the *New American Bible* says that "Gethsemani," meaning "oil press," denoted an olive tree grove situated across from the Jerusalem temple. Reese Dubin identifies "Gethsemane" as "an olive orchard at the foot of the Mount of Olives."[17] (The original Hebrew word is *Gatshamanim*.)

We learn that, after a day of teaching, Jesus would ordinarily pass the nocturnal hours "lodged on the mount called Olivet" (Luke 21:37, *RSV*) and that it "was his custom" to go "to the Mount of Olives" (Luke 22:39, *RSV*); these two names are therefore synonymous. His conduct seems designed to instruct us with the lesson of blending the active and contemplative lives in a balanced manner. Confirmed Catholics cannot be content with just work, but must also withdraw periodically from the world into private prayer.

We are further told (in Matthew 24:3 and Mark 13:3-4) that Jesus delivered His eschatological discourse on the Mount of Olives. The site of this somber message reinforces the theme of a spirit of detachment from "this passing world," as St. Paul calls it in 1 Corinthians 7:31, *RSV* (and to which St. John alludes in 1 John 2:17, *RSV*). Hence, the confirmed Catholic should cultivate a long-term, elevated perspective on things, as St. Paul advises in Colossians 3:1-4.

Of course, the earthly disengagement or separation of Christ from His beloved Apostles began after the Last Supper, when "they went out to the Mount of Olives" (Matthew 26:30, *RSV*, and Mark 14:26, *RSV*; see again Luke 22:39). There, at the foot of the Mount, abandoned by the weakness of His friends, He underwent His Agony (wrenchingly recorded in Matthew 26:36-46; Mark 14:32-42; Luke 22:39-46). The "foot" of the Mount represents an ignoble situation, throwing into bold relief the infinite condescension of His Incarnation — the abasement of the *kenosis* eloquently preached by St. Paul in Philippians 2:6-8.

Now here is where the meaning of "Gethsemani" (or "oil press") enters. The word "agony" comes from the Greek noun *agonia*, which means "contest." In the olive grove garden, Jesus endured a monumental struggle beyond our comprehension. St. Thomas More writes that He beheld the imminence of the excruciating ordeal about to unfold around Him: in particular, "the treacherous betrayer, the bitter enemies, binding ropes, false accusations, slanders, blows, thorns, nails, the cross, and horrible tortures stretched out over many hours. . . , tormented by the thought of His disciples' terror, the loss of the Jews, even the destruction of the very man who so disloyally betrayed Him, and finally the ineffable grief of His beloved mother."[18]

According to the admirably heroic English martyr, "Christ . . . was overwhelmed by mental anguish more bitter than any other mortal has ever experienced. . . . For who has ever felt such bitter anguish that a bloody sweat broke out all over his body and ran down in drops to the ground?" But Christ freely allowed this extraordinary phenomenon to happen "in order to prefigure the blood that future martyrs would be forced to pour forth on the ground, and at the same time to offer this unheard-of, this marvelous example of, profound anguish as a consolation to those who would be so fearful and alarmed at the thought of torture that they might otherwise interpret their fear as a sign of their downfall and thus yield to despair."[19]

In the same vein, St. Thomas Aquinas writes: "Christ grieved not only over the loss of His own bodily life, but also over the sins of all others. And this grief in Christ surpassed all grief of every contrite heart, both because it flowed from a greater wisdom and charity, by which the pang of contrition is intensified, and because He grieved at the one time for all sins."[20]

We know that Christ emerged victorious from the inner tumult of this *agonia*, but only after He was squeezed (as it were) in an "oil press." If it were not for the olive trees there, it would otherwise seem strange that the garden in which He began to shed blood was not named "wine press." Indeed, the latter designation would have seemed an apt fulfillment of Gideon's "beating out wheat in the wine press" in Judges 6:11, *RSV*. On the other hand, the location with its actual meaning of "oil press" lends added significance to Numbers 28:5, which mandated (we recall) "beaten oil" or "oil of crushed olives" for Israel's daily sacrifice. This divine prescription constitutes a spiritual prefigurement: the grace of the Holy Spirit ("olive oil") was not fully poured out until Pentecost — after Christ (the "Olive" of Israel) had been "beaten" or "crushed" (see also Isaiah 53:5, 10, *NAB*) through His passion commencing in Gethsemani. There is again Trinitarian symbolism here: namely, the procession of the Third Person ("olive oil") from the Second Person (the "crushed olive").

Or else, in divine providence, it seems odd that there was no vineyard garden within walking distance of the Last Supper room as *prima facie* more appropriate scenery for this drama. Perhaps once again the Holy Sacrifice of the Mass is being profoundly signified in a veiled fashion: through the power of the Holy Spirit (symbolized by the "olive oil press"), acting first on Christ's flesh ("mixing with fine [wheat] flour"), the Precious Blood of Christ is then poured out on the altar. With regard to the Sacrament of Confirmation, the meaning may be that the presence of the Holy Spirit (symbolized by the surrounding olive trees) strengthens the recipient to withstand the trials of a witness ("martyr" from the Greek) to the Faith. For martyrdom demands the ultimate detachment from mundane affairs. Moreover, the "consolation" to which St. Thomas More refers may explain why the Holy Spirit is called the "Comforter." Although Jesus suffered intensely, the olive grove was also the scene of heavenly aid (see Luke 22:43).

The Mount of Olives and the Ascension

Yet another connection arises via Christ's post-resurrection departure. In Zechariah 14:4, *RSV*, the prophet foretold: "On that day his [the Lord's] feet shall stand on the Mount of Olives which lies before Jerusalem on the east." In fact, we learn from Acts 1:12 (compare Matthew 28:16) that Jesus ascended into heaven from Mount Olivet, which Dubin identifies as the Mount of Olives.[21] Actually, in anticipation of this ultimate exaltation, He had entered the Mount of Olives prior to His triumphal procession into Jerusalem attended by the (temporary) acclamation of His Davidic kingship (see Matthew 21:1-11; Mark 11:1-10; Luke 19:29-38). Some typology is at work here. For 2 Samuel 15:30-32 records the ascent of King David up the Mount of Olives while contending (prayerfully, courageously, and eventually victoriously) against his bitter sorrow over the betrayal by his beloved son Absalom.

But this site appears to have a dual significance for the Sacrament of Confirmation.

First, the presence of Christ standing on the Mount itself symbolically reverses His earlier state of humiliated submission kneeling at its foot. The act of ascension from the Mount of Olives represents His monarchical authority over all those who are sealed with the chrism of the Holy Spirit. He holds the summit of priestly and royal power — a reign in which His anointed subjects share.

Second, the setting seems to teach that confirmed Catholics should gaze upward, fixing their final hopes on the heavenly things disclosed by the Holy Spirit, whose Wisdom imbues them with the unction of supernatural insight. (See Acts 1:10-11; Romans 6:8-9; 8:11, 21-23; 1 Corinthians 2:9-16; 12:4-11; 15:19, 53-58; Philippians 4:8; Colossians 3:1-3; 2 Timothy 2:11-12.)

Olive Trees and the Blessed Trinity

In a fascinating vision described in Zechariah 4:1-3, 11-14, *RSV*, olive trees are intimately conjoined with the divine majesty and sovereignty displayed in Christ's Ascension: "And the angel who talked with me came again, and waked me, like a man that is wakened from his sleep. And he said to me, 'What do you see?' I said, 'I see, and behold, a lampstand all of gold, with a bowl on the top of it, and seven lamps on it, with seven lips on each of the lamps which are on the top of it. And there are two olive trees by it, one on the right of the bowl and the other on its left.' . . . Then I said to him, 'What are these two olive trees on the right and the left of the lampstand?' And a second time I said to him, 'What are these two branches of the olive trees, which are beside the two golden pipes from which the oil is poured out?' He said to me, 'Do you not know what these are?' I said, 'No, my lord.' Then he said, 'These are the two anointed who stand by the Lord of the whole earth.' " (For alternative translations of several words, note that "lips" is rendered as "tubes" in the *NAB* and as "funnels" in the *D-R*; "pipes" as "channels" in the *NAB* and as "beaks" or perhaps "funnels" again in the *D-R*; and "the two anointed" as "the two sons of oil" in the *D-R*. Also the *NAB* modifies the noun "oil" with the adjective "fresh" and the verb "pour" by the adverb "freely.")

Without claiming a definitive exegesis of this passage, we venture a mystical interpretation (subject, of course, to the Magisterium's correction). The "lampstand all of gold" symbolizes the sublime Godhead, especially God the Father, the pure unbegotten source of all being, truth, and goodness. The "bowl" (a feminine image) represents the one true Church established and supported by God. The "seven lamps" signify the seven sacraments received by the Church from God. (See also Numbers 8:1-4.) The "[olive] oil" that is "poured out" indicates the ever vital, invigorating, and generously abundant grace conveyed (or properly funneled as if by "lips" or "tubes") through the sacraments. The presence of seven lips on each of the seven lamps may indicate that each sacrament is somehow connected with the other sacraments. The "two olive trees" (or "two branches of the olive trees") responsible for the transmission of this gratuitous unction symbolize God the Son and God the Holy Spirit. Indeed, Christ is the "anointed" Savior (see Acts 10:38; Psalm 89:19-29) and the Spirit is the "anointed" Paraclete, both of whom proceed from the Father ("stand by the Lord of the whole earth") with equal dignity in the unity of the Blessed Trinity. Both are sent to build and nourish the Church with their own gracious divine missions ("golden pipes" or "golden channels"), and both are "sons of oil."

At any rate, the Church does not contradict the above exegesis, telling us that the Father always sends "his Breath" with "his Word" (see John 3:34): "In their joint mission, the Son and the Holy Spirit are distinct but inseparable. To be sure, it is Christ who is seen, the visible image of the invisible God, but it is the Spirit who reveals him. Jesus is Christ, 'anointed,' because the Spirit is his anointing, and everything that occurs from the Incarnation on derives from this fullness" (*CCC*, nn. 689-690).

For an alternative (and subordinate) possible fulfillment, the "olive tree" on the "right" side represents Jesus, since He ascended to the right hand of the Father, as we recite in the Nicene and Apostles' Creeds. On the other hand, the "olive tree" on the "left" could signify the reigning pope, since, as the Vicar of Christ on earth, he has been guaranteed the special assistance of the Holy Spirit protecting him from teaching error in his capacity as chief pastor of the flock; in addition, because he has been entrusted with jurisdiction over the sacraments, he acts as a subsidiary channel for the operation of the Holy Spirit.

Olive Trees and Christian Witness

We learn from 1 Kings 6 that, although the interior woodwork of Solomon's temple was derived mainly from cedar, the inner sanctuary (housing the ark of the covenant) featured entrance doors and two cherubim all constructed of olivewood overlaid with gold. These angelic statues were of gigantic proportions: each approximately fifteen feet tall, with a wingspan of fifteen feet as well. Now the cedar tree certainly presents an image of physical strength. But, since angels are pure spirits, the representation of their essential immutability demands an even more durable material. Furthermore, God's firm covenantal commitment requires a material of symbolically incomparable endurance. Therefore, the fact that olivewood was reserved for the very center of the holy place signifies the peerless permanence of the olive tree. (A point of additional interest: Jean Barilla calls olive oil "green gold."[22])

From a strictly natural viewpoint, the olive tree is extraordinarily hardy. Reese Dubin states: "Some of the original trees at Gethsemane — which was an olive orchard at the foot of the Mount of Olives — have been there since the time of Christ, or at least spring from the original roots. For even though the Romans tried to destroy the orchard in A.D. 70, it is almost impossible to kill the roots, from which many new sprouts arise."[23]

Barilla agrees that the olive tree is almost miraculously prolific, adding that olive wood itself is "resistant to decay."[24] From a supernatural perspective on the olive tree, the meaning is evident. Since Christ is the "Root" of God's kingdom, symbolized by the durable olive tree, the Church shares in her Divine Founder's own indefectibility: unlike a merely human institution, she can never be utterly vanquished. (See Matthew 16:18, *D-R*: "Upon this rock I will build my church, and the gates of hell shall not prevail against it.") Any attempt to eradicate the Christian spirit from one part of the world will only lead to growth of saplings elsewhere, for the blood of martyrs is proverbially the seed of faith.[25]

In other terms, the virtual indestructibility of the olive tree signifies the spiritual invincibility of confirmed Catholics resulting from the power of the Holy Spirit: "These [my two witnesses] are the two olive trees and the two lampstands which stand before the Lord of the earth. And if any one would harm them, fire pours from their mouth and consumes their foes" (Revelation 11:3-5, *RSV*; see also Matthew 5:14-16). Whether the historical personages represented by the olive trees/lampstands in this passage are literally Moses and Elijah, or Enoch and Elijah, or Peter and Paul, the verses can apply to all Catholics whose souls ("lamps") are fueled by the grace ("olive oil") of the Holy Spirit. According to Matthew 10:17-19, when they bear witness to the truth in the courts of godlessly inimical political regimes, they need not fret in advance over the content and manner of their speech. At the opportune moment, they will be inspired with the searing words of the "Spirit of truth" to incinerate the lies of their accusers. For, as Christ promised in Matthew 10:20, *RSV*, "it is not you who speak, but the

Spirit of your Father speaking through you." (Compare Mark 13:11 and Luke 12:11-12.)

Other verses (e.g., Mark 13:9-10, Luke 21:12-15, John 15:27, Acts 1:8, and 1 Timothy 6:12) show that all followers of our Lord must witness before the world to Him and His doctrine. Yet the archetypal witnesses sent by the Father to reveal the truth are Jesus Christ and the Holy Spirit, as proved by John 15:26; 16:7-15; 18:37 together with 1 Timothy 6:13. Hence, the two human "witnesses" of Revelation 11:2-12, who prophesy with great power for "forty-two months" or "one thousand two hundred and sixty days" (see also Daniel 12:11), are regal proxies or viceroys for Jesus and the Spirit — Divine Persons on whom they depend totally. Thus, our preceding exegesis of Zechariah 4:1-3, 11-14 does not conflict with this eschatological interpretation. On the contrary, our spiritual explorations of Zechariah 4:1-3, 11-14 and Revelation 11:3-5 are complementary: the Old Testament passage cryptically explains the heavenly causation or exemplarity of "witness" and the New Testament passage delineates its practical earthly effects.

The sturdiness of the olive tree also symbolizes the indomitable (virtually unshakable) faith of the confirmed Christian, as Psalm 52:8, *RSV*, declares: "But I am like a green olive tree / in the house of God. / I trust in the steadfast love of God / for ever and ever." Only someone who is firmly rooted in the sacramental life of the Church ("the house of God") can truthfully utter such a simile in the sorrowful desert of this earthly vale. Despite drought and heat amidst the vicissitudes of life, this olive tree remains supernaturally young and productive: "Like a tree planted by water, / that sends out its roots by the stream, / . . . its leaves remain green" and do "not wither," while "it does not cease to bear fruit" in "its season" (Jeremiah 17:7-8, *RSV*, together with Psalm 1:1-3, *RSV*).[26] Its spiritual fertility enables it to procreate, in the order of grace, other olive trees: "Your children will be like olive shoots around your table" (Psalm 128:3, *RSV*). In other words, the confirmed Catholic must spread the Faith to others (i.e., evangelize) by faithfully living out a vocation that admits engagement in some form of apostolate. The joy of these "children" in the Faith is a reward of the olive tree's growth to spiritual maturity. (See Ephesians 4:11-16.) We relate here Barilla's assertion that the olive tree "symbolizes longevity, fertility and maturity."[27]

John Heinerman furnishes more corroboration on the natural level: "The olive tree is an evergreen, commonly found in all of the Mediterranean countries, but widely cultivated in tropical climates as well. The hard, yellow wood of the gnarled trunk is covered by gray-green bark. . . . The leathery leaves are dark green on top and have silvery scales underneath. The tree yields fragrant white flowers and an oblong or nearly round type of fruit."[28]

Symbolically, therefore, its "evergreen" and tough ("leathery") leaves mean permanence of vigorous life, while its "fragrant white flowers" signify a sweet innocence that eventually burgeons with fruitfulness. According to St. Thomas Aquinas, olive oil symbolizes the Holy Spirit better than any other oil, since the evergreen olive tree represents "the refreshing and merciful operation of the Holy Ghost."[29]

Olive Oil, the Holy Spirit, and Peace

We have encountered several symbols for the Holy Spirit: fire, dove, and olive oil. There are, of course, others. For instance, in Chapter 1 we saw the connection between water and the Spirit. Another symbol for the Holy Spirit is wind, air, or breath (see Genesis 1:2 and John 3:6-8; 20:22). But the three images of fire, dove, and olive oil indicate virtues particularly attached to Confirmation. Fire signifies both fervent charity and zealous witness, as exemplified by the boldness of the formerly timorous Apostles in proclaiming the truth about salvation after the descent of the Holy Spirit under the form of fiery tongues at Pentecost (see Acts 2:1-4). The dove connotes innocence and purity (see Matthew 10:16, in light of James 3:17 and 2 Peter 1:3-7), as well as gentleness, meekness, forbearance, and kindness (see James 1:19-20; 3:5-6, 17; 1 Peter 3:15-16) — which ought to temper ardor lest it flare into fury.[30]

According to St. Thomas Aquinas, fire and oil are closely related, since oil is the combustible matter that fuels incendiary power
and activity.[31] Whereas fire represents the mighty, forceful action
of the Holy Spirit, olive oil signifies the placid peace of the Spirit
(see Ephesians 4:3); for restoration of the harmony on earth between God and man was signaled when a dove brought Noah an
olive leaf upon the recession of the punitive flood waters, as narrated in Genesis 8:11. (The olive branch as a sign of peace also
appears in 2 Maccabees 14:4.)

But note that this peace arrived at a terrible cost. Indeed, the
same Jesus who proclaimed in Matthew 5:9 that the "peacemakers"
are "blessed" also announced in Matthew 10:34 and Luke 12:49, 51
that He did not come to bring peace at any price, but rather to highlight in sharp contrast the division between good and evil. The peace
He gives does not emanate from the absence of conflict with the
unbelieving world (see John 14:27 and Philippians 4:7). Instead, as
St. Augustine defined it, peace is "the tranquillity of order."[32] When
the prophets foretold that Christ would "command peace to the nations," that He would be the "Prince of Peace," and that He would in
fact "*be* peace" itself, they also described His dominion as established
in *righteousness* and confirmed in *justice*. (Compare Zechariah 9:9-
10, *RSV*; Isaiah 9:6-7, *RSV*; and Micah 5:3-4, *NAB*.) Reading in
Micah that "He shall stand firm . . . / by the strength of the LORD"
should elicit the image of a robust olive tree.

Thus, genuine peace will not emerge until society is ordered
under divine law, until righteousness prevails. Peace and justice are
inextricably linked; peace cannot be purchased at the expense of
justice — justice in every way for everyone. (See James 3:18, *NAB*,
and Augustine's *City of God*, Book XIX, Chapter 12. A major theme
of Plato's *Republic* is the construction of a peaceful civic realm
through the well-ordered harmony that he defines as "justice.")
Therefore, the recipient of Confirmation, sealed with the chrism
of the Holy Spirit and faithful to the grace of witness, must be
prepared to meet opposition from a world at war against God's
definition of justice, in order to attain the inner peace of conscience,

which is the gift of the Spirit (compare 2 Timothy 1:7, 14; Ephesians 4:3; Philippians 4:7).

Along these lines, addressing from the thirteenth century our modern "multiculturalist," or "pluralist," reluctance to speak the untarnished truth lest someone of a different opinion be "offended," St. Thomas Aquinas instructs us by taking Jesus as a model:

> The salvation of the multitude is to be preferred to the peace of any individuals whatsoever. Consequently, when certain ones, by their perverseness, hinder the salvation of the multitude, the preacher and the teacher should not fear to offend those men, in order that he may insure the salvation of the multitude. Now . . . Christ's doctrine . . . was the only way to salvation. . . . For which reason our Lord, undeterred by their taking offense, publicly taught the truth which they hated, and condemned their vices.[33]

In short, peace cannot be bought with a cheaper metal than the mettle that lubricates the muscles of the Christian soul. Olive oil is expensive, especially the extra-virgin grade.

PART II

In the Sacrament of the Anointing of the Sick, "the Church commends to the suffering and glorified Lord the faithful who are dangerously ill so that He may support and save them," according to the *Code of Canon Law*, Can. 998. This sacrament is conferred "by anointing them [the seriously ill or aged] on the forehead and hands . . . — saying, only once: 'Through this holy anointing may the Lord in His love and mercy help you with the grace of the Holy Spirit. May the Lord who frees you from sin save you and raise you up' " (*CCC*, n. 1513). Since it serves as a kind of "medicine" of the soul, its principal purpose is to remedy residual spiritual weaknesses resulting from the "sickness of sin." Consequentially, however, because grace and sin are mutually exclusive, it also removes the guilt of any sin (venial or mortal), provided the recipient has contrition (a state of free will that this sacrament facilitates).[34]

In this sacrament the Holy Spirit bestows many gifts: inner peace, courage amidst the adversities of sickness or old age, fortification against temptations to succumb to disheartenment, invigorated faith and trust in God, and the fruitfulness of a configuring union with the Savior's redemptive passion (participation in Christ's work of sanctifying the Church and mankind). It supports the recipient in the agony of the last leg on the heavenward road, thereby completing the consecration for combat initiated at Baptism and intensified at Confirmation.[35]

The Sacrament of the Sick restores bodily health only to the extent that "it is conducive to the salvation of the soul."[36] This effect, though, occurs only "by assisting natural causes, not after the extraordinary manner of a miracle."[37] The result is indirect — that is, due to the repercussions of the soul's spiritual revitalization on the body.[38] Unlike Baptism, whose spiritual cleansing also washes the body by the natural power of its matter, Extreme Unction would not alleviate physical affliction in virtue of the matter applied.[39]

Valid Matter

Of course, this brings us to the question of the matter for the Sacrament of the Sick. The *CCC*, n. 1513, and the *Code of Canon Law*, Can. 847, both state that the anointing uses "duly blessed oil — pressed from olives or from other plants." According to Ludwig Ott, the requirement of oil referred to by St. James is *de fide*. (See James 5:14-15, *RSV*: "Is any among you sick? Let him call for the elders of the church, and let them pray over him, anointing him with oil in the name of the Lord; and the prayer of faith will save the sick man, and the Lord will raise him up.") Ott then concludes that this means *olive* oil, but he does not classify this more specific point as also belonging to the sacred deposit of revealed Faith. Rather, he merely cites the *Decretum pro Armenis* of 1439, which taught: "*cuius materia est oleum olivae per episcopum benedictum* [whose matter is olive oil blessed by a bishop]."[40] Similarly, Heribert Jone asserts that "valid matter is olive oil," but without even considering the issue whether other oils could also serve as valid matter.[41]

We have seen, however, a relaxation in the kind of oil allowed, although olive is still accorded prominence, since it is the only plant oil specifically mentioned in Canon Law. In fact, St. Thomas Aquinas writes:

> The spiritual healing, which is given at the end of life, ought to be complete, since there is no other to follow; it ought also to be gentle, lest hope, of which the dying stand in utmost need, be shattered rather than fostered. Now oil has a softening effect, it penetrates to the very heart of a thing, and spreads over it. Hence, in both the foregoing respects, it is a suitable matter for this sacrament. And since oil is, above all, the name of the liquid extract of olives, for other liquids are only called oil from their likeness to it, it follows that olive oil is the matter which should be employed in this sacrament.[42]

According to the Angelic Doctor, as we have seen before, olive oil symbolizes the Holy Spirit better than any other oil, since the evergreen olive tree represents "the refreshing and merciful operation of the Holy Ghost."[43] As a careful theologian, he does not aver that olive oil is the *only* possible valid matter for Extreme Unction; he merely proposes that it is the most ideally suited oil for this sacrament.

As Aquinas indicates, oil in itself has key attributes making it eminently fit for the Sacrament of the Sick. According to the *CCC*, n. 1293, "oil is a sign of abundance and joy; it cleanses (anointing before and after a bath) and limbers (the anointing of athletes and wrestlers); oil is a sign of healing, since it is soothing to bruises and wounds; and it makes radiant with beauty, health, and strength." These symbols derive from natural properties of oil: smooth texture, capacity to retain heat (thus warming the body), somewhat sweet in taste, and shiny in appearance on the skin. It is appropriate for the seriously ill to be spiritually treated with a substance that represents healing of the sores of sin, soothing of its residual abrasions, comforting in bitter sorrow, imparting a pure glow of grace to the soul, endowing with flexible strength to resist diabolical onslaught in the final combat, and promising the overflowing happiness of eternal life.

Why Olive Oil?

But why, beyond what Aquinas argues, is *olive* oil truly the most favorable kind of oil to employ? Reese Dubin declares: "Olive oil . . . is the symbol of goodness, purity, and — especially — long life." As we learned previously, the association with longevity stems at least partly from the ability of olive trees to survive and maintain their sturdiness for countless years. Moreover, olive oil was Biblically renowned for its ability to assuage neuro-muscular-skeletal pain and restore a limber strength. Dubin contends that olive oil safeguards the integrity of the cardiovascular system and can perhaps help avert death from other diseases, too.[44] These salient features of olive oil symbolize spiritual prowess, perseverance, and prevention of dis*heart*enment while engaging in the last strenuous battle against infernal forces.

The Consolation of the Holy Spirit

Alongside hardy endurance, olive oil symbolizes consolation. H.C.A. Vogel reports one researcher's claim that "the composition of the fat molecules of olive oil compare the closest [among all oils] to those found in mother's milk," rendering olive oil "probably the most acceptable kind [of oil] for human consumption, because the body will find it the easiest to process for assimilation."[45] Now mother's milk is associated with pacifying comfort or consolation: "Oh, that you may suck fully / of the milk of her [Jerusalem's] comfort, / That you may nurse with delight / at her abundant breasts! . . . / As a mother comforts her son, . . . / in Jerusalem you shall find your comfort" (Isaiah 66:11-13, *NAB*). Here Jerusalem represents our mother the Church, whose sacramental graces pour forth profusely. If the claim about the biochemical affinity of mother's milk to olive oil proves correct, it would reinforce the symbolic aptness of olive oil for the sacramental anointing of the sick — the sweet and consoling pledge of everlasting life upon gaining victory over the enemy. In addition, it would furnish a basis on the natural level for linking the Holy Spirit with olive oil. Indeed, the Holy Spirit is traditionally called the "Comforter" or the "Consoler," reminding us of the ephemeral character of this world's sorrow, to be replaced by everlasting happiness. (See John 14:16-18, 26; 16:13, 20-22 and Revelation 22:17, which unites the Holy Spirit with the "Bride," the Church, in pleading for her reunion with Christ in eschatological glory.)

The Holy Spirit also advocates our cause before the tribunal of divine justice ineffably better than we can help ourselves in our abject debility (see Romans 8:26-27). It is indeed consoling for an impoverished beggar to have a powerful intercessor. The words of the hymn "Come, Holy Ghost," attributed to Rabanus Maurus (c. 776-856) and translated by Edward Caswall (1814-1878), accompanied by the well-known music of Louis Lambillotte (1796-1855), are germane: "Come, Holy Ghost, Creator blest, / And in our hearts take up thy rest; / Come with thy grace and heav'nly aid / To fill the hearts which thou hast made. / O Comforter, to thee we cry, / Thou heav'nly gift of God most high; / Thou font of life, and fire of love, / And sweet anointing from above. / Praise be to thee, Father and Son, / And Holy Spirit, with them one; / And may the Son on us bestow / The gifts that from the Spirit flow."

Unction of Mercy and Healing

Two Old Testament narratives presenting oil (most probably olive) as a merciful blessing for the poor occur in the two books of Kings. In 1 Kings 17:7-24 we learn that Elijah, associated with the Holy Spirit due to the fiery chariot snatching him from earth in a heavenly whirlwind, worked the miracle of perpetuating the presence of oil for a widow and then later raised her son from the dead (certainly an "extreme" unction). Similarly, in 2 Kings 4:1-7, Elisha performed the miracle of multiplying vessels of oil to assist a widow in paying off debts owed to her deceased husband's creditors and to help her with living expenses for her children. In 2 Kings 4:8-37 this illustrious successor of Elijah (with a "double share of [his] spirit," according to 2 Kings 2:9, *RSV*) also brought another woman's dead son back to life. These passages corroborate the connection of the Holy Spirit, "the Lord and Giver of life" (*Nicene Creed*), with the symbolically soothing qualities of oil in assuaging the misery of suffering.

In the New Testament, besides the definitive James 5:14-15, we discover early evidence of a sacramental anointing of the sick in Mark 6:13, *RSV*: "And they [the twelve] cast out many demons, and anointed with oil many that were sick and healed them." Although the Apostles "went out and preached that men should repent" (Mark 6:12, *RSV*), their anointing of the sick here does not seem to constitute the authentic sacrament that is accompanied by forgiveness of sins, because Christ did not bestow on His first priests the power of absolution until after His resurrection (see John 20:21-23). Nevertheless, we find another association between oil (again, probably olive) and the alleviation of illness.

There are some Scriptural texts in which the main bodily area anointed in Extreme Unction is mentioned prefiguratively, for example Psalm 23:5, *RSV*: "Thou anointest my head with oil, / my cup overflows." This signifies the abundance of grace available due to God's generous mercy. Moreover, Psalm 133, *RSV*, depicts "precious oil upon the head" as an image of peace, prosperity, and the promise of unending life. Again, it is virtually beyond doubt that "oil" in these verses means "olive oil"; indeed, according to Jean Barilla, the olive tree is a "symbol of immortality."[46]

In Part I of this chapter, we quoted in full an important passage about the olive from St. Paul's Letter to the Romans 11:16-24. Here is an exegesis of this text that differs somewhat from the earlier one given; it is perhaps more appropriate for the Sacrament of the Sick.[47] Since the (natural) olive tree is Israel (Romans 11:17, 21, 24), since "salvation is from the Jews" (John 4:22, *RSV*), and since Jesus *is* this salvation (see Matthew 1:21; Acts 2:36; 4:11-12; 2 Corinthians 5:14-15, 21; Colossians 1:20-22; Hebrews 9:14-15, 28; 10:12; 1 John 4:14), it follows that Jesus is *the fruit* of the olive tree. Hence, He must be the principal source of "olive oil" (metaphorically speaking). But, because He is the "fullness of grace" (see John 1:14, 16, *D-R*), it is fitting that olive oil should symbolize sanctifying grace. The fact that olive oil is "rich" signifies the lavish anointing of the Comforter, the Holy Spirit, who imparts grace to the soul.

Ultimately, therefore, Jesus provides the healing unction that cures spiritual wounds. He is the "Good Samaritan" who pours spiritual oil on our disfigured souls (see Luke 10:34), even at His own expense, as indicated by Luke 10:35, along with Matthew 8:17 and Isaiah 1:6; 53:4-5. (Dubin opines that the oil in the "Good Samaritan" parable is olive oil.[48]) His powerful mercy is the soothing unguent that loosens and frees paralyzed spiritual limbs (see Acts 3:6-9, 16). He desires that our spiritual blindness be cured so that we may achieve clear insight into the truth of human existence and our everlasting destiny: "I counsel you to buy from me . . . salve to anoint your eyes, that you may see" (Revelation 3:18, *RSV*). That is, repair your vision and "keep your eyes open" (Matthew 25:13, *NAB*); you will then be able to view the approach of the light of glory. (Compare Psalm 36:9, *RSV*, Ephesians 5:14, 1 John 3:2, and Revelation 2:17; interpreting "see" in a spiritual sense, compare Ephesians 3:16-19, Philippians 1:9-11; 3:7-11, Colossians 1:9, and 1 Timothy 2:4.) In view of Deuteronomy 28:40 (and 1 Samuel 8:13-14, *NAB*, or 1 Kings 8:13-14, *D-R*), the ocular "salve" would probably be based on olive oil. Dubin recites anecdotal evidence vindicating the naturally therapeutic value of olive oil for healing the eyes — and ears, too.[49] (This is not intended as medical advice, but rather as information for the reader's edification.) Another resource speculates that the "tree of life" whose "leaves . . . were for the healing of the nations" (Revelation 22:2, *RSV*) may refer to (what else?) the olive.[50] At any rate, the foregoing citations collectively imply the propriety of olive oil for anointing the sick.

The Oil Lamp

Being filled with "olive oil," Christ is the "lamp" lighting the way to eternal life — a metaphor contained in three salient Scriptural verses:

1. Psalm 119:105, *RSV*: "Thy word is a lamp to my feet / and a light to my path."
2. John 8:12, *D-R*: "I am the light of the world."
3. Revelation 21:23, *RSV*: "And the [heavenly] city has no need of sun or moon to shine upon it, for the glory of God is its light, and its lamp is the Lamb."

We observe that Exodus 35 repeatedly juxtaposes "anointing oil" with "oil for the light," where "oil" means "olive oil." The significance for Extreme Unction of the parable about the wise virgins and the foolish ones in Matthew 25:1-13, *RSV*, with their bargaining over the matter of oil, then becomes luminous. The individual "lamps" here represent human souls, which are lit when in the state of grace and thus have the supernatural capacity to discern the road to heaven. The (olive) oil symbolizes the indwelling of the Holy Spirit who keeps the soul-lamps alive with His sanctifying grace. Without vigilant (or "wise") recourse to the Christ-Lamp Himself for the blessed unction of this gracious fuel, the soul is in peril of losing its flame (i.e., falling into mortal sin) and hence its way to everlasting life (see Ephesians 5:14 and Psalm 112:4). The Sacrament of the Sick is intended to keep the "lamps burning" (Luke 12:35, *RSV*) for negotiating the passage to the next life. Perhaps it is from this parable that the designation "virgin" olive oil arose. Indeed, regarding the policy of the ancient Greeks, Barilla informs us: "Only virgins and chaste men were entrusted with tending olive groves."[51]

O Lord, give us this pure oil for our lamps and keep them burning! Lead us to the glory of the Olive!

APPENDIX

As we said at the outset of this chapter, although anointing with blessed oil plays a customary ancillary role in Baptism, oil is not this sacrament's essential valid matter, which is water (covered in Chapter 1). Nevertheless, for the sake of completeness, we now very briefly discuss the symbolic purpose of olive oil for Baptism.

According to the *CCC*, n. 1237 (emphasis in the original paragraph): "Since Baptism signifies liberation from sin and from its instigator the devil, one or more *exorcisms* are pronounced over the candidate. The celebrant then anoints him with the oil of catechumens, or lays his hands on him, and he explicitly renounces Satan. Thus prepared, he is able to *confess the faith of the Church*, to which he will be 'entrusted' by Baptism."

Because the rubrics for this rite permit an alternative, the anointing with oil here is optional.

The *CCC*, nn. 1241-1242, goes on to elaborate that the usual rite in the Roman liturgy involves a "post-baptismal anointing" with "*sacred chrism*, perfumed oil consecrated by the bishop." This chrismation "signifies the gift of the Holy Spirit to the newly baptized" and "announces a second anointing with sacred chrism to be conferred later by the bishop — Confirmation, which will as it were 'confirm' and complete the baptismal anointing." But note that the *CCC* calls this chrismation "*post*-baptismal"; in other words, it is not an essential part of the Sacrament of Baptism considered in itself, for Baptism is validly administered using water accompanied by the required Trinitarian formula.

So why is baptismal chrismation performed at all? In n. 1241 the *CCC* explains that the new Christian has become "incorporated into Christ who is anointed priest, prophet, and king." Thus, the newly baptized individual shares in the salvific office of Christ as "one 'anointed' by the Holy Spirit" also.

We learned in Part I of this chapter that Jesus is metaphorically the Olive Tree Root, hence symbolically filled with its oil, like an inexhaustible reservoir. Since He is the "King of kings and Lord of lords," the eternal high priest, and the "Messiah" or "Anointed One," it follows that *His* regal oil should be the proper oil of anointing. Now, as the *CCC* amplifies in n. 1546, Christ has fashioned out of the Church's members "a kingdom, priests to his God and Father" or "a kingdom and priests to our God" (Revelation 1:6; 5:10, *RSV*). Therefore (we continue to cite the *CCC*, n. 1546), the "whole community of believers is, as such, priestly," and all the

"faithful exercise their baptismal priesthood through their participation, each according to his own vocation, in Christ's mission as
priest, prophet, and king." Because baptismal chrismation represents initiation into the New Covenant's common "holy priesthood" of all baptized persons, consecrated as "a chosen race, a royal
priesthood, a holy nation" (1 Peter 2:5, 9, *RSV*), its matter is most
fittingly the oil derived from the olive tree.

chapter five

WHY MALE PRIESTS?

The next two debates would never have gained currency except for the widespread refusal to acknowledge or accept the deep supernatural significance of the natural differences between male and female. We first examine the controversy over ordination of women to the priesthood and then, in the next chapter, devote our attention to the topic of so-called homosexual "marriage."

The Catholic Church is a hierarchical society, consisting of members (united under Jesus Christ, the invisible Head of the Body) who assist one another as participants in an ordered structure with various capacities. Holy Orders is the sacrament of integration into an ecclesiastical rank whose purpose is to serve the Church through the exercise of a special sacred power, thus perpetuating for all time the mission delegated by Christ to His Apostles. (See the *CCC*, nn. 1536-1538.) It is true that all the faithful, by virtue of their Baptism, form a "holy royal priesthood" (see 1 Peter 2:5, 9 and Revelation 1:6; 5:10); however, according to the *CCC*, n. 1547, the office of the ordained priest differs essentially from the common priesthood of the laity, since it is directed to the spiritual origin and development of members of Christ's Mystical Body. The *Code of Canon Law*, Can. 1008, asserts: "By divine institution some among Christ's faithful are, through the sacrament of order, marked with an indelible character and are thus constituted sacred ministers; thereby they are consecrated and deputed so that . . . they fulfill, in the person of Christ the Head, the offices of teaching, sanctifying and ruling, and so they nourish the people of God."[1]

Hence, Holy Orders elevates the recipient above a universally shared status, initiating the ordained individual into a consecrated office ultimately under the authority of the pope (the successor of

Peter and Vicar of Christ as visible head of the Church on earth) and locally under a diocesan bishop (one of the successors of the twelve Apostles). Therefore, the sacred priestly ministry has a special communitarian aspect that makes it *collegial*. But by its very nature it is also *personal*, because each priest receives the vocation to this sacerdotal service from Christ, in whose name the priest functions (see the *CCC*, nn. 874-883). The priest "truly represents" the God-Man Jesus Christ, acting "in the power and place" of His very Person (see the *CCC*, n. 1548). This condition occurs through a spiritual configuring of the priest to Christ; the soul of the priest is sealed with an indelible (everlasting) sign called a sacramental *character* (see the *CCC*, nn. 1563, 1581-1582).[2]

The two chief tasks for which each priest has been ordained are preaching the Gospel and administering the sacraments — culminating in the supreme offering of the Holy Sacrifice of the Mass. There, mystically assuming the role of Jesus, the priest represents and applies (for the benefit of the faithful) Christ's unique oblation to God the Father on the cross in atonement for humanity's sins (see the *CCC*, nn. 1563, 1564, 1566).

Valid 'Matter'

Now comes the thorny issue. We are not concerned so much with the details of the ordination rite itself, the "form" of the Sacrament of Holy Orders (although we will touch on a pertinent point later). Rather, in keeping with the overall running theme of this book, we ask the same question once again — applied to this new context. *What* is the proper "matter" (in the sense of "recipient subject") of the Sacrament of Holy Orders? *Who* may be legitimately ordained to the sacred or ministerial priesthood? The *Code of Canon Law*, Can. 1024, asserts unequivocally: "Only a baptized man can validly receive sacred ordination." (The *CCC*, n. 1577, makes basically the same statement.[3]) Pope John Paul II solemnly reaffirmed this constant traditional teaching of the Church in his Apostolic Letter *Ordinatio Sacerdotalis*: "Wherefore, in order that all doubt may be removed regarding a matter of great importance, a matter which pertains to the Church's divine constitution itself, in virtue of my ministry of confirming the brethren (cf. Lk 22:32) I declare that the Church has no authority whatsoever to confer priestly ordination on women and that this judgment is to be definitively held by all the Church's faithful."[4] Hence, this pronouncement is a doctrine of the Catholic Faith — not merely a discipline subject to change (contrary to the wishful thinking of some).

Why the discrimination between the two genders here? *Why* can only males be priests? To answer this somewhat complicated question, we devote the rest of the chapter. Initially, our argumentation will consist primarily in philosophical reflections on human biology — though not exclusively, since the existence and nature of the priesthood is unknowable apart from faith in divine revelation. Subsequently, our apologetic for the all-male priesthood will rest on Sacred Scripture alone.

PHILOSOPHICAL ARGUMENTS

Of the two irreducible types of human (hence embodied) persons, we must decide which one (male or female) is the more suitable vehicle for executing the priestly office.[5] It would be inexcusably facile to dismiss the very question as unworthy, inconsequential, or even absurd on the grounds that men and women can perform the same social and occupational functions — implying the apparently logical conclusion that both genders are equally adapted for serving in the role of priest. Over and again the claim is made that women can do as good a "job" as men at serving in the ranks of the ordained clergy, as though there were nothing more to the priesthood than doing a "job." But this sort of superficial and simplistic attitude (betraying a functionalist repudiation of human ontology) permeates the secular gnostic mentality. On the contrary, adverting to the profound sacramental principle that the natural order of things reflects supernatural mysteries, we ought to contemplate some pertinent divine attributes, since the God-Man Jesus Christ is the eternal high priest.

Divine Transcendence

In order to explain the changeable universe of contingent (nonnecessary) being, sound metaphysics demonstrates the existence of a necessary Being (called "God") who is pure actuality, free from any limiting passive potentiality.[6] It follows that in His creative activity God gives without needing to receive from anything outside Himself. Thus, His being is utterly transcendent: infinitely beyond and wholly other than the domain of creation. Because the universe of both spiritual and material entities depends for its existence entirely on His sustaining efficient causality, His own substance cannot in any way be immersed in it. Otherwise, He would be producing His own reality out of nothing, as well — a blatant violation of the law of noncontradiction.[7] (God is simply a self-sufficient, though not self-causing, subsistent Being.) In short, the Divine Essence in Itself is devoid of any trace of immanence. This complete lack of *entitative* intertwining with the world is therefore a necessary corollary of God's absolutely total involvement in His transitive *action* upon the world.

Gender Symbolism

Next, let us ponder the natural roles of the sexes in propagating the species. In the procreative event, the male supplies from his surplus without receiving anything substantive from the female, who remains initially passive in the sense of awaiting fertilization by the male. The following analogy is not perfectly precise but must be taken relatively on account of the disproportion between the finite and the infinite. Despite its inexactitude, we dare to assert (undoubtedly to the vexation of feminist gnostics and their sympathizers) that in his initiative action of begetting offspring the man mirrors God's transcendence, whereas in her incipiently receptive state of conceiving offspring the woman images cosmic immanence.[8] Of course (let us stress to avoid engendering any misunderstanding), in essence God is pure Spirit. Christ Himself said so verbatim in John 4:24, *D-R*: "God is a spirit," although this assertion is a philosophically conclusive corollary of God's pure actuality, since matter would introduce passive potentiality into the Divine Essence.[9] Therefore, God is "without sexuality, which as such belongs only to creatures"; yet, though "not male," God is "infinitely masculine."[10]

Nevertheless, observing the natural roles of the two genders does lead to some grasp of their inner significance with respect to the relation between God and the universe. This deduction of the philosophy of biology is already an intuition at the heart of primeval metaphors (explaining their pervasive occurrence among ancient cultural myths) comparing the masculine element to Father-sky and the feminine factor to Mother-earth. Indeed, just as the heavens pour down vital waters upon the ground, awakening its potentiality to burgeon forth in vegetation, so also does the male *qua* paternal transmit living seed to stir up dormant forces issuing in the birth of progeny from the female *qua* maternal.[11]

Of course, in the global scheme of things, males also contain an inescapably receptive feature of cosmic immanence: their act of begetting is merely ephemeral. Yet this evanescence does not nullify the fact that males, unlike females, *cannot* conceive within their bodies, but produce solely outside themselves. Hence, male fertility participates, however dimly and feebly, in the transcendence of God's continuously active creativity more than the reproductive capability of females, who *can* conceive within themselves but *never* beget outside their bodies.[12]

We finally pass to the supernatural realm, drawing parallel connections with the foregoing. When Holy Orders is conferred upon someone, that person's body assumes a sacramental condition (correlative to the spiritual *character* impressed upon the soul of the ordained). Since all the sacraments effect what they signify, the body of the ordained person ought to be of a nature that has adequate symbolic value for the sacerdotal task. Now a priest serves as a conduit between heaven and earth, between God and humanity, *begetting* the new life of grace in the soul (via Baptism and Penance) and conveying an increase of spiritual vitality in the soul (via the other sacraments). As Jesus declares in John 3:3, *NAB*: "No one can see the

reign of God / unless he is *begotten* from above" (emphasis added).
The commentary accompanying this verse in the *New American Bible*
informs us that the Greek verb employed by St. John "primarily
means" " 'begotten' by a male principle," just as in John 1:13, *NAB*,
which refers to believers "who were *begotten* . . . by God" (emphasis
added). In this respect, then, the priest bestows without receiving,
sharing in a lofty manner in the boundless generosity of the transcendent divine agency. Therefore, such an individual must have the
natural capacity (or obediential potency) to be elevated as a channel
for work in the supernatural arena. Only a man, however, possesses
the physical qualifications to fittingly represent the prototypical priesthood of the Father's eternally *begotten* Son, who Himself *begets* spiritual offspring (born from the womb of the Church). A woman is not
suited for priestly ordination precisely on account of her natural constitution manifesting the receptivity of cosmic immanence in its openness to conception — not due to any inferiority of her individual
person.

It is not a question of whether a particular woman can do a
better "job" than a particular man in clerical ministry to the Church's
members. Those who pose this superficial objection fail to grasp
the importance of physical, and hence sacramental, symbolism.
Their protestation misses the whole point. For male biology, with
its essentially exterior directedness, *more naturally represents* divine
transcendence than female biology, with its fundamentally interior
dimension. Hence, the priesthood consists, not exclusively or even
primarily in a professional occupation, but instead in a supernatural state of *being* rooted in significant natural attributes. A priest
does not merely *do* what Christ did; rather, a priest *is* another Christ,
so that Christ can then act through him.

Papa and the Papacy

Here is a similar argument, one still based on natural biological
symbolism, but a bit more theological. One of the pope's titles is
Pontifex Maximus, or "Supreme Pontiff"; however, every other priest
subordinately shares in this office of *pontifex* (Latin for "bridge-

builder"), because each priest mediates between God and humanity, functioning as a key link between heaven and earth. The priest's gestures themselves at Mass emphasize this role, especially at the elevation of the Host and chalice (after, respectively, each part of the Consecration, as well as at the Doxology). Now only an adult male possesses the intrinsic physical capacity corresponding to this spiritual service, as manifested by the carnal extension required for the procreative act, wherein the husband literally bridges the gap between his flesh and his wife's flesh. The incongruity of a purportedly ordained woman attempting to mimic the Consecration at Mass, accompanied by the requisite bodily posture, borders on an absurd parody of the sacred — the very negation and obscene inversion of the sacramental order. Consequently, only a man can participate in the ordained priesthood of Christ, performing papally (like a pope, since *Papa* means "father" in the familiar form of the term).

The wife, of course, symbolizes the Church (the Bride of Christ) — the Body to whom an ordained man (acting in the Person of the Groom, the Lord Jesus) ministers in a sacerdotal manner. (See Revelation 21:2, Ephesians 5:22-33, Matthew 9:14-15, Mark 2:18-20, Luke 5:34-35, John 3:26-30.) The representation of God as the Groom and Israel as His bride began in the Old Testament with several prophets. (See, for example, Hosea 1-2, Jeremiah 2, and Isaiah 62.)

SCRIPTURAL ARGUMENTS

Under the following three subheads, we give some strictly theological proofs grounded in Scripture and what can be safely inferred from Biblical texts.

Mary Never Ordained Priestess

Let us contemplate the virtues of our Lady. Our Lord endowed His most holy Mother, Mary, with the summit of all appropriate gifts. He preserved her from original sin in the Immaculate Conception, bestowing on her the fullness of grace, as revealed by the traditional formulation of the angelic salutation ("Hail, full of grace") in Luke 1:28, *D-R*, and foreshadowed in Song of Solomon 1:8; 4:7, *RSV* ("fairest among women" having "no flaw"). He designated her the "Woman" predestined to crush the proud Serpent's head (see Genesis 3:15 and John 2:4; 19:26). He protected her from the corruption of the grave by her Assumption into heaven, crowning her Queen of heaven and earth (see Psalm 45:9-15, *RSV*, and Revelation 12:1). In addition, He worked the miracle of maintaining her virginity before, during, and after His conception and birth, although she was wife (true spouse of St. Joseph) and mother. Now many women have been virgins, but none of them have simultaneously been legal wives and biological mothers. (Religious sisters and nuns are mystically brides of Christ and are spiritually mothers for humanity, but their virginity precludes their being legal wives and biological mothers.) And, of course, even more women have been legal wives and biological mothers, but the latter condition cancels virginity. So the Virgin Mary is singular among all women for also being a most blest Mother.

Therefore, after all these extraordinary privileges, far exceeding in excellence those benefits granted all other women, our Lord certainly would have adorned our Lady with any further appropriate dignities. In particular, if the ordained priesthood were an office befitting a woman, how could He, as an infinitely loving and devoted Son, have failed to confer it upon her? Yet in fact He did not, despite her incomparably greater worthiness to receive such an honor than any man's — if Holy Orders were really a question of "worthiness" or "honor." The logical conclusion is that the issue of "worth" or "honor" is irrelevant for this sacrament as such. What matters is the symbolic aptness for executing the purpose of Holy Orders: to serve as a mediator between God and humanity, offering sacrifice to God in the role of Jesus and channeling God's grace to us through sacramental signs. Hence, if it was not suitable for even the Mother of God to perform these tasks, then *a fortiori* no other member of the female gender can be ordained a priest.

Moreover, since Christ is "seed of woman" (see Genesis 3:15, *D-R*), no human person in history could pronounce the formulas of the Consecration ("this is my body; this is my blood") over bread and wine with greater veracity than Mary.[13] Indeed, as we saw in Chapter 2 (Song of Solomon 7:2), Jesus is the "heap of wheat, encircled with lilies," taking His flesh from the "belly" of His virgin Mother. But this ineffably lofty stature of our Lady did not matter when our Lord instituted the Sacrament of Holy Orders and decided on the gender of His priestly ministers.

One can anticipate the usual response: namely, that Jesus was constrained in what He could do by the limitations of His time and place. This counterargument stems from ignorance. To entertain the idea that the Lord of history and geography, the Eternal God who transcends space and time, was imprisoned by the conventions of a particular era and locale is preposterous. He did whatever He wanted to do — period. He spoke with peerless confidence and authority (see Matthew 7:28-29; 10:1; 28:17-20, especially 18; Mark 1:22; Luke 2:47-49; 4:32; John 7:15-17). He acted audaciously to upset the *status quo* — for instance, by driving merchants from the temple (see Matthew 21:12-13; Mark 11:15-17; Luke 19:45-46; John 2:13-17). He certainly could have ordained women to the hierarchical priesthood if He had wished it. For one thing, priestesses were part of the scene of religious cult in the ancient world, in certain lands around the Mediterranean Sea (e.g., Greece).

But, the objector may reply, Jesus was a Jew, forcing Him to obey Jewish customs. Even this is false. For example, the *Jewish* Jesus declared Himself "Lord of the Sabbath" (see Matthew 12:1-8 along with John 5:16-17), and reprimanded the Pharisees for their extremist interpretations in scrupulously abiding by Mosaic rituals (see Matthew 12:9-12 and John 5:18). In addition, He explicitly violated Jewish custom by conversing publicly with a foreign woman, as recorded in John 4:7-9, 27-28. Since women sometimes accompanied Him on His travels (see Luke 8:1-3) and since He sometimes dined with women present (see Matthew 26:6-13; Mark 14:3-9; Luke 7:36-39; John 12:1-3), He could very easily have invited them to the Last Supper (the first Mass), when He instituted both the Blessed Sacrament of the Holy Eucharist and the Sacrament of Holy Orders. Yet He did not, for only the twelve Apostles were there, according to the accounts of Matthew 26:17-29; Mark 14:12-25; Luke 22:7-20. Surely His independent way of fulfilling the Old Law, though not entirely abolishing it (Matthew 5:17), precludes any verdict of so-called "ethnocentric sexism" on His part. The hubris of such an accusation should be countered by quoting Isaiah 55:8-9 regarding the superiority of divine wisdom to human thinking.[14]

Furthermore, contrary to feminist hermeneutics, the "Sophia," or "Wisdom," of the Old Testament (in Proverbs 1-4, 8-9; Wisdom 6-10; Sirach 24) is portrayed with a feminine *persona* only by mystical assimilation of the Blessed Virgin Mary (the "Seat of Wisdom") and the Catholic Church ("the pillar and ground of the truth") to the God-Man Jesus Christ, who is primarily "the Wisdom of God." They are "wisdom" only derivatively or by participation, however exalted; He is Wisdom ("the Word" of God) essentially or by His very nature. We discussed this matter at some length in Chapter 2. Mary's intimate relationship with Christ as co-redemptrix of humanity (and mediatrix of all graces[15]) no more rendered her a viable candidate for priestly ordination than Eve's role as "mother of all the living" (Genesis 3:20) made her capable of mimicking Adam's role as the father who begot their offspring. And, as we know, a priest is a spiritual *father* — a state of being and acting that neither our Lady nor any other woman is suitable for signifying. Since the Church is the Bride of Christ and our mother, our Lord (like His heavenly Father) is also in the truest sense our *father* (see John 14:7-11; 17:21). Since Mary is our spiritual mother (see John 19:26-27) and the Mother of Christ, Jesus is also in some sense our *brother*. But both relationships (fatherhood and brotherhood) are male, and cannot be naturally represented (and thus sacramentally symbolized) by a female.

Old Testament Typology

Hence, the all-male priesthood of the Old Testament was a true *type* of the New Testament priesthood. This is certainly the case for the mysterious priesthood of King Melchizedek (see Genesis 14:18-20) perfectly fulfilled and perpetuated in Christ, as intimated in Psalm 110:4 and elaborately elucidated in Hebrews 5:5-6; 7:1-28. It is even the case for the Levitical priesthood of Aaron that was, as such, finally annulled. Note that Leviticus 6-8 restricts hierarchical participation in the sacred rites (which God commanded of Moses) to males: specifically, "to Aaron the priest and to his sons, as a perpetual due from the people of Israel . . . throughout their generations" (Leviticus 7:34, 36, *RSV*; see also Numbers 18). Indeed, despite the formal termination of the Aaronic priesthood, Isaiah 66:21, *RSV*, employs Levitical language to prophesy about the dimly foreshadowed New Covenant priesthood: "And some of them also I will take for priests and for Levites, says the LORD." Now if it were merely an arbitrary Hebrew cultural artifact that males alone could function as priests, Christ would undoubtedly have abrogated the practice upon the establishment of His new priesthood — just as the early Church changed the official day of community worship from Saturday to Sunday.

In particular, the divine mandate that the Passover lamb be a "male without blemish" (see Exodus 12:1-28, especially verse 5, and Leviticus 1:10-11), whose sacrificial blood would save from wrath those obedient to God's ritual command, is an allegory for the divine mission of the "Lamb of God" (see Isaiah 53:7; John 1:29, 36; Acts 8:32; 1 Peter 1:18-19; Revelation 5:6-8, 12-13; 7:9-10, 13-17; 21:9, 14, 22-23; 22:1, 3), whose bloody death redeemed mankind from the grip of hell. The insistence that the Paschal lamb be male cannot be dismissed. It bears profound significance for the sacrament of Holy Orders, whose purpose is a sacrificing priesthood — prolonging through the ages the Lamb's unique atonement to God for our sins under the unbloody appearances of bread and wine (offered according to the lineage of Melchizedek).

It may be objected that, since the anointing with oil of priests and kings in the Old Testament prefigures the Confirmation chrismation of a "royal priesthood" discussed in Chapter 4, the fact that females can be confirmed in the New Covenant should likewise permit their presbyterial ordination (regardless of the Old Mosaic Law). We reply as follows. Although the Levitical sacerdotal consecration in the Old Testament does adumbrate the common "holy priesthood" of all the baptized faithful in the New Covenant (see the *CCC*, n. 1546), nevertheless this ordinary rite according to the order of Aaron was eventually abolished in favor of the everlasting priesthood of Jesus Christ according to the order of Melchizedek. But just as Melchizedek was mysteriously consecrated a priest without the common Mosaic ritual using oil, so also the essential ordination rite of Catholic priests takes place without the oil of anointing — rather, solely by "the bishop's imposition of hands on the head of the ordinand and in the bishop's specific consecratory prayer asking God for the outpouring of the Holy Spirit and His gifts proper to the ministry to which the candidate is being ordained" (*CCC*, n. 1573). Ludwig Ott asserts with a high degree of certitude (doctrinally proximate to direct revelation itself) that priestly ordination is materially conferred by "the imposition of hands alone."[16] (See especially 2 Timothy 1:6 and Acts 14:23, along with Acts 6:6, although the latter text may refer only to the first rank of Orders — namely, the Diaconate.) Thus, there is no intrinsic nexus between the two sacraments of Confirmation and Holy Orders, except that a precondition for Orders is Confirmation (*Code of Canon Law*, Can. 1033). In any event, the initial objection founders on the rock-solid datum that all priests (whether in the line of Aaron or Melchizedek) were necessarily male.

The Priest as Spiritual Father

A related Scriptural narrative supporting an all-male priesthood occurs in the story of Micah and the Levite in Judges 17:7-13. This tale records the search of a young Levitical tribesman from Bethlehem (literally meaning "the house of bread") for another residence. During his travels he encountered a layman named Micah who offered to take him into his house like a son, furnishing him with food, clothing, and a stipend, in exchange for spiritual service. Micah entreated the young man (Judges 17:10, *RSV*): "Stay with me, and be to me a father and a priest." The strange thing here is that the foster father requested that his adopted son also be his "father"! The key to unlocking this apparent reversal of relationships lies in the role of *priest*. Micah recognized that the Levite's religious function raised him to the status of spiritual fatherhood, notwithstanding the difference in the chronological ages between the two men. A later episode centering on this young Levite is recounted, in which he eventually consents (under duress from an envoy of invaders) to leave Micah's home and serve as "father and priest" for "a tribe and family in Israel" at a different place (see Judges 18:1-27, especially verse 19, *RSV*). The principal lesson is that the priesthood is being intimately connected with fatherhood and hence masculinity.

Nevertheless, there are some subordinate points to ponder, as well. The young man, though descended from the tribe of Levi, had been living in a town of the tribe of Judah: namely Bethlehem, later to be renowned as "the city of David" (Luke 2:4, 11; see also 1 Samuel 16:1, 4). Yet he journeyed from there, only to be called to priestly service elsewhere for other tribes of Israel. His departure and subsequent spiritual elevation can be interpreted as an allegory of Christ's universal redemptive mission, since these events strongly evoke the prophecy in Micah 5:2, *RSV* (see also Matthew 2:4-6, *RSV*): "But you, O Bethlehem-Ephrathah, / who are little to be among [or "by no means least among"] the clans of Judah, / from you shall come forth for me / one who is to be ruler in Israel, / whose origin is from of old, / from ancient days." (See also 2 Samuel 5:2 and John 7:42.) The young man seems to be a sort of transitional *type*-figure, still a descendant of the Levitical line of priests, yet mystically partaking in and foreshadowing to some degree the new priesthood of Jesus Christ, the "Son of David," born in Bethlehem (see Matthew 1:1; Mark 11:10; Luke 20:41-44), which is thus the original earthly abode of the "Heavenly Bread of Life" (see John 6:35, 51, 58).

In fact, another Scriptural passage (different from the Abraham-Melchizedek incident) interweaves the notions of "bread" and "priesthood," namely Psalm 132:13-16, *RSV*: "For the LORD has chosen Zion; / he has desired it for his habitation: / 'This is my resting place for ever; / here I will dwell, for I have desired it. / I will abundantly bless her provisions; / I will satisfy her poor with bread. / Her priests I will clothe with salvation, / and her saints will shout for joy.' "

Interpreted in a spiritual sense, "Zion" means the Catholic Church, the New Israel or the kingdom of God on earth[17]; the "bread" is the Body of Christ in the Eucharist, which is abundantly available for the faithful Catholics ("saints") who are "poor in spirit" and who rejoice in the wine of the Blood of Christ; and the "priests" are, of course, the Catholic clergy who bring the sacraments of salvation. It is impossible to treat the priesthood apart from the sacraments and especially the Holy Eucharist, for priests (as "other Christs") are "bread to be broken" in their self-sacrificing service to the Church (that is, groomlike ministry to the Bride of Christ).

Another point to stress about the Micah-Levite story is the title "father" itself accorded to a priest. This designation has been Catholic tradition for all priests — especially the pope ("Papa"), who is affectionately addressed as the "Holy Father." At any rate, the priesthood is inextricably intertwined with the symbolism of fatherhood, which can be represented (and hence sacramentally symbolized) only via maleness.

No Injustice in All-Male Priesthood

Feminist-inspired agitators for female ordination have accused the Church of condoning a so-called "sinful structure" by listening only to the spiritual wisdom of men and failing to cherish the spiritual gifts of women. This charge veers off target for two reasons: it is factually false and, even if it were true, is irrelevant to the matter of female ordination.

First, the Church down through the centuries has always valued the contributions of women to various ministries, such as staffing schools, hospitals, orphanages, and other charitable agencies (not to mention the lofty vocation of motherhood). The Church has canonized many women as saints for their holy lives dedicated to the service of Christ, whether in convents or in society at large. Moreover, the Church treasures the spiritual literature produced by orthodox Catholic women, particularly those declared "doctors of the Church."

Second, this criticism evades the issue at hand by begging the question: it assumes without proof the equation of personal spiritual wisdom (or other virtues) with fittingness for priestly ordination. But these are two distinct things. In fact, the latter condition is a matter of natural (in this case, biological) symbolism; it is not based on an evaluation of subjective character, where a particular woman may indeed surpass in spiritual "worth" a particular man. As we have demonstrated, even the "Seat of Wisdom" herself could not have been an apt candidate for sacerdotal ordination in the Church of her Divine Son.

Some writers have justified the noninjustice of excluding women from Holy Orders using comparisons based on the other sacraments. For example, Mark P. Shea, in a concise article,[18] treats the topic of the Church's sacramental perspective on reality, connecting it with the male priesthood. His main premise is that the sign-values of objects on the natural level vary, depending on the sacred purpose for which they are intended on the spiritual level. Nevertheless, their symbolizing differences do not necessarily imply any absolute superiority with regard to their inherent worth. Shea employs the usual example of water for Baptism, but in addition he draws a contrast with wine for confecting the Precious Blood of Christ in the Holy Eucharist. Each of these two substances (water and wine) is perfectly proportioned to its own sacramental end. Therefore, it would be absurd to claim that one is inferior to the other simply because it lacks the relative appropriateness possessed by the other. The point of this analogy, of course, is that the natural suitability of men for representing the priesthood of Jesus Christ (the paternal Bridegroom everlastingly espoused to His Bride, our Mother the Church) does not detract one scintilla from the equal intrinsic dignity of women as human persons. Hence, the restriction against female ordination perpetrates no injustice.

But the advocates for female ordination content themselves with expressing their feelings of victimhood (in the case of disaffected women) or else feigned emotional pain (in the case of dissident men) about a network of supposed "patriarchal oppression." They do not present persuasive rational arguments in favor of their position, because they cannot intellectually refute the logic of the Church's sacramental system — which recognizes the inexorable objective significance of material things.

Joseph Cardinal Ratzinger warns that "one cannot struggle against nature without undergoing the most devastating consequences. The sacrosanct equality between man and woman does not exclude, indeed it requires, diversity."[19] To deny the significant repercussions of the material differences between man and woman for this supernatural sphere risks blurring the distinction between divine transcendence and created immanence, inevitably leading to Gaia-goddess worship.[20] Absorbing priestesses would effectively neutralize the ontological symbolism of a "feminine" Church in relation to the supremely "masculine" Creator by relegating men to an effete superfluousness and enshrining women as simultaneously conceivers and begetters (hence all-encompassing). Paradoxically, neo-gnostic dualism can, by a circuitous route, unwittingly wind up in the engulfment of a materialistic pantheism.[21] To prevent this metaphysical confusion, God (through the Church's Magisterium) has providentially ordained that her hierarchy must remain exclusively male.

But the incarnation (or corporation) and governance (or management) of a human family must be shared by man and woman, as the final chapter argues.

chapter six

WHY MALE AND FEMALE SPOUSES?

In the last chapter we saw that the resolution of the question about the all-male priesthood depends ultimately on faith in divine revelation. But this faith does not entail an irrational acceptance of a brute fact or a blind act of trust in the dark night of arbitrary Church policy. For, proceeding from the assent of faith, our minds can logically vindicate this Catholic dogma by philosophical reflections on the nature of God and gender dichotomy.

The issue of Matrimony, however, is essentially different. In order to demonstrate the marital requirement of two persons of distinct gender, we do not need any reliance on faith in divine revelation (whether promulgated through Sacred Scripture or Church Tradition codified in Canon Law). By contrast, here we enter a domain fully accessible to unaided human reason. We must add, though, that we insist on open-minded and logical thinking unencumbered by prejudice stemming from emotional distress or from false compassion for those afflicted with a psychological disturbance. Although our treatment in this chapter is primarily philosophical, for the sake of symmetry with the book's other chapters we will append some relevant Scriptural verses.

Why Are Certain Acts Immoral?

Why are homosexual liaisons not really "marriages"? Why are they objectively immoral? Well, why are any deeds, which are traditionally deemed wrong, immoral? Why is murder, the deliberate killing of an innocent human being, wicked? Why is stealing (furtive theft or armed robbery) wrong? Why is rape (sexual assault) evil? The usual response is that murder, stealing, and rape harm others, whereas consensual homosexual activity does not hurt anyone (with the possible exception of the partners, who willingly risk infection by a disease). Well, is this "harming" criterion a rigorous standard by which to judge morality?

Let us leave aside the question whether in fact no one in society (except perhaps the consenting partners themselves) would be harmed by homosexual unions. We reply as follows to the customary response invoking the "harm-to-others" that certain acts involve. Why should it be immoral to injure others? After all, we destroy plants and animals when we eat them. So what makes human cannibalism evil? Maybe it is just a nice social convention that people should not consume other people. Like the precepts against murder-in-general, stealing, and rape, perhaps social strictures against cannibalistic indulgences merely make life more pleasant (or at least endurable), when we know that the force of legal sanctions will be brought to bear on anyone who attempts to commit such allegedly heinous deeds.

Is there some basic reason why harming fellow human beings is wrong? The answer depends on one's view of reality (one's basic metaphysical perspective). If one holds the position of *nihilism* (that ultimately nothing matters and that reality is senseless or absurd), then why should the chaos that would ensue upon unrestrained behavior be bad? It would simply be the result of a power struggle from which the (temporarily) strong would emerge (temporarily) victorious before battles for supremacy begin anew. In particular, if one embraces the tenet of *materialism* (that human beings are fundamentally reducible to energized collections of material particles, with no essential superiority over other animals), then what would it matter if human beings are subjected to domination by other human beings? It would simply be a reflection of the pecking order operative everywhere in the wild kingdom. Anyway, we all eventually wind up dead, just like the supposedly "lower" animals — totally annihilated when the corpse rots in the grave and its chemical constituents revert to the earth. Since no single human being's life would matter, why would it be wrong to use individuals in accordance with the way the controlling group sees fit?

Any relativistic version of "morality" in principle ends up in the same predicament of materialistic nihilism. In order to justify solidly the stance that harming other human beings is wrong, one must adhere to absolute principles of a deeper order. Otherwise, moral values are rooted only in subjective and superficial opinions, which (unfortunately) are easily eroded when challenged by "liberalizing" anticultural tendencies.

Essential Immutability of Human Nature

The explanation why *any* moral principles have uniform validity is the constancy of a transcendent human nature. All human beings of whatever time and place are composed of the same kind of body animated by the same kind of soul — a spiritual soul, endowed with intellect and free will, destined for immortality. This truth need not be accepted on faith. It can be philosophically demonstrated by invoking the principle "*operatio sequitur esse*": we know the *kind of being* that something is by observing the characteristic ways in which it tends to *operate*. (This is perhaps the theoretical version of the practical precept "You will know them by their fruits" or "The tree is known by its fruit" (Matthew 7:16, 20; 12:33, *RSV*; see James 3:11-12.) We know from personal experience that we can engage in abstract thought using universal concepts, which (unlike sensory impressions) are not limited by concrete particularities (such as a determinate color, sound, odor, flavor, temperature, pressure, size, or shape); instead, general ideas contain all members of a potentially infinite class. Since human intellectual operations (conceptualizing, judging, reasoning) transcend the confining restrictions of bodily processes in space and time, they are essentially removed from matter — whether by dint of their indefinite range of applicability (e.g., the notions "tree," "dog," and "house") or by their inherent nonapplicability to material entities (say, "virtue," "God," and "angels"). Thus, the human mind cannot be reduced to the brain (no matter how complex and uncharted biochemical science tells us the cerebral cortex is), because it is logically impossible for a physical organ to produce immaterial ideas, as though they were electrochemical secretions.

(The contrary supposition would contradict the necessary proportion between an effect and its alleged cause.) Hence, since we can engage in activity that is *spiritual* (i.e., intrinsically independent of matter), each of us must possess a *spiritual soul* as the substantial inner source or foundation of this nonmaterial mental faculty. Consequently, the animating human soul (unlike the life principle, or "soul," of animals) is naturally incorruptible (i.e., *immortal*). Concomitant with the ability to think in universal terms is the power to deliberate among alternatives or weigh options — in other words, to enjoy freedom of will attended by moral responsibility. (This sort of argumentation goes back to philosophers such as Plato, Aristotle, Augustine, Boethius, and Aquinas.)

This specifically identical soul-body structure shared by all mankind implies that what is good (objectively perfective and truly fulfilling) for human beings does not vary over time and place. Likewise for what is evil (or contrary to the objective welfare of human persons). Therefore, actions done with sufficient knowledge and free consent of will have everlasting repercussions for each person and for human society as a whole. Now, if there were no ultimate sanctions (rewards and punishments) in an afterlife for deliberate actions committed on earth, then morality would indeed be without adequate foundation. It would not really matter what anyone did to or with anyone else in this life, because no one would have to pay any lasting price. Nihilism would reign as the supreme truth about reality, if there were no eternal repercussions consequent on human actions.

Skin color and other ethnic characteristics are incidental to human nature. The only difference among (mature adult) human persons containing any moral relevance is the gender distinction. All males are basically the same as each other and all females are basically the same as each other, but every male is basically different from every female — not in specific human nature, but in the dichotomized *manner* of propagating members of the human species (along with its concomitant psychological and symbolical facets). Of course, the same gender differences prevail among the inferior species of the animal genus. But, since the lower animals lack intellect and free will, they are not responsible for harnessing their drives. In fact, their instincts generally lead them to what is really good for them. Lacking free will, they cannot rebel (like man) against the essential constitution with which they are endowed.

Indeed, the intricate patterns evident throughout the cosmos manifest the work of a supremely intelligent Designer, who fashioned all things according to a definite plan, giving things their natural order and end. Let us be careful, though: the term "natural" is often used equivocally. In one sense it means whatever actually occurs in the animal world. According to this usage, some attempt to justify homosexual behavior as "natural" (hence not "deviant"), because it allegedly occurs within some animal groups. Whether it does or not, however, is irrelevant. It may be an anomalous result of the Fall of man, whose Original Sin caused the "natural" (i.e., physical) world to go awry; it does not mean that the Creator initially ordained things this way. But the correct understanding of "natural" in the context of ethics is "that which harmonizes with the objective perfection of human nature" — in other words, what *ought* to be the case for human beings, regardless of what might actually happen among some human or animal groups. In this sense of the term we speak of the "natural moral law" by which to judge the objective goodness or evil of human acts. Here, human nature, considered as the proximate or immediate norm of morality, must be understood in a complete manner; that is, it must be grasped in all its relations (to God and to other members of society in their diverse roles), and not be taken in isolation according to what seems attractive for individual satisfaction.[1] The most fundamental reason, then, why it matters what kind of bodies are paired in marriage is that human beings are not merely material, but instead have the virtually infinite dignity of incarnate spirits who will exist forever.

Procreative Purpose of Sex

With regard to homosexual unions, it is self-evident to anyone morally sane, who accepts the premise of the fundamental procreative meaning for the division of all animal species into two genders, that same-sex "marriage" transgresses and subverts the natural order based on such material distinction. Human arrangements between two members of identical sex contrived to simulate the norm may yield various gratifications (e.g., filling a psychological vacuum through erotic pleasure), but obviously cannot of themselves (apart from the intervention of Tower-of-Babel technologies striving to supplant divine sovereignty) generate the fruit of children. Anyone for whom all this does not constitute a patent platitude is afflicted with intellectual blindness emanating either from a falsely compassionate relativism or from a perversely stubborn will coarsened by concupiscence. To any of these people we can only address some rhetorical questions. If the basic purpose of sexual congress is not procreation, why is it that the energies of the reproductive cells are always actually aroused in adult males and at least tendentially stimulated in adult females? Do not these physiological phenomena bespeak an inherent demand for bodily difference, since germ cells from the same sex of themselves possess no complementary unitive dynamic?

Homosexual relations are morally corrupt because they contradict the principal point of sexual unions: the marital bond between one man and one woman that is the foundation of the family, the basic unit of society. Even the unintentional infertility of a wedded heterosexual couple is incidental to the ethical goodness of their communion, because the essential reality of their complementary physiology remains. If their inability to procreate were cured, they would maintain the same stance as before: namely, openness to begetting and conceiving children. Thus, even in their state of barrenness, their wills are radically fruitful, since their opposite gender guarantees their abiding possession of the fundamental potentiality (albeit unactualized) for generating offspring through their loving intimacy. This is not the case for two people of identical gender, whose sterility is irremovable: their very sameness presents an ontological impediment to the natural origin of a family.

Disparaging these facts tacitly endorses nihilism — that the world is not rationally ordered and is fundamentally devoid of purpose. Then the gnostic disregard for material differences is free to run untrammeled at the whim of individual desires.

Besides traditional natural law arguments showing that homosexual unions are intrinsically immoral due to their frustration of the finality (or ordered tendency) built into the very structure of the two genders, a more contemporary Catholic approach to questions of sexual morality goes by the name of "integral personalism." But, since our elaboration of this approach will involve references to so-called "Kantian ethics," we must first explain this terminology.

Kant's Criterion of Morality

A notable attempt to ground an absolute ethic is due to the eighteenth-century philosopher Immanuel Kant, who advocated what he called the "Categorical Imperative." One version of this basic law undergirding all morality is the following. Whenever we are weighing a decision to act, we must be sure that our proposed action is rationally "universalizable." In other words, we must be able to convince ourselves logically that the precept guiding our action could be reasonably applied by anyone in the same circumstances. That is, we must be able, while willing the action for ourselves, to will at the same time (without contradiction) that such a rule of conduct (or "maxim") become a general norm (or law) for everyone.[2]

Kant's categorical imperative immediately brands certain deeds as immoral. For example, someone cannot logically desire to commit murder while remaining alive himself to enjoy its consequences (such as the pleasure of revenge or eliminating an obstacle to success or indulging in cannibalism), because he would have to be able to will simultaneously that anyone else could justify a similar deed — including killing him for the same motives. Since every potential murderer would be caught in the same contradiction, murder is absolutely unjustifiable. For a second example, someone cannot rationally wish to steal another's goods while retaining his own possessions, because he would have to be able to will simultaneously that anyone else could engage in the same action with respect to him. This blatant inconsistency means that taking another's goods without permission is always wrong. Again, one cannot coherently will to lie to others while preserving the truth inside one's own mind, because one would be implicitly granting others permission to deceive oneself — an unwanted state of mental distortion. Kant adduces other examples, as well (among them, suicide and borrowing money with an insincere promise to repay the loan).[3]

And so it goes. Invoking Kant's categorical imperative, we can exclude from the sphere of morally good actions any deed that "harms" others, because we would be unable to will that such a deed be perpetrated against ourselves. Although the formulation is different, it sounds like the "Golden Rule" articulated in Matthew 7:12, *RSV*: "So whatever you wish that men would do to you, do so to them; for this is the law and the prophets."

A disclaimer or note of caution to the reader is in order before we proceed any further. In examining Kant's (first) version of his categorical imperative, the author intends to furnish some historical background for understanding Karol Wojtyla's references to it, as well as to point out that it has some plausibility and applicability in its favor. The author does not mean to imply endorsement of Kant's ethical system, which as a whole is inadequate. In fact, it has been criticized on several grounds: (1) for its strictly negative approach to morality (excluding, most assuredly, some acts as wrong, but providing no positive motivations or inducements to do good); (2) for its over-emphasis on "formal" duty (sheerly for its own sake), with an outright disparagement of virtue practiced for the reward of happiness; and (3) for the potential loopholes in its universalizability criterion, which may render any proposed deed capable of rationalization, given enough cleverness in describing it.[4] It appears to this author that the second version of the categorical imperative (mentioned below), which Kant claims is equivalent to the first, nevertheless does not suffer from the same defects in its formulation, and hence seems preferable for expressing the philosophical content of the "Golden Rule."

Application to Homosexual 'Unions'

What about sexual behavior? Nonconsensual acts, as nearly everyone except a hardened (and probably suicidal) nihilist would agree, would be subsumed under the above precepts. But how about so-called "consenting activity in private between two adults"? Using Kant's categorical imperative, could we, for instance, will that everyone bond in same-sex pairs? Well, if this sort of arrangement were universalized, after a very short period the human race would be extinct. There would be no people at all remaining to link up (of same or opposite sex), because homosexual acts are intrinsically nongenerative or unfertile. (They are sterile with regard to fertility, though frequently unsterile or septic in their execution.) The same verdict cannot be rendered of heterosexual marriage: willing its universalization implies no inconsistency. Therefore, since homosexuality is parasitic on the fruits of heterosexuality (namely, human offspring), homosexual couples cannot logically desire its universalization. According to the Kantian law of morality, it follows that homosexual unions are immoral.

Of course, the rejoinder from the "gay activists" and their sympathizers will be that, in our "Brave New World" of *in vitro* fertilization, it does not matter whether all real-time human coupling is homosexual. Our medical technocrats can harvest reproductive cells to induce vicarious "mating" in the laboratory, and then "grow" children by implantation in natural or artificial wombs. There are two flaws in this thinking, however.

First, we would have to be able to will that the husbandry of human children (as though they were farm animals) be universalizable. But do most people really believe that it is a good thing for human procreation to become merely another commodity offered by modern industry? Would each of us not really care whether *we* were conceived in a test tube or petri dish by the intervention of officious technicians in white coats, who have virtually invaded the intimate privacy of the bedroom? Would not most people prefer that all children be conceived in an act of love between a husband/father (male) and wife/mother (female) who are committed to each other and to the inviolable enclosure of their marital bed? Are we all prepared to embrace the assembly-line baby factories of Aldous Huxley's *Brave New World*? To dismiss this concern as irrelevant reeks of a gnostic disdain for the way human biological processes naturally occur.

Second, this appeal to updated technology is dangerous. It assumes that morality is historically relative, hostage to time and place, subject to fundamental revision when scientific power reaches a feasible stage of development. This would mean that homosexual unions may once have been morally deficient because non-universalizable in previous eras, but (with the advent of efficacious alternative reproductive methodologies) they are now as morally good as traditional heterosexual marriages. The peril latent in this rationalization is an open-ended road toward an abyss: we cannot count on any permanent moral anchor if some unforeseen "breakthrough" is lurking in the future to unfasten our purportedly secure moorings. For the sake of our sanity and our very lives, we must take the stand that moral principles are essentially unchanging and that they can be known with certitude to apply to all human beings at all times and places, regardless of scientific advances.

The contrary position that assails the universal validity of moral precepts can be sustained only by a nihilist who cares nothing about contradiction or by someone who is suicidal. Yet, if this irrational perspective were to gain ascendancy (as is possible should the allure of passion and sentiment triumph), the human race, viewing its very own existence as meaningless in an obscure outpost of an incomprehensible universe, could not survive the catastrophe stemming from self-destructive impulses.

Wojtyla's Integral Personalism
This horrific prospect goads us to seek refuge in a brighter and more viable ethical vision. This brings us to a discussion of "integral personalism,"[5] whose chief proponent is the ethician Karol Wojtyla (who later took the name John Paul II when he became pope). His thought, representing an endeavor to formulate natural

law ethics by emphasizing human personal dignity, begins with the fundamental intuition that no person may "use" another person merely as an instrumental "means to an end." This maxim is based on the very nature of personhood and is "an inherent component of the natural moral order," since each human being is by nature endowed with freedom of will in setting his own goals.[6] He recasts Kant's categorical imperative as follows: "Whenever a person is the object of your activity, remember that you may not treat that person as only the means to an end, as an instrument, but must allow for the fact that he or she, too, has, or at least should have, distinct personal ends."[7] As hinted above, this norm was already anticipated by Kant in his second version of the categorical imperative, although he gave only a negative formulation.[8]

Wojtyla then enunciates the cardinal postulate of his ethical system, the "personalistic norm," which, negatively put, asserts that "the person is the kind of good which does not admit of use and cannot be treated as an object of use and as such the means to an end"; stated positively, it affirms that "the person is a good towards which the only proper and adequate attitude is love."[9] This canon applies even to instrumental use by mutual consent,[10] since such a condition doubly partakes of the utilitarianism that he denounces as antagonistic to the personal good.[11] He maintains that the personalistic norm is the natural basis of morality — "the 'natural' content of the commandment to love, that part of it which we can equally well understand without faith and by reason alone."[12]

The personalistic norm finds its crucial application in the domain of sexual morality, which, Wojtyla declares, is profoundly ensconced in "the laws of nature."[13] The central "problem of sexual ethics is how to use sex without treating the person as an object for use"[14]; indeed, exploitation in the realm of sexual conduct consists in the isolation and pursuit of erotic pleasure as a "distinct aim" in itself,[15] always (to some extent) apart from the value of the other person as a whole. The personalistic standard, however, demands that sensual enjoyment be "subordinated to love."[16]

According to Wojtyla, the only way to preclude the ever-present possibility of egoistically reducing the other person to the level of a mere sexual object (a plaything for bodily gratification) is love incarnated in (heterosexual) marriage with its inherent tendency to procreativity.[17] After all, the essential purpose of sexual differentiation is generation, whose object is the primary and fundamental good of existence itself.[18] Now it is the task of philosophy (and not the province of biological science) to treat of being under its universal aspects. Hence, the subject matter of human sexuality properly pertains to that subdivision of metaphysics called "philosophical anthropology" and thus, as well, to ethics.[19] Moreover, the philosophy of human nature can articulate what empirical biology cannot even discover: namely, that the "proper end" and "natural orientation" of the "full productive power of love" is the procreation and education of children.[20]

Wojtyla censures both the "rigorist" and the "libidinist" attitude toward the human person. The first, while avoiding using the person for physical delight, winds up objectifying him or her as a mere means to reproduction, thereby excising the unitive purpose of sexual intercourse as a loving union of spouses from its procreative end. This attitude not only imbues the antiquated theologies of Jansenism and Puritanism, but also especially and pervasively characterizes the modern resort to *in vitro* fertilization, which annihilates the person as such, reducing the individual to the status of a breeding animal. This form of utilitarianism must, instead, learn to embrace the joyous fruition of love along with its usefulness, in order not to fracture the integrity of the person.[21] On the other hand, the second version of reductivist utilitarianism, more sinister because it is a more common, routine, and ever-present danger in ordinary human relationships, detaches the procreative purpose of sexuality from the unitive end,[22] suppressing procreation entirely and transmogrifying a supposedly loving "union" into mere lustful recreation[23] (whether through heterosexual contraception or homosexual perversion).

Nevertheless, the three purposes of marriage (procreation, mutual aid, remedy for desire) are ordered by an objective and rational schema in accordance with the personalistic norm — a hierarchy of ends that is "natural to man" and therefore "binding." To assault any of these ends or subvert their order of priority through either type of utilitarianism would be tantamount to violating the dignity and intrinsic value of the person, since sexual morality depends on a certain "stable and mature synthesis of nature's purpose with the personalistic norm."[24] In other words, virtue requires a harmonious reconciliation or integration of individual person with nature.[25] In fact, "the rejection of natural law in ethics leads to . . . [the] consequences . . . of arbitrary individualism . . . [which] threaten to destroy the ontic and ethical balance of the person."[26] That is, the failure to conform to the demands of human nature (considered totally, in all its ramifications for the good of self and others) leads to the dire straits of rampant egotism and unfettered appetite, along with both internal and external chaos.

Thus, Wojtyla proposes an ethics in which the sexuality of the person is integrated with or subordinated to the value of the person as such.[27] But although the person as a whole must be the principal focus of human relationships according to "integral personalism," nonetheless, particular attributes of attractiveness need not be ignored. For a "healthy empiricism" posits a pyramid of values, with the value of the entire person as its summit, under which are subsumed lesser features that are surely important, but that must never absorb the ultimate value of the person as a whole.[28] The enriching, all-embracing fullness of "integral personalism" is therefore contrary to the dry and merely dutiful "formalistic personalism" of Kant.[29] It also opposes, at the other extreme, the subjectivist utilitarian attitude, which, via its primary occupation with sensual pleasure,[30] repudiates a basic component of the person (namely, fertility), reducing the person to the level of a thing to be manipulated for enjoyment.[31] Integral personalism therefore strikes a balance between angelism (ignoring the emotions with their psychosomatic character) and bestialism (treating people as barnyard animals).

In order to ensure an "integral respect for the person"[32] in matrimony, every conjugal act "must have its own internal justification."[33] To this end, the "willingness to accept parenthood" (at least by never thwarting its very possibility) is required, lest indulgence in venereal relations degenerate from acceptance of each person's totality into the "reciprocal egoism" of mutual exploitation.[34] For in marriage the natural order (whose primary objective aim is procreation) and the personal order (whose milieu is the expressive dimension of love) must converge in an intimate synthesis. Loyalty to the person's value demands adherence to nature's inner tendencies, since transgressing natural boundaries entails objectifying the person,[35] as the negative formulation of the personalistic norm indicates.

Application to Homosexual 'Unions'

Although Wojtyla is overtly discussing the issue of contraception in traditional (i.e., heterosexual) marriage, his critique applies just as forcefully (if not more so) to homosexual "marriages." Such unions, which from the start irremediably sunder the unity of person with physical nature, epitomize the idolization of sexual attributes to the exclusion of their inherent function. Moreover, as in heterosexual contraceptive intercourse, the purported "union" in same-sex coupling embodies a falsehood by pretending to donate the gift of the whole self, yet in reality withholding an essential part of the person (namely, the procreative power).[36] It "contradicts the language of love by a lie," by altering the intentionality of total self-surrender and thereby degrading sex to the level of a tool solely for carnal immersion.[37] But we can discover with certitude what the natural moral law teaches in this regard by reading with right reason (which presupposes an open, honest mind) the "language of the body," whose very structure and function communicate its objective meaning to the unbiased thinker.[38] The "body language" of same-sex encounters shows that (objectively speaking) they amount to mutual exploitation, thereby violating the personalistic norm.

Cardinal Ratzinger echoes this analysis when he says (emphasis in the original):

For the Church the *language of nature* (in our case, two sexes complementary to each other yet quite distinct) is *also the language of morality* (man and woman called to equally noble destinies, both eternal, but different). It is precisely in the name of nature — it is known that Protestant tradition and, in its wake, that of the Enlightenment mistrust this concept — that the Church raises her voice against the temptation to project persons and their destiny according to mere human plans, to strip them of individuality and, in consequence, of dignity. To respect biology is to respect God himself, hence to safeguard his creatures.[39]

Wojtyla has expounded at great length on his thesis of the "nuptial meaning of the body." The human body, in its masculine and feminine complementarity, bears the signature of a gift intended for the unification of one man and one woman in a true communion of persons. This mutual self-donation should be free from the interior domination of sexual turbulence (i.e., concupiscence) and open to the blessing of fertility.[40] It is patently evident that homosexual unions preclude or nullify the very possibility for realizing this nuptial meaning, whose significance is so profound on the natural plane that Christ could fittingly elevate Matrimony to a sacrament. (See Matthew 19:3-6; Mark 10:6-9; Ephesians 5:22-33.)

Objective Disorder of Homosexuality

Homosexual eroticism exhibits a gnostic rejection of the material dynamics embedded in human persons. In exalting the superior spiritual realm of personal consciousness and willful desire, homosexual liaisons subjugate the lower material order and harness it for merely subjective gratification. But when an individual's trajectory is dissevered from its roots in the natural domain, personal integrity is fragmented and an already shattered self-image cannot help but be perpetuated.

This personality disruption is classifiable as a neurosis instead of a psychosis, due to anxiogenic emotional disturbance affecting the sphere of gender identity, rather than severe cognitive distortions about reality. From a psychological perspective, its causes are almost invariably linked with adverse early childhood experiences. These could be acutely traumatic (as happens in episodes of abuse that may negatively rewire nervous system responses to stimuli) or more subtle (such as chronic detachment or alienation, for various reasons, from the same-sex parent and peers). Much psychological literature exists on this subject.[41]

Paul Quay has some deep insights on the natural and supernatural significance of homosexuality, portraying it as the antithesis of conjugal love in its symbolic spurning of what is not the same as oneself, of what is "different."

By its nature, both physiologically and psychologically, sexuality is directed to another who attracts precisely because of the very "otherness" embodied there (both somatic and psychic differences). According to Quay, however, homosexual activity exhibits "a fear of sexuality as such": that is, insofar as it is "something open to such difference." There is an implicit disavowal of the sexually other as "not needed" and "not desirable." Other persons are alluring and are pursued due to their sameness as the self[42] — probably on account of feelings of insecurity about one's own gender identity, leading one to seek in those of the same sex what is perceived as lacking and to internalize these seemingly missing qualities.[43] (To the extent that the latter psychological account revolves around feelings of inferiority or inadequacy, it appears to apply more to males than females, since males are more prone to measurement on grounds of competence of various kinds.)

Quay proceeds to give a brilliant theological analysis of male homosexuality:

> Male homosexual activity, then, symbolizes at the supernatural level man as in love with one like himself, enamored of the strength of the state, seeking from it the strength to be savior of himself. It is a refusal of the femininity of the Church, her weakness in human terms. It

signifies secular humanism, for which "the only God of man is man himself," refusing to accept the true otherness of God. The state, its technology, its power for war, its attempt to solve all problems independently of God or His Church, its taking all initiative to itself — this is indeed a male principle. But we know that Christ has not wedded himself to the state, to technology, to secular "progress," or to war — however good these things may be in themselves when not loved but only rightly used. Christ is wedded only to His Church.[44]

Quay's trenchant analysis explains, for example, why homosexuality was so prevalent and appealing among the upper echelons of the Nazi regime, with their cult of masculine prowess, their ideology of auto-racial durability, their glorification of scientific technology (for medical, industrial, and military purposes), and their deification of the state — in short, their adoration of the Nietzschean will-to-power.

On the other hand, Quay offers an equally incisive religious analysis of the female side of the homosexual disorder:

> Lesbianism, then, signifies a Church who would turn away from the Lord to embrace what is like herself: created, dependent for fruitfulness on union with Another who is *not* like herself, lovely with a beauty given by that Other, incapable of initiative with regard to God. What lesbianism symbolizes is not a Church at all but nature-worship, a worship of Isis or the Earth-Mother rather than Christ.[45]

This explains the infatuation with lesbianism among certain congregations of dissident nuns who remodel after their own feminist image the Church's Trinitarian/Christological dogmas and who fabricate neo-pagan/New-Age "liturgies" centering on earthly elements and sometimes goddesses.[46] Their obsessive lashing out at the Church's established patriarchal hierarchy and their screaming for female ordination to the priesthood are temper-tantrum tactics staged to build support for a church refashioned wholly like themselves, from which a masculine transcendental order would be banished because unwanted. (Psychologically, they suffer from hatred of men, probably due to traumatic childhood or adolescent experiences perpetrated by abusive fathers or brothers.)

Biblical Background

Although our approach in this chapter is primarily philosophical, for the sake of symmetry with the book's other chapters we now briefly discuss some relevant Scriptural passages. The first (negative) group consists of texts denouncing homosexual behavior as intrinsically evil (or "objectively disordered" in contemporary ecclesiastical parlance). The second (positive) group is comprised of texts affirming the sanctity of heterosexual marriage.

Against Homosexual Relations

In several crucial verses of both the Old and New Testaments, homosexual conduct is strictly forbidden according to God's plan for the human race.

We read in Leviticus 18:22, *RSV*: "You shall not lie with a male as with a woman; it is an abomination." And in Leviticus 20:13, *RSV*: "If a man lies with a male as with a woman, both of them have committed an abomination." These citations cannot be critiqued on the grounds that they are historically conditioned or contingent proscriptions susceptible to abrogation (such as dietary restrictions or outmoded ritual specifications), for they occur primarily in a context of divine anathema against what any decent civilization (though not degenerate pagan cultures) would recognize as inherently wicked deeds: infant sacrifice, incest, adultery, and bestiality.

St. Paul excoriates sexual perversions in the well-known graphic passage found in Romans 1:24-27, *RSV*: "Therefore God gave them up in the lusts of their hearts to impurity, to the dishonoring of their bodies among themselves, because they exchanged the truth about God for a lie and worshiped and served the creature rather than the Creator. . . . For this reason God gave them up to dishonorable passions. Their women exchanged natural relations for unnatural, and the men likewise gave up natural relations with women and were consumed with passion for one another, men committing shameless acts with men and receiving in their own persons the due penalty for their error." Moreover, in 1 Corinthians 6:9, *RSV*, St. Paul explicitly includes "homosexuals" in the list of "the unrighteous [who] will not inherit the kingdom of God." (The term "sodomites" appears in the *NAB* translation, while the *D-R* renders the corresponding term in verse 10 there as "the effeminate" or "liers with mankind.")

Speaking of "Sodom," we now come to an event in Genesis 19:1-29 (with contextual backdrop Genesis 18:16-33) that has been subjected to a grievously tendentious, or biased, interpretation. The revisionist exegetes have thinly disguised their agenda for sexual revolution via a campaign either to dismiss (in the case of Leviticus) or discredit (in the case of St. Paul) or obfuscate (in the case of Genesis 19) any and all Biblical texts that *prima facie* condemn what they devoutly wish society to meekly accept by being "sensitive," "compassionate," and thus "politically correct." These practitioners of so-called "queer hermeneutics" claim that the sin for which Sodom and Gomorrah were destroyed by divine wrath was "lack of hospitality to strangers." Let's investigate whether there is any solid textual evidence to support this view.

We learn from Genesis 19:4-11, *RSV*, that "the men of Sodom, both young and old, all the people to the last man, surrounded [Lot's] house [where two angels disguised as men were staying as guests]; and they called to Lot, 'Where are the men who came to you tonight? Bring them out to us, that we may know them' [or, as the *NAB* translates it, 'that we may have intimacies with them']. Lot went out of the door to the men, shut the door after him, and said, 'I beg you, my brothers, do not act so wickedly. Behold, I have two daughters who have not known man; let me bring them out to you, and do to them as you please; only do nothing to these men, for they have come under the shelter of my roof.' But they said, 'Stand back!' And they said, 'This fellow came to sojourn, and he would play the judge! Now we will deal worse with you than with them.' Then they pressed hard against the man Lot, and drew near to break the door." Fortunately, the two angels rescued Lot, who was at this point threatened himself, by pulling him into the house and closing the door, while striking the mob outside with a certain blindness, which rendered them unable to see and open the door.

Now there is no doubt that the men of Sodom showed a crude "lack of hospitality" to Lot's overnight guests; however, to character-ize the lewdness they attempted to commit as mere "inhospitable-ness" is like castigating a burglar for leaving litter at the scene of his crime. In other words, this slanted eisegesis ignores the enormity of the Sodomites' chief transgression by conveniently focusing on a comparatively less flagrant aspect of their behavior. If it were mere "lack of hospitality to strangers" of which they were guilty, then why did Lot call their attempted assault on the male guests "wicked" while offering them his very own virgin daughters to satisfy their urges? Surely he knew that such an overture on his part (though predictably declined) was itself wrong. He must have reasoned that heterosexual fornication (essentially rape in this situation) was the lesser of two evils in a dilemma where he felt trapped; that is, he figured that the homosexual lust driving the Sodomites, if successful at achieving its aim, would have exceeded in moral vileness (or unnaturalness) what-ever indignities they might have inflicted on his female children. Moreover, this so-called "inhospitality" took place only after the Lord was already offended "because the outcry against Sodom and Gomorrah is great and their sin is very grave" (Genesis 18:20, *RSV*). The angels could have endured the alleged "inhospitality" in the first place only if they had been sent to devastate the two cities for *another* and *prior* reason. In addition, Lot's use of the term "wicked" regard-ing the Sodomites' projected indulgence recalls the same language God employed about the two cities when his uncle Abraham was bargaining for clemency in Genesis 18:22-33. As it turned out, there were not even ten "righteous" adult males in all of Sodom; it seems that the sole exceptions were Lot and his prospective sons-in-law, two men who were buried in fiery rubble with the rest of the citizens on account of their refusal to take seriously Lot's warning to flee the impending chastisement (see Genesis 19:12-25).

Our examination of Genesis 19 has clearly established the proper interpretation of the disputed passage. This obvious understanding of the text can be attacked only by a mendacious methodology seeking to justify disoriented activities in order to ward off the reproach of conscience.

In Favor of Heterosexual Marriage

The inspired word of God prohibits homosexual relations because they contradict the very purpose of sexual unions: the marital bond between one man and one woman that is the foundation of the family, the basic unit of society. Several key texts can be adduced to support this tenet.

The verses in Genesis 1:27-28 and 2:24, *RSV*, inform us that, at the dawn of human history, the Creator ordained one purpose for carnal union: "God created man in his own image. . . ; male and female he created them. And God blessed them, and God said to them, 'Be fruitful and multiply, and fill the earth and subdue it. . . .' Therefore a man leaves his father and his mother and cleaves to his wife, and they become one flesh." Christ reaffirms this teaching in Mark 10:6-9, *RSV* (compare Matthew 19:4-6): "But from the beginning of creation, 'God made them male and female.' 'For this reason a man shall leave his father and mother and be joined to his wife, and the two shall become one.' So they are no longer two but one. What therefore God has joined together, let not man put asunder." One cannot logically interpret a man's "wife" as admitting the possibility that this "wife" could be another male, for several reasons. First, the context here involves "male and female." Second, two people of the same gender cannot in themselves "be fruitful and multiply." Third, it is biologically impossible for two males (or two females) to attain the genuine unity of "one flesh."

Contemporary proponents of "homosexual marriage" would dispute this last assertion. But St. Paul emphasizes this truth in 1 Corinthians 6:16, *RSV*, by repeating the main point: "Do you not know that he who joins himself to a prostitute becomes one body with her? For, as it is written, 'The two shall become one.' " The two bodies that become merged into one here are clearly of opposite gender. Hence, a male can "prostitute" himself for another male only in an equivocal sense. This is still more obvious in the case of two females. A woman can be cemented in an interpersonal unity of flesh solely by the regular administration of a man's bodily substance. Conversely, a man can use his masculine effusion to establish a salubrious sexual bond only with a woman.

Further, in 1 Peter 3:7, *RSV*, St. Peter implies (contrary to current debased homosexualist jargon) that only a man can be a husband and only a woman can be a wife: "Likewise you husbands, live considerately with your wives, bestowing honor on the woman as the weaker sex."

On a more positive note, in 1 Corinthians 7:2-3, 8-9, *RSV*, St. Paul strongly commends heterosexual relations under the appropriate circumstances: "But because of the temptation to immorality, each man should have his own wife and each woman her own husband. The husband should give to his wife her conjugal rights, and likewise the wife to her husband. . . . To the unmarried and the widows I say that . . . if they cannot exercise self-control, they should marry. For it is better to marry than to be aflame with passion."

Moreover, in 1 Timothy 4:1-4, *RSV*, he censures the foreseen Manicheanism, latent or incipient in gnostic thinking, that would reprehend and proscribe heterosexual marriage as evil: "Now the Spirit expressly says that in later times some will depart from the faith by giving heed to deceitful spirits and doctrines of demons, through the pretensions of liars whose consciences are seared, who forbid marriage and enjoin abstinence from foods which God created to be received with thanksgiving by those who believe and know the truth. For everything created by God is good, and nothing is to be rejected if it is received with thanksgiving." As the

Archangel Raphael (no gnostic spirit) encouraged Tobias (in Tobit 6:17, *RSV*) about marrying Sarah, "Do not be afraid, for she was destined for you from eternity. You will save her, and she will go with you, and I suppose that you will have children by her."

Finally, we reproduce the beautiful and celebrated passage (Ephesians 5:21-32, *RSV*) where St. Paul draws an analogy between the human marital covenant and the bond that weds Christ to the Church, in light of which the Apostle harks back to and amplifies on the explanation for marriage in Genesis:

> Be subject to one another out of reverence for Christ. Wives, be subject to your husbands, as to the Lord. For the husband is the head of the wife as Christ is the head of the church, his body, and is himself its Savior. As the church is subject to Christ, so let wives also be subject in everything to their husbands. Husbands, love your wives, as Christ loved the church and gave himself up for her, that he might sanctify her, having cleansed her by the washing of water with the word, that he might present the church to himself in splendor, without spot or wrinkle or any such thing, that she might be holy and without blemish. Even so husbands should love their wives as their own bodies. He who loves his wife loves himself. For no man ever hates his own flesh, but nourishes and cherishes it, as Christ does the church, because we are members of his body. "For this reason a man shall leave his father and mother and be joined to his wife, and the two shall become one." This is a great mystery, and I mean in reference to Christ and the church; however, let each one of you love his wife as himself, and let the wife see that she respects her husband.

Thus, God ordained Matrimony to be a natural symbol (elevated by Jesus to the supernatural dignity of a sacrament) for the love He bears the Church, which is feminine in relationship to Him. (See also Hosea 1-2, Jeremiah 2, Isaiah 62, Matthew 9:14-15,

Mark 2:18-20, Luke 5:34-35, John 3:26-30, Revelation 21:2, along with the *CCC*, nn. 1601-1605.) We observe that Christ began His public ministry (at His Mother's behest) at a wedding feast (see John 2:1-11), highlighting (so to speak) with His active approval the importance of the solemn marital commitment between one man and one woman. This first wedding feast publicly attended by the Lamb of God also has Eucharistic significance. For the miraculous transformation of water into wine at Cana prefigures the second transubstantiation at Mass, when our Lord, acting through his priest, converts grape wine to His Precious Blood. And just as the male-female couple at Cana were united in one flesh to each other, so also we become spiritually one with Christ by receiving His Body and Blood physically (under the appearances of bread and wine) in Holy Communion. As a wife's reproductive system is activated by her husband's bodily substance (the seed of life), so is the spiritual growth of the Church's members actualized by the Groom Christ's flesh (the Bread of Life). The Mass therefore takes on the aspect of a wedding banquet where the gracious Host is simultaneously the Victim and Groom, and the worshiping guests have the symbolic value of brides.

Deleterious Consequences of Legalizing Same-Sex 'Unions'

In actual practice there is no way that society could recognize homosexual "marriages" without opening a Pandora's box of every conceivable "union" clamoring for official acknowledgment. Bryan Rudnick has written persuasively about this inevitable downward slide. Suppose the government were to approve homosexual "marriage" as equivalent to traditional heterosexual marriage, with all the same benefits and privileges. There would in principle be no logical and legal means for stopping there. If challenged, the restriction of officially sanctioned "marriage" to just two homosexuals could not be sustained. Several same-gender people could live together claiming to be sexual partners, and the government would be forced to legitimize such an arrangement on the usual grounds of "nondiscrimination" (that tiresome mantra of decadent democracy). But then groups of heterosexual partners would start to agitate for the legalization of polygamy (whether polygynous, polyandrous, or some combination of bisexual cohabitation). And why should mutually consenting incestuous relationships be denied access to the public seal of respect?[47] Would we be able to halt the disgusting farce even when confronted with a lawsuit by someone who claims to passionately love his pet dog?[48] These not implausible scenarios demonstrate the importance for social order of maintaining the traditional institution of marriage as an exclusive (and indissoluble) union between one man and one woman. As even the Vermont Supreme Court warned while granting civil recognition to homosexual unions, its own decision could "destabilize" the traditional institution of marriage and harbor "disruptive and unforeseen consequences." What havoc is being wrought in yet another proud endeavor to show that man knows better than God how to play the Creator's part in the cosmic drama?

Marital "matter" (i.e., the embodied persons bonded together) matters for the social, cultural, and political common good. George Gilder, for example, has strenuously advocated the thesis that heterosexual marriage provides a way for society to subordinate the barbaric sexual impulses of males to the stability of female rhythms and family life[49] — something that homosexual partnering can never accomplish.

Moreover, it is hard to fathom how the absence of a parent of either gender, with their complementary physical and psychological nature, can be a beneficial situation for children. William Oddie, citing the work of Stephen Clark[50] among others, provides interdisciplinary evidence (from psychology, sociology, and cultural anthropology) demonstrating the virtually universal sets of qualities making men (in general) more fit for governing a society in light of the common good oriented to the future, and women (in general) more suited for the fine details of present domestic management.[51] Children need both kinds of humanly embodied authority: paternal objective discipline (tempered by caring love) and maternal nurturing warmth (elevated by the goal of character development). In the opinion of this author, given the leftist propaganda promoted by the public school system and even many nominally "Catholic" schools, the best way (if feasible) to educate children both in the Faith and in the classical disciplines is to home-school them, with the joyful burden of supervising this instruction shared between father and mother (according to their respective talents). A natural balance ought to prevail. Of course, a circumstance of deprivation is sometimes tragically unavoidable. But this defect from the ideal condition does not warrant raising "two mommies" or "two daddies" to a socially equivalent status in order to satisfy the demands of homosexual unionists for civic recognition.

Some individuals with psychological and emotional disorders will find it difficult or impossible to adjust to the time-hallowed norm. Although these afflicted people should be accorded genuine empathy (accompanied by concerned assistance, if appropriate), for the sake of civilization itself their chosen "lifestyles" cannot be transported into the public square of legal protection — despite the discomfort liberal sympathizers feel about "imposing" moral norms on the citizenry (which they hypocritically have no qualms about doing anyway, so long as it is a question of their own favorite anti-traditional causes). Christopher Derrick has written a lengthy critique lamenting the way sex (the powerful primordial force symbolized by "Venus") has been trivialized and profaned (or "desacralized") in recent times. But a casual treatment of something that inherently blazes with fury can only backfire with a vengeance.[52]

To underestimate or disregard the crucial physical, psychological, and therefore symbolic differences between the two sexes would be disastrous for either sacramental vocation, whether stemming from Holy Orders or Holy Matrimony. Paul Evdokimov brilliantly summarizes the overall "callings" of man and woman:

> Men . . . express themselves in the world through instruments and acts. . . . Left to himself man loses himself

in abstraction and objectifications; when degraded he becomes degrading and invents a dehumanized world. The vocation of every woman is to protect the world and men like a mother, as the new Eve, and to protect and purify life as the Virgin. Women must reconvert men to their essential function, which is priesthood; the function of the spirit is to penetrate the elements of this world sacramentally and to sanctify them, to purify through prayer the work of the scientist, and to show that matter is the expression of the spirit.[53]

This concludes our study, in Chapters 5 and 6, of how the dialectic of "the same and the different" apply to the sacraments of Holy Orders and Holy Matrimony. Yes, as Evdokimov says, "matter is the expression of the spirit." But it is an organically truthful expression of the human spirit in its humble integrity. For, as we hope these six chapters have demonstrated, matter is not the plastic playground of a gnostically capricious human spirit. We finish these reflections in the Epilogue.

EPILOGUE

We cannot finish without some commentary on the ruinous havoc wrought by gnostic attitudes toward the embodied human being in our time. Often the implementation of the gnostic project is justified by compassion for suffering or by an appeal to alleged benefits projected to accrue from following a certain course of medical technique. This so-called "compassion," however, can be a false and ultimately *cruel* response to someone's misery, because somebody else is compelled to submit to murderous debasement. And the utilitarian rationalization winds up doing the same thing: enslaving a weak and depersonalized minority to the vaunted needs of a dictatorial majority who hold power over life and death. Three salient examples of this diabolical ethic follow.

First, artificial means of preventing or causing fertilization commit the error of dismissing the relevance of material methods to our well-intentioned actions. (We suppose for the sake of argument that contraception and artificial conception could occur with no loss of human life. In practice, this would be a generous hypothesis, since most contraceptives are abortifacient and since laboratory reproduction often entails trial-and-error with deadly consequences.) To declare that any means whatsoever can be licitly employed to realize a noble objective is to propose a thesis that is not at all obvious; in fact, it is counterintuitive. For instance, no one with a modicum of moral maturity would maintain the legitimacy of robbing banks to achieve the admittedly desirable aim of a comfortable lifestyle. Therefore, since the general maxim that "the end justifies the means" fails, it begs the question and amounts to special pleading to claim that it *does* hold in the cases of artificial contraception and reproduction. Granted that human procreation occurs normally in only one way, a presumption in favor of not altering the physical processes entailed ought to prevail. The burden of proof rests on an opponent to demonstrate why it is not morally degrading (i.e., treating human subjects as though they were objects for laboratory manipulation) to bypass these evidently normative human biological pathways. Indeed, scientists who arrogate unto themselves the prerogative of molding human constituents in any technically feasible fashion exhibit gnostic disdain (and even contempt) for matter in its most egregious (not to say monstrous) guise. Of course, affirmative arguments beyond this negative criticism should be, can be, and have been expertly advanced and defended, employing both the natural moral law approach[1] and the integral personalist approach.[2]

Next, abortion and euthanasia intrinsically demean the human person by assailing the human body as a commodity for disposal in the name of exalting the freedom of choice of the autonomous individual will. These deeds are consonant with the gnostic aversion for imprisoning spirits in lowly burdensome matter: preferable to release the souls of unwanted preborn children and other miserable people from potentially or actually agonizing enfleshment. Contrary to gnostic hubris, though, finite wills do *not* have unlimited dominion over matter when that matter is an integral part of our own or someone else's personhood (see Wisdom 12:2-7). The fatal tissue harvesting in contemporary embryonic stem-cell research (like the human experimentation in the Nazi era) entails executing wicked deeds subject to the same condemnation.[3]

A blatant assertion of the so-called "right" of the human will to trample on the existence of the defenseless (who have become obstacles to self-liberation) appears in the U. S. Supreme Court's 1992 *Planned Parenthood* v. *Casey* decision refusing to overturn the infamous 1973 *Roe* v. *Wade* decree (which had basically legalized unlimited abortion, despite the ruling's ludicrously arbitrary trimester division): "At the heart of liberty is the right to define one's own concept of existence, of the meaning of the universe and the mystery of human life." Nothing could be further from the truth than this infernally audacious (even blasphemous) metaphysical slap-in-the-face at divine sovereignty over human life.

Lastly, gnostic minimalization of natural differences among things plummets to absurdity with the convergence of the extremist environmentalist and so-called "animal rights" movements. Both groups (especially the first) present a palatable front to the public, advertising their façade of sensitivity to nonhuman forms of existence. Their misguided zealotry, however, conceals a latent and menacing materialism that would reduce mankind to the level of beasts. In the name of "protecting endangered species," the government agencies under their control "reclaim" (or seize) land and withhold irrigation from family farms — all for the sake of aquatic creatures such as suckerfish and bull trout fingerlings.[4] Federal law prohibits destruction of bald eagle eggs (never mind the birds themselves), yet human zygotes (not to mention embryos and fetuses) are wantonly discarded as trivialities.[5] Under the aegis of "biodiversity" treaties and "sustainable development" commissions, public officials must tender priority consideration to the spotted owl, kangaroo rat, and Delhi Sands flower-loving fly — the latter species holding hostage even construction of schools, hospitals, sanitation projects, and electrical stations.[6] Taxpayer subsidies for depopulation programs, involving both contraception and sterilization, are promoted under the mendacious and propagandistic guise of overpopulation scares, when in fact the earth is underpopulated with the attendant threat of economic collapse.[7]

We read in Genesis 1:28, *RSV*: "And God blessed them, and God said to them, 'Be fruitful and multiply, and fill the earth and subdue it.'" But when preserving whales, seals, bald eagles, spotted owls, kangaroo rats, exotic fish and flies, together with all their wildlife habitats, takes precedence over family livelihoods, human offspring, and the right to procreate, gnosticism clashes with itself. For, although it claims to extol the intelligent spirit over merely physical entities, it ends up placing brute animals on a par with rational human beings — at least on a par with certain human beings deemed insufficiently valuable (either lacking consciously productive capacity or else too resistant to higher "enlightenment") for the gnostic masters to abide. In fact, protecting the biosphere from pollution serves merely as a strategic pretext for their ultimate goal of ridding the world of independent and nonsubservient men. The overlords are not interested in conservation for its own sake, but rather in global control, with eco-socialism as a convenient tactical tool. Their agenda is precisely the dislocation or elimination of human masses that would interfere with their project to build a new planetary regime under their omnivigilant eye.[8]

In Genesis 1:26-28 and 2:18-20, the first human beings alone are created in the divine "image and likeness," and given dominion by God over all other animals. But the truth of humanity's essential superiority can be philosophically demonstrated by invoking the principle "*agere sequitur esse*": we know the *kind* of thing a being is by observing the characteristic ways it tends to act. Indeed, there is no solid and incontrovertible evidence to warrant the conclusion that animals other than man can engage in abstract thought using universal concepts. Their abilities to communicate and to be trained can be parsimoniously explained by recourse to sensory perception (the five external senses and the internal senses of imagination, instinctive judgment, and experiential memory), as well as emotive reactions — all associated with conditioning by environmental stimuli. By contrast, since human intellectual operations transcend the restrictive confines of space and time, they cannot be exhaustively explained by sensory faculties localized in the brain — no matter what their degree of complexity and sophistication (because a physical organ cannot produce immaterial ideas). Hence, man alone can possess a spiritual and immortal soul, along with free will and moral responsibility. This proves that subhuman animals cannot have "rights" in the proper sense of the term.

Some so-called "radical" professors in academia do not deserve their prestigious positions, since they are enemies and not guardians of civilization (blinded hindrances to truth rather than torchbearers for ignorant and impressionable students). Instead of excavating to the "roots" of reality, they superficially accuse those who uphold mankind's virtually infinite superiority to animals as guilty of the alleged crime of "speciesism"; yet they commit the sin of ecolatry —

worshiping primitive geocratic systems. What's more, they contravene the Creator's plan that the human race should "*fill* the earth and subdue it." Truly, it is God, and not they, who loves people (see Wisdom 11:26 and 1 John 4:7-11, 16).[9] The final irony: the very same Church so often libeled as antiscience (e.g., the Galileo canard, artificial reproduction, embryonic experimentation) is blamed for the depredations of technology alleged to follow as a consequence of God's Genesis command.[10] These contradictory censures remind one of the passage where Jesus exclaims the equivalent of "You can't win!" (See Matthew 11:16-19 and Luke 7:31-35.)

In today's neo-pagan (or post-Christian) climate, there often seems (once again in human history) a chilling aversion of the mighty to identify with the weak and an appalling indifference to their exploitation. We are reminded of the words of Jesus in Matthew 24:12, *RSV*, "Because wickedness is multiplied, most men's love will grow cold." (See also Matthew 25:40, 45, in which *He* identifies Himself with the marginalized.) Indeed, as we insisted in the Introduction, when man's delicately woven biological and spiritual fabric is not respected, then might makes right and the vulnerable are manipulated or destroyed. When the Creator's sovereign rights are usurped rather than revered, when man refuses to answer to the divine tribunal under the just and gentle reign of Christ the King (the Prince of Peace,[11] Lord of Life,[12] and Light of the world[13]), then he must submit to the horrifying tyranny of the father of lies and murder[14] (the prince of darkness[15]), as diabolical insanity erupts to foment hellish catastrophe on earth.

We live in an age of enormous moral degeneracy abetted by superficial thinking. Most people are not fully cognizant of our calamitous predicament, because the benighted slide down the proverbial "slippery slope" (from legalized divorce, contraception, abortion, fetal experimentation, assisted suicide, to impending euthanasia) has been gradual enough throughout the past century to accustom, numb, and inure the populace to the grievous evil surrounding us. The strange thing is that it does not take an immense amount of skilled acumen to discern that most items on the agenda of increasing licentiousness are blatantly wrong. Even a moderately decent epoch would possess the intuitive moral sense to appreciate this fact — or at least possess the humility to recognize that it ought to consult and ponder the wisdom deposited in traditional Western philosophy and theology.

But superficial thinking — the refusal to grapple by reason with the objective nature of things — makes it impossible to stop the juggernaut of the sinister questions "Why not?" and "Who's to say?" Examples are easy to cite. *Why not* substitute rice cakes for wheat wafers in Holy Communion for those with celiac disease? *Why not* ordain women to the priesthood, since they can do as fine a "job" as men? *Why not* legally approve homosexual unions for those devoid of attraction to the opposite sex? *Why not* manufacture babies (even to customer specification) if parents are unable to procreate in the normal way? *Why not* harvest stem cells from fetal tissue if someone else may benefit from a touted therapy? Aren't all these approaches to solving problems the "compassionate" things to do? *Who's to say* what's normal? *Who's to say* what's right or wrong? *Who's to say* that the answers don't merely depend on one's own subjective values?

Thus, beneath the current moral morass lies a turbid swamp of relativism (whether sentimental, apathetic, or militant) that relentlessly eclipses those glimmers of moral light still flickering.[16] Sadly, we have few prophets of the caliber of Elijah, Jeremiah, and John the Baptist; nevertheless, the popes of the past two centuries do stand out as voices crying in the wilderness. For instance, Pope Paul VI, although directly addressing the issue of contraception, can be construed as prophetically warning against all gnostic intervention in the structural underpinnings of human nature:

> If the mission of generating life is not to be exposed to the arbitrary will of men, one must necessarily recognize insurmountable limits to the possibility of man's domination over his own body and its functions; limits which no man, whether a private individual or one invested with

authority, may licitly surpass. And such limits cannot be determined otherwise than by the respect due to the integrity of the human organism and its functions.[17]

As Cardinal Ratzinger puts it: "To respect biology is to respect God himself, hence to safeguard his creatures."[18] For the most part, however, human "respect" of the wrong sort has dealt a severe blow to countercultural witness, which has probably been in short supply for most of mankind's history, anyway.

As a result, resurgent gnostic challenges to the Church's moral and sacramental doctrines now confront us with their ghastly ramifications. Many people refuse to acknowledge (for whatever subjective reasons) that "matter matters." The cultural factors at play, undermining the serious consideration of this truth about human reality, emanate (as we said) from a deeply entrenched relativism. Yet those who criticize the Church for "intolerance" toward "diversity" because of her unwavering stance on valid sacramental matter (especially for the Eucharist, Holy Orders, and Matrimony), not only manifest a gnostic dismissal of material differences, but also unwittingly (perhaps) promote a totalitarian ideology. For if the Church were to surrender to secular demands for "pluralism," she would ironically be swallowed up in a "monistic" mass uniformity that deifies the collective will-to-power of pressure groups. (*Monism* is the philosophical thesis that all is ultimately reducible to one thing; in other words, that everything basically coalesces into a single substance.) Although gnosticism overtly posits an extreme dualism of spirit (considered as good) versus matter (regarded with suspicion as dispensable and perhaps evil to the extent that it obstructs personal freedom), in practice it can paradoxically tend toward the monism of atheistic materialism (the dominant elites styling themselves godlike owners of a farm of disposable human bodies). In opposition, the Church's stalwart defense of the rights of God and the noninterchangeable integrity of material substances ensure a corresponding respect for each individual human person, created in the spiritual likeness of God with specific physical requirements displayed in the psychosomatic realm of symbolism. Matter matters because man (who is partly composed of matter arranged in a unique and irreducible manner by an informing rational soul) matters.

About this contentious issue of the Church's alleged "judgmentalism," Pope John Paul II writes:

> The Church, one hears, is lacking in understanding and compassion. . . . In fact, genuine understanding and compassion must mean love for the person, for his true good, for his authentic freedom. And this does not result . . . from concealing or weakening moral truth, but rather from proposing it in its most profound meaning as an outpouring of God's eternal Wisdom, which we have received in Christ, and as a service to man, to the growth of his freedom and to the attainment of his happiness. . . . The Church's firmness in defending the universal and unchanging moral norms is not demeaning at all. Its only purpose is to serve man's true freedom. Because there can be no freedom apart from or in opposition to the truth, the categorical — unyielding and uncompromising — defense of the absolutely essential demands of man's personal dignity must be considered the way and the condition for the very existence of freedom.[19]

With regard to *moral* truth, the pope's words would obviously apply much more to the topic of Chapter 6; nonetheless, they still have some relevance for the earlier Chapters 1-5.

In particular, it is a sorry commentary on the tragic state of our times that a defense of the traditional institution of marriage should seem necessary. Who would seriously have entertained an opposing view until fairly recently? What could be simpler than the idea that Matrimony entails one man and one woman? One is tempted to summarize the entire long-winded argumentation of Chapter 6 (or at least its thesis) in a single brief sentence: "It's so obvious."

Probably many people would agree with this assessment, but most of them have been neutralized by pressure-group intimidation and by the indoctrination of the mass media: conform to ways of thinking and talking that we (the illumined monitors of thought-crimes[20]) condone.[21] Although at least some bear no guilt for direct complicity with the waves of moral error inundating us, they lack the courage to vocalize indignant protest against the raging storm assaulting our moral shores and devastating our culture, for fear of being branded by the labels currently most lethal in their paralyzing potency: "intolerant" and "judgmental." But some situations in human history are so egregiously intolerable that, for the good of mankind, they ought to be judged and denounced. As Archbishop Fulton J. Sheen diagnosed, we are suffering from a surfeit of "broadmindedness."

Therefore, whatever naïveté we may still have clung to about our popular culture has been vaporized. Our wide-open eyes see how the left-leaning mainstream media (with the complacent docility of a poorly informed, half-educated, and thus unwittingly prejudiced citizenry) purveys a sappy picture of God, as though He were made in the image and likeness of a typical so-called "liberal" — permissive and "nonjudgmental" toward the agenda of "diversity," like a politically correct talk-show host (or audience) nodding sympathetic approval of a guest's justification for the latest infringement of a traditional taboo. The modern mind-set, spurning logic and submerged in relativistic emotionalism, interprets God's infinite love and mercy in an overly sentimental way. But we must exercise great care *not* to interpret God's boundless compassion in an excessively emotional way, for *not* every precept is a question of mere custom or arbitrary convention (hence changeable regulations).

In particular, it clearly matters to the Creator of matter what materials are used for what purposes. Jesus announced (in Luke 12:51 and Matthew 10:34, *RSV*) that He Himself had come to bring "division," not necessarily "to bring peace on earth"; indeed, at His birth the angels specifically proclaimed (in Luke 2:14, *D-R*) "on earth peace to men of good will" (only). In this context, we might add the commentary that Christ came to reveal the significance of the distinctions among earthly matters. Peace will reign only when mankind puts various matters in their rightful place: that is, when we "learn to value the things that really matter" (Philippians 1:10, *NAB*). This conversion includes a repudiation of the errors of materialism itself (especially its Communist incarnation) — a programmatic doctrine that (as our Blessed Lady predicted at Fátima in 1917) has engulfed the world, provoking interminable persecutions and wars to consolidate politico-economic power. For objective truth encompasses an authentic *metaphysical* (not ideologically driven) pluralism — one that recognizes the utter priority of allegiance to God and the immortal human soul, while not neglecting physical matters and the real differences among them (see Matthew 23:23). Perhaps God manifests His love for us in a special manner by setting absolute standards to root us in the objective nature of things, lest we lapse into gnostic indifferentism.

We began this book with a Scriptural epigraph (Jeremiah 31:12, *NAB*) intended to set the tone for the sequel:

> Shouting they shall mount the heights of Zion,
> they shall come streaming to the LORD's blessings:
> The grain, the wine, and the oil, . . .
> They themselves shall be like watered gardens,
> never again shall they languish.

These remarkably prophetic lines compactly encapsulate everything we have been trying to convey. We venture to interpret them as follows. The "heights of Zion" represent the Catholic Church, the New Israel.[22] The multitudes who approach to ascend her lofty citadel rejoice,[23] because, as it is written in Isaiah 11:9; 65:25, *RSV*: "They shall not hurt or destroy / in all my holy mountain." In other words, the elect find therein an abundance of spiritual sustenance and protection from "hurt": namely, the sacraments, symbolized by the material substances enumerated. Initially regenerated by the "waters" of Baptism, they will never experience the desert of fruitless debility so long as the "waters" of grace continue to flow into the "gardens" of their souls through the mighty channels of the other sacraments. They are nourished by eating the Bread of Life ("grain") and refreshed by draughts of the Precious Blood ("wine") in the Holy Eucharist. They are strengthened by the chrism ("oil") of Confirmation and comforted by the unction ("oil") of the Anointing of the Sick.

Concerning the relation between Baptism and the other sacraments, we read in Genesis 2:10, *NAB*: "A river rises in Eden to water the garden." In 2:11-12 we are told that, after dividing, the first of this river's branches (called the "Pishon") winds through a land of "excellent *gold.*" Interestingly, Sirach 24:23, *NAB*, employs the name of this very same tributary in a simile that involves "overflow[ing] . . . with wisdom." We proffer a possible spiritual interpretation. After Baptism restores the soul to a state of pristine purity, it opens the soul up to the other sacraments that continue to convey grace. The preeminent among these sacraments is the Holy Eucharist, containing the fountainhead of wisdom — the Incarnate Wisdom of God, the "Wheat of Life" symbolized by *gold* (as discussed in Chapter 2). Further supporting this exegesis of Genesis 2:10-12, we read in Psalm 72:8, 15, 16, *RSV*: "May he [Christ] have dominion . . . / from the River to the ends of the earth! . . . / Long may he live, / may gold of Sheba be given to him! . . . / May there be abundance of grain in the land; / on the tops of the mountains may it wave." The grain waving from the mountaintops is golden wheat, symbolizing the Eucharistic reign of Christ from the high throne of wisdom in the Catholic Church (see Isaiah 2:2-3) after a baptismal flood of repentance and regeneration has subjugated the nations to the Lord.

The state of spiritual well-being signified by the prodigious availability of all the sacramental materials in Jeremiah 31:12 presages the total eschatological fulfillment of body and soul in the literal resurrection of the flesh. Isaiah 25:6-8, *RSV*, foretells: "On this mountain the LORD of hosts will make for all peoples a feast of fat things, a feast of wine on the lees, of fat things full of marrow, of wine on the lees well refined. And he will destroy on this mountain the covering that is cast over all peoples, the veil that is spread over all nations. He will swallow up death for ever, and the Lord GOD will wipe away tears from all faces"; and Isaiah 66:13-14, *RSV*, adds: "You shall be comforted in Jerusalem. / You shall see, and your heart shall rejoice; / your bones shall flourish like the grass." In like manner, Revelation 21:1, 4, *RSV*, presents the parallel prophetic vision: "Then I saw a new heaven and a new earth; . . . he will wipe away every tear from their eyes, and death shall be no more, neither shall there be mourning nor crying nor pain any more, for the former things have passed away." And Philippians 3:20-21, *RSV*, adds: "We await a Savior, the Lord Jesus Christ, who will change our lowly body to be like his glorious body." A similar passage about the immortalized body (too lengthy to quote) is 1 Corinthians 15:42-49, 51-52. Finally, the Beatific Vision in a resurrected world is suggested in Job 19:26, *RSV*: "Then from my flesh I shall see God," along with Ezekiel 36:35, *RSV*: "This land that was desolate has become like the garden of Eden."

A passage cognate to Jeremiah 31:12 about the Creator's provision for humanity through the sacramental substances of water, bread, wine, and oil, occurs in Psalm 104:14-16, *RSV*: "Thou dost cause . . . / to grow . . . / plants for man to cultivate, / that he may bring forth food from the earth, / and wine to gladden the heart of man, / oil to make his face shine, / and bread to strengthen man's heart. / The trees of the LORD are watered abundantly." Likewise, there is the promise in Joel 2:19, 23, 24, *RSV*: "Behold, I am sending to you / grain, wine, and oil, / and you will be satisfied. . . . / Be glad, O sons of Zion, / and rejoice in the LORD, your God, / for he has given the early rain for your vindication, / he has poured down for you abundant rain. . . . / The threshing floors shall be full of grain, / the vats shall overflow with wine and oil." In context, Joel 1:10-11, *RSV*, explicitly equates grain with "the wheat and the barley" (in that order of priority), whereas Joel 1:5, *NAB*, specifies "the juice of the grape" (and 1:10 mentions "must"). On account of the overall agricultural imagery here and from what we learned in Chapter 4, the "oil" in 1:10 and thus in 2:19, 24, must be olive.

These excerpts all display the identical substances that we have seen repeatedly and ubiquitously in our Scriptural exploration throughout this book: the simple basics of water, bread, wine, and oil. We would render the same sacramental interpretation of these texts as the one we gave our epigraph. As 1 John 5:8, *RSV*, summarizes: "There are three witnesses, the Spirit, the water, and the blood; and these three agree." The "water" here is a *metonym* representing Baptism, the sacrament with which it is most closely associated. The "blood" is a *synecdoche* — a part standing for the entire Eucharistic Body of Christ. And the "Spirit" (metonymous with olive oil) is received upon the anointing in Confirmation. They operationally converge in the integral sacramental life of the practicing Catholic.

A skeptic may still protest that the specific composition of bread, wine, and oil does not really matter; Christ may have selected wheat, grapes, and olives for the sacraments only because they happened to be in plenteous supply in the Middle East of His earthly time. But this objection ignores the fact that the man Jesus is also God — the First Cause for whom no circumstance is accidental. The Father's infinite Wisdom is exquisitely particular. From all eternity He chose to make wheat, grapes, and olives prolific in the Middle East precisely because He knew His incarnate Wisdom would be laboring there in a sacramental manner. Christ testified to this fact in John 5:17, *RSV*: "My Father is working still, and I am working." In any event, these foods have become universal (or *catholic*): where they may not grow natively, they are nonetheless not difficult to procure. As St. Thomas Aquinas averred about the Eucharistic elements: "Although wheat and wine are not produced in every country, yet they can easily be conveyed to every land, that is, as much as is needful for the use of this sacrament."[24]

Once again, it is the Catholic (or *Universal*) Church that furnishes all the needs of mankind — neither disparaging material things with a gnostic condescension nor forsaking any individual person in favor of the anonymous herd. Ultimately, of course, she owes all her sacramental symbols and their efficacy to her Divine Founder, who (while remaining immutable, eternal, infinite Spirit as the Second Person of the Holy Trinity) in His physical nature represented Himself as a fountain of water, wheat bread, a grape vine, an olive tree, priest, and groom.

ENDNOTES

Introduction

1. *Metaphysics*, Bk. II, Ch. 1.
2. *The Republic*, Bk. VII.
3. Thomas Aquinas, *Summa Theologiae*, Pt. I, quest.1, art. 9. All citations from this monumental work are based on the translation by the Fathers of the English Dominican Province (the "Blackfriars"), reprinted by Christian Classics (Westminster, Md.) in 1981.
4. *CCC*, n. 1114.
5. *Summa Theologiae*, Pt. III, quest. 60, art. 4, and quest. 61, art. 1.
6. *Summa Theologiae*, Pt. III, quest. 62, art. 2.
7. *CCC*, n. 1121.
8. See also 1 Peter 1:3-5 and *Summa Theologiae*, Pt. III, quest. 62, art. 1.
9. C. S. Lewis, *The Abolition of Man* (New York: Macmillan Publishing Co., 1947/1955), especially pp. 67-91 (Ch. 3).
10. See, for example, Karl Keating, *The Usual Suspects* (San Francisco: Ignatius Press, 2000), p. 69.
11. *Summa Theologiae*, Pt. III, quest. 84, art. 2.
12. For pertinent references, see Augustine's renowned *Confessions*, Bk. VII, Chs. 12, 13, 16, 17; his influential *City of God*, Bk. XI , Chs. 9, 22, and Bk. XII, Ch. 6; also, *Concerning the Nature of Good*, Chs. 6, 17, 18; finally, *Enchiridion*, Chs. 11-14.
13. See Plato's *Theaetetus* (155d) and Aristotle's *Metaphysics*, Bk. I, Chs. 1-2.
14. On God's deciding the matter of the sacraments, see *Summa Theologiae*, Pt. III, quest. 60, art. 5.
15. *Summa Theologiae*, Pt. I, quest. 1, art. 10. The *CCC* describes "typology" in nn. 128-130.
16. For a far deeper study of this fascinating area of "Symbolic Theology," see Edith Stein (St. Teresa Benedicta of the Cross), "Ways to Know God," in *Knowledge and Faith*, trans. Walter Redmond (Washington, D.C.: Institute of Carmelite Studies Publications, 2000), pp. 83-134. On p. 108, she lucidly captures the essence of God's disclosure of Himself to us through symbols, with her concise assertion: "What the prophet hears and sees is as it were the great school of symbolic theology where images and words become available to the

sacred writer so that he may say the unsayable and make the invisible visible."

Chapter 1

1. Ludwig Ott, *Fundamentals of Catholic Dogma*, trans. Patrick Lynch, ed. James C. Bastible (Rockford, Ill.: TAN Books and Publishers, 1974), p. 352.

2. See also the *CCC*, n. 1215.

3. For a fascinating account of the therapeutic value of water, see H.C.A. Vogel, *The Nature Doctor: A Manual of Traditional and Complementary Medicine* (Teufen, Switzerland: Verlag A. Vogel, 1991), English ed. Harry Selbert (New York: Instant Improvement Inc., 1993, with permission of Keats Publishing, New Canaan, Conn.), pp. 424-434.

4. *Fundamentals of Catholic Dogma*, p. 352.

5. Heribert Jone, *Moral Theology*, trans. Urban Adelman (Westminster, Md.: The Newman Bookshop, 1945), par. nn. 464-465, p. 337.

6. *Fundamentals of Catholic Dogma*, p. 250.

7. Christopher Derrick, *Sex and Sacredness* (San Francisco: Ignatius Press, 1982), pp. 67-73.

8. See the *CCC*, n. 1220, although the particular episode in question is not explicitly mentioned.

9. *Summa Theologiae*, Pt. III, quest. 39, art. 1.

10. *Summa Theologiae*, Pt. III, quest. 39, art. 4.

11. *CCC*, n. 696.

12. *Summa Theologiae*, Pt. III, quest. 39, art. 4.

13. *Summa Theologiae*, Pt. III, quest. 39, art. 5.

Chapter 2

1. *Instruction Concerning Worship of the Eucharistic Mystery (Inaestimabile Donum)*, Sacred Congregation for the Sacraments and Divine Worship, Approved and Confirmed by His Holiness Pope John Paul II, April 17, 1980 (English edition reprinted with permission from *L'Osservatore Romano* by Pauline Books and Media: Daughters of St. Paul, Boston), n. 8, p. 7.

In *Summa Theologiae*, Pt. III, quest. 74, art. 4, St. Thomas Aquinas distinguishes between the universally valid matter for Eucharistic confection and the licit matter depending on liturgical custom in a particular rite: "It is necessary that the bread be wheaten, without which the sacrament is not valid. . . . It is not, however, necessary for the sacrament that the bread be unleavened or leavened, since it can be celebrated in either." He goes on to explain that there are reasons why unyeasted bread is suitable (pertaining to the Passover tradition of Exodus 12:15-20, to the significance of Jesus' noncorrupting conception in His Mother's integrally unimpaired body, and to the symbolism of "the unleavened bread of sincerity and truth" found in 1 Corinthians 5:7-8 by contrast with Matthew 16:5-12, where our Lord denounces the hypocritically distorted and manmade doctrines of the corrupt Pharisees). Nevertheless, Eastern rites can also justify the use of leavened bread (relating to the imagery of the Eternal Word's assuming the "leaven" of human flesh in the Incarnation — see, as well, Matthew 13:33 and Luke 13:20-21, where "leaven" represents the expansive growth on earth of the Church, the Mystical Body of Christ).

2. *Fundamentals of Catholic Dogma*, p. 391. According to *Moral Theology*, par. n. 493, p. 358, in order for bread to be licit matter it must be "made without the admixture of any other substance besides wheat flour and water," although the Consecration will still be valid if "only a relatively small quantity of another substance is added." Also see *Summa Theologiae*, Pt. III, quest. 74, art. 3, especially reply to objection 3.

3. From the start people had trouble believing in the very possibility of this miracle, even aside from gnostic suspicions about divine action through material things. John 6:52, *RSV*, reports: "The Jews then disputed among themselves, saying, 'How can this man give us his flesh to eat?' " For an attempt at a philosophical justification, see David P. Lang, "The compatibility of the Eucharist with reason," *Homiletic and Pastoral Review* (December, 1995), pp. 18-24.

4. *Summa Theologiae*, Pt. III, quest. 74, art. 1, where Aquinas explicitly cites 1 Corinthians 10:17.

5. *Summa Theologiae*, Pt. III, quest. 74, arts. 1, 3.

6. *Summa Theologiae*, Pt. III, quest. 74, art. 3.

7. John Heinerman, *Heinerman's Encyclopedia of Fruits, Vegetables and Herbs* (West Nyack, N.Y.: Parker Publishing Co., 1988), p. 165.

8. David L. Vise brought to my attention the symbolic relations between wheat, gold, and God.

9. See, as an undoubtedly partial list, the following additional Scriptural references: Exodus 25-26, 28, 37; Numbers 8:4; 31:50-52; 1 Kings 6:19-22, 30-35; 7:48-51; 2 Chronicles 3:4-9; 4:7-8, 19-22; 13:11; Psalm 45:9, 13, *RSV*; Psalm 72:15; Tobit 13:16; Job 23:10; Wisdom 3:6-7; Zechariah 4:2; Isaiah 60:6; 1 Maccabees 4:56-57; 11:57-58; Matthew 2:11; 1 Peter 1:6-7; 1 Corinthians 3:10-15; Hebrews 9:3-4; Revelation 1:12-13; 3:18; 4:4; 8:3; 21:15-21.

10. Isaiah 53:5, *NAB*, prophesies that He was "crushed for our sins." The same verb, "crush," occurs in verse 10 of the *NAB* translation, con-

noting the fragmentation and pulverization of grain, especially wheat.

11. *CCC*, nn. 1331, 1391, 1396, 1416; see also 1 Corinthians 10:16-17; 12:12-27; Ephesians 4:4; Psalm 122:3.

12. *Heinerman's Encyclopedia of Fruits, Vegetables and Herbs*, p. 165.

13. *Inaestimabile Donum*, n. 8, p. 7.

14. This quotation is the Communion antiphon for his feast day (October 17), taken from the sixth of his seven letters addressed to different local churches, written en route from Antioch to his impending death in Rome.

15. The word "holocaust" is derived from Greek, meaning "wholly burnt."

16. This associative chain linking *types* and their fulfillments is due to David L. Vise.

17. The Passover ritual is initially described in Exodus 12:1-20 but decreed again in both Leviticus 23:5-14 and Deuteronomy 16:1-6.

18. *Summa Theologiae*, Pt. III, quest. 74, art. 3, reply 1.

19. Reese Dubin, *Miracle Food Cures from the Bible* (Paramus, N.J.: Prentice Hall, 1999), p. 125.

20. *Miracle Food Cures from the Bible*, p. 189.

21. Vogel confirms the biological basis of this symbolism by explaining the nutritional benefits of whole wheat germ for normalizing the energy of the reproductive system. See *The Nature Doctor*, pp. 451, 466-467, 519-523. Moreover, according to Genesis 30:14, *D-R*, "Ruben [the firstborn son of Jacob], going out in the time of the wheat harvest into the field, found mandrakes," which he then brought to his mother Lia (Leah), who in turn gave them to her sister Rachel, who (after a long period of barrenness) later conceived her firstborn son, Joseph. Now the European mandrake (*Mandragora officinarum*) is a plant with a long segmented fleshy root vaguely resembling the human shape, and hence legendarily represents procreative potency (see also Song of Solomon 7:13, *RSV*). According to the herbalist John Lust, in some locales "mandrake root is believed helpful in promoting conception." See *The Herb Book* (Benedict Lust Publications, Simi Valley, Calif., 1974; reprinted by Bantam Books, New York, 1978), pp. 264-265. On the other hand, exactly how Rachel employed this botanical is debatable, since Lust also avers that the "European mandrake is poisonous"; it can be safely taken only in "homeopathic preparations" (used for certain respiratory ailments, although in ancient times it served as a surgical anesthetic and an emetic). At any rate, this explicit association of the wheat harvest with the mandrake, found also in the *RSV* and *NAB* translations, suggests a similar connection between wheat and fertility.

22. *Summa Theologiae*, Pt. II-II, quest. 45, art. 2.

23. See also Psalm 110:1-4, *NAB/RSV,* or Psalm 109:1-4, *D-R,* for an identical notion.

24. See also Revelation 19:13, *D-R* ("his name is called, THE WORD OF GOD"). Note further that John 1:14, *RSV* ("And the Word became flesh and dwelt among us") corresponds to Sirach 24:8, 11, *RSV* ("Make your dwelling in Jacob, / and in Israel receive your inheritance, . . . / In Jerusalem was my dominion").

25. This is not (yet) a defined dogma of the Catholic Faith, but it has been widely accepted as worthy of belief. In fact, as far back as the eleventh century, a prayer (ascribed to Hermanus Contractus, 1013-1054) was composed, titled *"Salve, Regina Caelitum"* (a hymn now called in English "Hail, Holy Queen Enthroned Above"), whose second stanza reads: "The cause of joy to us below, O Maria. / The spring *through which all graces flow,* O Maria" (emphasis added).

26. Many of these insightful interpretations connected with 1 Samuel 4-6 are due to David L. Vise, from personal communications with the author.

27. See the entry for "Mandrake" in *The New World Dictionary Concordance to the New American Bible* (C. D. Stampley Enterprises, Charlotte, N.C., 1970), p. 407.

28. Again, the analytical exegesis in this paragraph comes from David L. Vise.

Chapter 3

1. *Fundamentals of Catholic Dogma,* p. 392. Also see *Summa Theologiae,* Pt. III, quest. 74, art. 5.

2. *Moral Theology,* par. n. 494, p. 359: "*Wine* is lawful matter if it is unadulterated, fermented, unspoiled and clear." If any extra alcohol be added "the better to preserve the wine," then "it is required . . . that the alcohol be derived from grapes." Moreover, the grapes must be ripe, according to par. n. 491 (b), p. 357.

There is a practically nonalcoholic beverage derived from grapes called *"mustum."* This term is defined in Sec. 2 (c) of the document *Norms for Use of Low-Gluten Bread and Mustum,* promulgated by the Congregation for the Doctrine of the Faith (August 22, 1994): "By *mustum* is understood fresh juice from grapes or juice preserved by suspending its fermentation (by means of freezing or other methods which do not alter its nature)." The prefect Joseph Cardinal Ratzinger issued a more precise clarification of *mustum* in a circular letter (dated June 19, 1995) addressed to presidents of episcopal conferences (see Protocol N. 89/78). He elaborated that, in order for grape juice to qualify as *mustum,* there must be no interference with its inherent tendency to ferment, even if the actual fermentation process is "arrested at an early stage." (This stricture would, for example, exclude pasteurization, which involves enzymatic destruction.) What matters is that it retain as nearly as possible the intrinsic characteristics of grape wine.

In *Summa Theologiae*, Pt. III, quest. 74, art. 5, reply to objection 3, St. Thomas makes a crucial distinction: "The juice of unripe grapes is at the stage of incomplete generation, and therefore it has not yet the species of wine: on which account it may not be used for this sacrament. *Must*, however, has already the species of wine, for its sweetness indicates fermentation which is the result of its natural heat; consequently this sacrament can be made from *must*." He goes on to caution, however, that the direct pouring into a chalice of juice pressed from grapes is prohibited unless truly necessary. Agreeing with Aquinas's assertions, the *New Commentary on the Code of Canon Law*, commissioned by The Canon Law Society of America (New York: Paulist Press, 2000), states: "Canonists and theologians have commonly held that *mustum*, or the unfermented juice of ripe grapes, is valid matter for the Eucharist but is gravely illicit except in necessity." Hence, a priest suffering from alcoholism, who wishes to employ this virtual or ersatz wine, must present medical documentation to the competent ecclesiastical authority in order to obtain a dispensation permitting its use. Otherwise, the matter is not lawful, because the usual licit matter is completely fermented grape juice — what is ordinarily meant by *wine*. But full fermentation affects only liceity of matter, and not its validity for confecting the Blood of Christ, since the second part of the Consecration can be accomplished with *mustum*. In any case, the normative value of wine, bearing the significance of a mature time element, still prevails despite such relatively rare exceptions.

3. *Summa Theologiae*, Pt. III , quest. 74, art. 1.

4. *Miracle Food Cures from the Bible*, pp. 209-225.

5. *Heinerman's Encyclopedia of Fruits, Vegetables and Herbs*, p. 178.

6. *Summa Theologiae*, Pt. III, quest. 74, art. 5.

7. *Heinerman's Encyclopedia of Fruits, Vegetables and Herbs*, p. 177.

8. See (as classic examples of similar texts that must refer to the Catholic Church) Psalm 48, Psalm 87, and Isaiah 2:2-3. Clues to this interpretation are found in Romans 9:25-26; 11:7, Galatians 3:23-29; 4:22-28, and 1 Peter 2:9-10, where St. Paul and St. Peter seem to imply that the Church is the New Israel or new Mount Zion.

9. *Summa Theologiae*, Pt. III, quest. 31, art. 5.

10. This is not (yet) a defined dogma of the Catholic Faith, but it has been widely accepted as worthy of belief, as indicated in Ch. 2.

11. In *Summa Theologiae*, Pt. III, quest. 74, art. 6, Aquinas offers several reasons for this mingling of water and wine, in the course of which he quotes Proverbs 9:5 as mystically applicable to the pre-Consecration rites.

12. By contrast, the separate flow of blood and water in John 19:34, after Christ's side is pierced with a lance, symbolizes the distinction between the two sacraments of Baptism and the Eucharist. But Aquinas associates this event with the mingling of water and wine, since it "harmonizes with the representation of our Lord's Passion." See *Summa Theologiae*, Pt. III, quest. 74, art. 6.

13. See Aristotle's *Nicomachean Ethics*, Bk. X, Chs. 7-8.

14. This is why the wine sometimes seems dry and even bitter.

15. I think in particular of friends or acquaintances who spend hours every week (often daily) before the Blessed Sacrament reserved in the tabernacle.

Chapter 4

1. *Fundamentals of Catholic Dogma*, pp. 361, 365, 366; see also *Code of Canon Law*, Can. 879, and the *CCC*, nn. 1302-1303.

2. *Moral Theology*, n. 487, p. 353; also see *Code of Canon Law*, Can. 880, and the *CCC*, n. 1289.

3. *Fundamentals of Catholic Dogma*, p. 363.

4. *Fundamentals of Catholic Dogma*, pp. 364-365.

5. *Summa Theologiae*, Pt. III, quest. 72, art. 2.

6. *Summa Theologiae*, Pt. III, quest. 72, art. 2.

7. *Miracle Food Cures from the Bible*, p. 227.

8. *Miracle Food Cures from the Bible*, p. 228.

9. Jean Barilla, *Olive Oil Miracle: How the Mediterranean marvel helps protect against arthritis, heart disease and breast cancer* (New Canaan, Conn.: Keats Publishing, 1996), especially pp. 8-11. She credits the International Olive Oil Council for furnishing historical information on the olive.

10. *Miracle Food Cures from the Bible*, pp. 228-231. The positive claims about olive oil's beneficial effects on both LDL and HDL cholesterol are also reported in *Heinerman's Encyclopedia of Fruits, Vegetables and Herbs*, p. 243, as well as the negative assertion that it does not "promote cancer."

11. As an exception, for instance, the Evangelists explicitly tell us that the anointing at Bethany in anticipation of Jesus' burial (according to His own prophetic verdict on the episode) involved the fragrant ointment of costly "pure nard" (i.e., probably spikenard or possibly lavender). See Matthew 26:6-13; Mark 14:3-9; Luke 7:36-38; John 12:1-8.

12. *Miracle Food Cures from the Bible*, pp. 231-232.

13. Many of the prescriptions in Numbers 28 are recapitulated in Ezekiel 45:13-25; 46:1-15.

14. As we observed in Chapter 2, there seems to be a pervasive Old Testament contrast between "fine flour" and "barley," indicating that the "fine flour" could very well mean *wheat*. (Note that Numbers 7 repeats the phrase "fine flour mixed with oil" twelve times and Numbers 15 three times.) See the textual glosses in Chapter 2 on Exodus 9:31-32; 29:2; 34:22, Leviticus 2, Numbers 28-29, Ezra 6:9-10; 7:21-22, Amos 8:5, Psalms 81:16; 147:14, as well as on Luke 16:7 versus Revelation 6:6; 18:13.

15. See John 14:26, *RSV* ("the Counselor, the Holy Spirit, whom the Father will send in my name"); 15:26, *RSV* ("when the Counselor comes, whom I shall send to you from the Father, even the Spirit of truth, who proceeds from the Father"); 16:7, *RSV* ("I will send him [the Counselor] to you"). Let these verses from the Gospel according to St. John suffice, without entering into the intricacies of the *filioque* controversy that divided the Eastern and Western Church.

16. This typologically mystical interpretation of "mixing" with oil is due to David L. Vise.

17. *Miracle Food Cures from the Bible*, p. 227.

18. St. Thomas More, *The Sadness of Christ*, trans. Clarence Miller, ed. Gerard Wegemer (Princeton, N.J.: Scepter Publishers, 1993), p. 7.

19. *The Sadness of Christ*, pp. 40-41.

20. *Summa Theologiae*, Pt. III, quest. 46, art. 6. Aquinas then cites Isaiah 53:4, *D-R*: "Surely he hath . . . carried our sorrows."

21. *Miracle Food Cures from the Bible*, p. 228.

22. *Olive Oil Miracle*, p. 11.

23. *Miracle Food Cures from the Bible*, pp. 227-228.

24. *Olive Oil Miracle*, p. 11.

25. This famous saying is attributed to Tertullian.

26. On the relative immunity of the olive tree to drought, see *Olive Oil Miracle*, p. 11.

27. *Olive Oil Miracle*, p. 8. On the olive tree's fecundity, see again *Miracle Food Cures from the Bible*, p. 228, along with *Olive Oil Miracle*, p. 11.

28. *Heinerman's Encyclopedia of Fruits, Vegetables and Herbs*, p. 242.

29. *Summa Theologiae*, Pt. III, quest. 72, art. 2.

30. St. Thomas Aquinas lists some appropriate symbolic characteristics of the dove in *Summa Theologiae*, Pt. III, quest. 39, art. 6.

31. *Summa Theologiae*, Pt. III, quest. 72, art. 2.

32. See Augustine's *City of God*, Bk. XIX, Ch. 13: "*pax omnium rerum tranquillitas ordinis.*"

33. *Summa Theologiae*, Pt. III, quest. 42, art. 2.

34. *Summa Theologiae*, Supplement, quest. 30, art. 1. See also James 5:15, *RSV* ("if he has committed sins, he will be forgiven"). The *CCC*, n. 1532, adds this qualification: "if the sick person was not able to obtain it [the forgiveness of sins] through the sacrament of Penance." Jone and Ott furnish a number of nuances. Because the primary effect of this sacrament is the "strengthening of the soul through . . . the infusion of sanctifying grace," also granting the soul "the right to those actual graces . . . necessary for final perseverance," it follows that "forgiveness of mortal sins is . . . only a secondary effect." Since it is a sacrament of the living, in itself presupposing the state of grace, mortal sin is absolved (*per accidens*, with imperfect contrition) only if confession is not possible. If absolution is imparted to an unconscious person who, after anointing, does not die, subsequent confession of any mortal sins is required. Remission of at least some temporal punishment due to sin ensues *ex opere operato*. See *Moral Theology*, n. 625, pp. 459-460, together with n. 631, p. 463, and *Fundamentals of Catholic Dogma*, p. 448.

35. *CCC*, nn. 1520-1523, 1532; also see *Fundamentals of Catholic Dogma*, p. 448.

36. *CCC*, nn. 1508, 1532; *Fundamentals of Catholic Dogma*, p. 449; *Moral Theology*, n. 625, p. 460; *Summa Theologiae*, Supplement, quest. 30, art. 2.

37. *Moral Theology*, n. 625, p. 460.

38. *Fundamentals of Catholic Dogma*, p. 449.

39. *Summa Theologiae*, Supplement, quest. 30, art. 2.

40. *Fundamentals of Catholic Dogma*, p. 447.

41. *Moral Theology*, n. 622, p. 457.

42. *Summa Theologiae*, Supplement, quest. 29, art. 4.

43. *Summa Theologiae*, Pt. III, quest. 72, art. 2.

44. *Miracle Food Cures from the Bible*, pp. 227-228.

45. *The Nature Doctor*, pp. 529-530.

46. *Olive Oil Miracle*, p. 9.

47. This chain of reasoning is due to David L. Vise, in a personal communication by letter with the author.

48. *Miracle Food Cures from the Bible*, p. 227.

49. *Miracle Food Cures from the Bible*, pp. 231-232.

50. See Robert Concoby, *The Olive Leaf: Unequalled Immune Support for Health and Longevity* (Kent, Ohio: The National Life Extension Research Institute, 1999).

51. *Olive Oil Miracle*, p. 9.

Chapter 5

1. *Fundamentals of Catholic Dogma*, pp. 450-451.

2. For a summary exposition, but nevertheless scholarly presentation, of the nature of the priesthood, see Thomas McGovern, "Priestly identity: Other Christs," *Homiletic and Pastoral Review* (April, 1992), pp. 21-29.

3. See also *Fundamentals of Catholic Dogma*, pp. 459-460, which gives the Scriptural references 1 Corinthians 14:34 ff. and 1 Timothy 2:11 ff. — though neither Biblical text is popular (or "politically correct") in our so-called "enlightened" and "liberated" age. Also see *Moral Theology*, n. 638, p. 468.

4. John Paul II, *On Reserving Priestly Ordination to Men Alone*, trans. *L'Osservatore Romano* (Boston: St. Paul Books and Media, 1994).

5. The author is indebted to both Louis Bouyer and Paul M. Quay for some pivotal insights — to Bouyer primarily for some reasoning in this chapter, and to Quay mainly for some ideas in the next chapter (as well as for general notions about symbolism pervading this book, especially its Introduction). See Bouyer's *Woman in the Church* (San Francisco: Ignatius Press, 1979) and Quay's *The Christian Meaning of Human Sexuality* (Evanston, Ill.: Credo House Books, 1985). Also recommended are Alice von Hildebrand and Peter Kreeft, *Women and the Priesthood* (Steubenville, Ohio: Franciscan University Press, 1994), and Manfred Hauke, *Women in the Priesthood?* (San Francisco: Ignatius Press, 1988).

6. *Summa Theologiae*, Pt. I, quest. 2, art. 3; quest. 3, arts. 1, 2; quest. 4, art. 1.

7. *Summa Theologiae*, Pt. I, quest. 3, art. 8.

8. *Woman in the Church*, pp. 53-54.

9. For a short but excellent article on masculine names for God (with repercussions for an all-male priesthood), see Christopher Kaczor, "Inclusive language and revealed truth," *Homiletic and Pastoral Review* (April, 1992), pp. 16-20.

10. *The Christian Meaning of Human Sexuality*, p. 44.

11. Chris Kaczor makes a similar point in "Inclusive language and revealed truth," p. 18.

12. *Woman in the Church*, pp. 34, 48-49, 51-52.

13. This is essentially a point made by Jason Evert, "Why Can't Women be Priests?," *This Rock* (January, 2002), p. 30.

14. Pope John Paul II, in his 1988 Apostolic Letter *Mulieris Dignitatem*, wrote that "Christ acted in a completely free and sovereign manner" when choosing men for His Apostles.

15. This is not (yet) a defined dogma of the Catholic Faith, but it has been widely accepted as worthy of belief.

16. *Fundamentals of Catholic Dogma*, p. 454.

17. This interpretation, as we saw in earlier chapters, derives from a synthesis of Psalm 48, Psalm 87, Isaiah 2:2-3, Romans 9:25-26; 11:7, Galatians 3:23-29; 4:22-28, and 1 Peter 2:9-10. We have been using passages of the Bible to understand the meaning of other Scriptural texts.

18. Mark P. Shea, "Ordination is not a Right," *This Rock* (May-June, 2001), pp. 22-23.

19. Joseph Cardinal Ratzinger with Vittorio Messori, *The Ratzinger Report: An Exclusive Interview on the State of the Church*, trans. Salvator Attanasio and Graham Harrison (San Francisco: Ignatius Press, 1985), p. 96.

20. See the essay by C. S. Lewis titled "Priestesses in the Church?," appended to *Woman in the Church*, pp. 123-132.

21. Chris Kaczor remarks on some pertinent matters, observed by other thinkers as well (for instance, C. S. Lewis and Peter Kreeft), in "Inclusive language and revealed truth," p. 18. Since "mother" (and "*Mutter*," "*madre*," "*mae*," or "*mère*") is etymologically linked to the Latin "*mater*," whence derives the Latin word "*materia*" for (in English) "matter," our Western languages reflect the fact that the whole material world is feminine in relation to the Creator-God. In reality, no one who refuses receptivity to divine "marriage" and "impregnation" can be spiritually fruitful. Religions that view God as "Mother" are not theistic but rather pantheistic, because they worship creation, confounding the sovereign Lord with His handiwork. The various New Age cults, like the Eastern religions inspiring them, have rejected the Father-God of Judaeo-Christian revelation in favor of a reversion to paganism.

Chapter 6

1. For an excellent detailed discussion of the fundamental principles of ethics, including the topics of good and evil acts, the norms of morality (both ultimate and proximate, subjective and objective), as well as the natural moral law, see Martin D. O'Keefe, *Known From The Things That Are* (Houston: Center for Thomistic Studies, 1987), pp. 71-170. Application to sexual issues (marriage, family, homosexuality, etc.) can be found on pp. 220-234.

2. Immanuel Kant, *Grounding for the Metaphysics of Morals*, trans. James W. Ellington (Indianapolis, Ind.: Hackett Publishing Co., 1981), pp. 15, 24-26, 30, 32-33, 42.

3. *Grounding for the Metaphysics of Morals*, pp. 30-32.

4. Alasdair MacIntyre, *A Short History of Ethics* (London: Routledge and Kegan Paul, 1967), pp. 197-198.

5. The champion of this school of ethics, Karol Wojtyla, began espousing this newer approach as a professor of ethics decades before his election to the papacy as Pope John Paul II. A series of his lectures given at the Catholic University of Lublin, Poland, during the academic year 1958-1959, was compiled and published in Polish in 1960, and later translated into English. See Karol Wojtyla, *Love and Responsibility*, trans. H. T. Willetts (New York: Farrar, Straus and Giroux, 1981). This book is highly recommended by the present author. Wojtyla has continued to write employing the principles of integral personalism since becoming pope. A noteworthy example is his series of Wednesday afternoon talks on the "theology of the body" in the late 1970s and early 1980s.

6. *Love and Responsibility*, pp. 25-27.

7. *Love and Responsibility*, pp. 27-28.

8. *Grounding for the Metaphysics of Morals*, pp. 35-37, 41-43.

9. *Love and Responsibility*, p. 41.

10. *Love and Responsibility*, p. 39.

11. *Love and Responsibility*, pp. 35-39, 43.

12. *Love and Responsibility*, p. 213.

13. *Love and Responsibility*, p. 179.

14. *Love and Responsibility*, p. 60.

15. *Love and Responsibility*, p. 33.

16. *Love and Responsibility*, p. 34.

17. *Love and Responsibility*, p. 30.

18. *Love and Responsibility*, pp. 51, 218.

19. *Love and Responsibility*, p. 52. See also John Paul II, *Original Unity of Man and Woman: Catechesis on the Book of Genesis* (Boston: Daughters of St. Paul Editions, 1981), p. 25.

20. *Love and Responsibility*, pp. 55-56.

21. *Love and Responsibility*, pp. 57-61.

22. *Love and Responsibility*, pp. 61-66.

23. John Paul II, *Blessed are the Pure of Heart* (Boston: Daughters of St. Paul Editions, 1983), pp. 126, 133.

24. *Love and Responsibility*, pp. 66-67.

25. Karol Wojtyla, *The Acting Person*, trans. Andrzej Potocki, Vol. X of *Analecta Husserliana*, ed. Anna-Teresa Tymieniecka (Dordrecht, Holland: D. Reidel Publishing Co., 1979), pp. 80-83.

26. *The Acting Person*, p. 165.

27. *Love and Responsibility*, p. 123.

28. *Love and Responsibility*, p. 133.

29. *Love and Responsibility*, p. 133.

30. *Love and Responsibility*, p. 155.

31. *Love and Responsibility*, p. 152.

32. *Love and Responsibility*, p. 151.

33. *Love and Responsibility*, p. 225.

34. *Love and Responsibility*, p. 230.

35. *Love and Responsibility*, pp. 226-230.

36. John Paul II, *The Role of the Christian Family in the Modern World* (Boston: Daughters of St. Paul), p. 23.

37. *The Role of the Christian Family in the Modern World*, pp. 51-52.

38. John Paul II, *Reflections on Humanae Vitae* (Boston: Daughters of St. Paul, 1984), pp. 8-9, 27, 42.

39. *The Ratzinger Report*, pp. 97-98.

40. *Original Unity of Man and Woman: Catechesis on the Book of Genesis*, pp. 83, 99-101, 106-119, 128-134, 141-145. See also *The Role of the Christian Family in the Modern World*, p. 33.

41. Some less technical, but very illuminating, treatments can be found in Leanne Payne, *The Broken Image* (Westchester, Ill.: Crossway Books, 1982), Elizabeth R. Moberly, *Homosexuality: A New Christian Ethic* (Cambridge, England: James Clarke, 1983, and Greenwood, S.C.: Attic Press), and Gerald Van den Aardweg, *Homosexuality and Hope* (Ann Arbor, Mich.: Servant Publications, 1985). A good overall perspective on diverse aspects (comparative psychological theories, theological and moral arguments, pastoral implications) of the problem can be obtained from John F. Harvey, *The Homosexual Person: New Thinking in Pastoral Care* (San Francisco: Ignatius Press, 1987).

42. *The Christian Meaning of Human Sexuality*, p. 70.

43. *The Christian Meaning of Human Sexuality*, p. 69.

44. *The Christian Meaning of Human Sexuality*, p. 79.

45. *The Christian Meaning of Human Sexuality*, p. 80.

46. That feminism has made damaging inroads into the Church through women's religious orders hardly needs documentation. But anyway, we give, as classic references for all the revolting details, these two works: William Oddie, *What Will Happen to God? Feminism and the Reconstruction of Christian Belief* (San Francisco: Ignatius Press, 1988) and Donna Steichen, *Ungodly Rage: The Hidden Face of Catholic Feminism* (San Francisco: Ignatius Press, 1991), especially pp. 174-176 (and passim) on lesbianism. See also *The Ratzinger Report*, pp. 99-100.

47. Bryan G. Rudnick, Letter on behalf of *Massachusetts Citizens for Marriage* (August, 2001).

48. Not long after this paragraph, with this particular sentence, was written, the author learned that Peter Singer, in a review of Midas Dekker's *Dearest Pet: On Bestiality*, has unequivocally come "out of the closet" (or

"doghouse") in favor of consigning the last sexual taboo to the old-fashioned past. Singer, who holds that the lives of young infants and the comatose (not to mention the unborn) have less value than some fully developed and healthy animals, is Professor in the Princeton University Center for Human [*sic*] Values. See Nick Felten, " 'Pollys' Spotlight PC Excess," *Campus* (Wilmington, Del.: Intercollegiate Studies Institute), Fall 2001, p. 18. The pace of decadence is accelerating so fast that one can hardly keep up with the latest travesties of what passes for respectable opinions.

49. George Gilder, *Men and Marriage*, revised edition (Gretna, La.: Pelican Publishing Co., 1986).

50. Stephen B. Clark, *Man and Woman in Christ* (Ann Arbor, Mich.: Servant Publications, 1981).

51. See *What Will Happen to God?*, pp. 62-73, on masculine-feminine differences.

52. *Sex and Sacredness*, passim.

53. Paul Evdokimov, "Ecclesia Domestica," in *A Voice for Women* (Geneva, 1981), p. 176, quoted in *What Will Happen to God?*, p. 70.

Epilogue

1. See, for example, Martin D. O'Keefe, *Known From The Things That Are*, pp. 148-153, 222-223, 227-232.

2. See, for example, Karol Wojtyla, *Love and Responsibility*, pp. 21-44, 224-248.

For an excellent article consolidating aspects of both approaches, see Joseph L. Doran, "Are contraception and artificial procreation sometimes permissible?," *Homiletic and Pastoral Review* (March, 1993), pp. 48-57.

3. For a sober philosophical analysis of arguments for and against abortion using natural law theory, see Martin D. O'Keefe, *Known From The Things That Are*, pp. 178-189. A comprehensive treatment of all the crucial facets of this issue can be found in Stephen Schwarz, *The Moral Question of Abortion* (Chicago: Loyola University Press, 1990).

4. Linda Bowles, "Time . . . to Declare Preborn's Right to Life," *The Wanderer*, August 23, 2001, p. 6.

5. Andrew Sullivan, "When Does Dignity Really Begin?," *The Wanderer*, August 23, 2001, p. 5. (Reprinted from *The New Republic*.)

6. Ted Flynn, *Hope of the Wicked: The Master Plan to Rule the World* (Sterling, Va.: MaxKol Communications, 2000), pp. 328, 345-346. He devotes a substantial chapter (pp. 328-346) to the "Green Movement," which espouses the gnostic "gaia ideology" that the earth is a superior living being, a goddess "worthy of worship" (p. 330).

7. Steven W. Mosher, President, *Population Research Institute*, asserts: "It's an amazing fact, for example, that every family in the world could be placed in a house with a front and back yard within the state of Texas. That's right. Everyone in the whole world would comfortably fit inside Texas. And the other 49 states and all the other countries of the world would be *completely empty of people!*" He insinuates, though, that this demographic fact does not deter the environmental fanatics from their nefarious goals. (See *The Wanderer*, August 23, 2001, p. 12.) An encyclopedic volume to consult on this subject is Jacqueline Kasun, *The War against Population: The Economics and Ideology of World Population Control*, revised edition (San Francisco: Ignatius Press, 1999). On p. 45, she credits the Texas calculation to the biologist Francis P. Felice, "Population Growth," *The Compass*, 1974.

8. *Hope of the Wicked*, pp. 328-329, 341.

9. For more on the occultist, pagan, nature-worshiping undercurrents within the feminist-environmentalist-New Age "green" axis, see *The War against Population*, pp. 230-232. These elitists seem to disdain most of the human race (at least everyone not in their networking circles) as a contemptible blight on the planet, which they have deified as "Gaia" (the earth goddess).

10. *Hope of the Wicked*, p. 330.

11. See Isaiah 9:5-6 and John 14:27.

12. See John 10:10; 14:6; 1 John 2:25; Psalm 36:10a; Wisdom 1:13-14.

13. See John 9:5; 12:35-36, 46; 1 John 1:5-7; Psalm 36:10b.

14. See Genesis 3:1-14; Wisdom 2:23-24; John 8:44; Revelation 12:7-9.

15. See Isaiah 14:12-15; Luke 10:18; John 12:31; 14:30.

16. For a superb discussion and demolition of relativism in general, see Francis J. Beckwith and Gregory Koukl, *Relativism: Feet Firmly Planted in Mid-Air* (Grand Rapids, Mich.: Baker Books, 1998). For an excellent treatment of ethical relativism, see Peter Kreeft, *A Refutation of Moral Relativism: Interviews with an Absolutist* (San Francisco: Ignatius Press, 1999). For a briefer but less adequate account, see David P. Lang, "Arguing against relativism," *Homiletic and Pastoral Review* (March, 1994), pp. 18-23.

17. Paul VI, Encyclical Letter *Of Human Life (Humanae Vitae)*, NC News Service Translation (Boston: Pauline Books and Media, 1968), n. 17 (excerpt).

18. *The Ratzinger Report*, p. 98.

19. John Paul II, Encyclical Letter *The Splendor of Truth (Veritatis*

Splendor), Vatican Translation (Boston: Pauline Books and Media, 1993), nn. 95, 96.

20. By now everyone should agree that George Orwell's novel *1984* was thematically prescient.

21. An astonishing manifestation of the arrogance of powerful sympathizers for the antifamily agenda of militant homosexuals appears in the following excerpt from a speech by the (radical feminist) Chief Justice of the Massachusetts Superior Court at a meeting in 2000 of the Massachusetts Lesbian and Gay Bar Association (quotation from Bryan G. Rudnick's Letter on behalf of *Massachusetts Citizens for Marriage*): "Vermont recognizes same-sex couples. And here we are in Massachusetts. Would you please? It's embarrassing. Could we get with the program a little bit?" Our supposedly impartial judges have been functioning for decades as social engineers with a pernicious "program" to mold our culture in their secular humanist image. Talk about gnostic contempt for the created physical order! And what is really "embarrassing" is the spectacle of these "liberal" and "nonjudgmental" tyrants competing with one another to impose their immoral vision of society by coercive taxation in order to fund benefits for same-sex "partners." What they really want is to criminalize and penalize verbal criticism of "alternative lifestyles," in the name of protective "safety" from sexual "harassment." (Freedom of speech ends at the point of disagreement with them.)

22. See Psalm 48, Psalm 87, Psalm 132:13-14, Isaiah 2:2-3, Romans 9:25-26; 11:7, Galatians 3:23-29; 4:22-28, and 1 Peter 2:9-10.

23. See also Isaiah 35:6, 7, 10.

24. *Summa Theologiae*, Pt. III, quest. 74, art. 1.

Our Sunday Visitor. . .
Your Source for Discovering
the Riches of the Catholic Faith

Our Sunday Visitor has an extensive line of materials for young children, teens, and adults. Our books, Bibles, booklets, CD-ROMs, audios, and videos are available in bookstores worldwide.

To receive a FREE full-line catalog or for more information, call **Our Sunday Visitor** at **1-800-348-2440**. Or write, **Our Sunday Visitor** / 200 Noll Plaza / Huntington, IN 46750.

- -

Please send me: ___A catalog

Please send me materials on:

___Apologetics and catechetics   ___Reference works

___Prayer books   ___Heritage and the saints

___The family   ___The parish

Name_____

Address_____Apt._____

City_____State_____Zip_____

Telephone (   ) _____

A29BBABP

- -

Please send a friend: ___A catalog

Please send a friend materials on:

___Apologetics and catechetics   ___Reference works

___Prayer books   ___Heritage and the saints

___The family   ___The parish

Name_____

Address_____Apt._____

City_____State_____Zip_____

Telephone (   ) _____

A29BBABP

- -

Our Sunday Visitor
200 Noll Plaza
Huntington, IN 46750
Toll free: 1-800-348-2440
E-mail: osvbooks@osv.com
Website: www.osv.com